Pitch Woman and Other Stories

Native Literatures of the Americas

Pitch Woman
and Other Stories

The Oral Traditions of Coquelle Thompson,
Upper Coquille Athabaskan Indian

Edited and with an introduction
by William R. Seaburg

Collected by Elizabeth D. Jacobs

UNIVERSITY OF NEBRASKA PRESS • LINCOLN AND LONDON

Set in Times and Form Lushootseed by Bob Reitz. ¶ Designed by R. W. Boeche.

Library of Congress Cataloging-in-Publication Data ¶ Thompson, Coquelle, 1848–1946. ¶ Pitch woman and other stories: the oral traditions of Coquelle Thompson, upper Coquille Athabaskan Indian / edited and with an introduction by William R. Seaburg; collected by Elizabeth D. Jacobs. ¶ p. cm. ¶ Includes bibliographical references and index. ¶ ISBN-13: 978-0-8032-4333-0 (hardcover: alk. paper) ¶ ISBN-10: 0-8032-4333-2 (hardcover: alk. paper) ¶ ISBN-13: 978-0-8032-4494-8 (paperback: alk. paper) ¶ 1. Coquille Indians—Folklore. ¶ 2. Athapascan Indians—Oregon—Folklore. ¶ 3. Oral tradition—Oregon. ¶ 4. Thompson, Coquelle, 1848–1946. ¶ 5. Coquille Indians—Biography. ¶ 6. Siletz Indian Reservation (Or.)—History. ¶ I. Seaburg, William R. ¶ II. Jacobs, Elizabeth Derr. ¶ III. Title. ¶ E99.C8742T4693 2007 ¶ 398.2089'972—dc22 ¶ 2006027329

So, take a listen to these,
    a few times
        and think about it,
            to these stories, and what I tell you now.
Compare them.
    See if you can see something more about it.
        Kind of plain,
            but it's pretty hard to tell you
                for you to know right now.
Takes time.
And then you will see.

> Harry Robinson,
> *Nature Power: In the Spirit of*
> *an Okanagan Storyteller*

Contents

List of Map, Illustrations, and Tables

Map

Illustrations

Tables

Foreword

Some Thoughts on Reading Oral Traditions

There is something ironic—some might argue perverse—about reading stories that were meant to be heard and seen as a live performance by an accomplished storyteller.[1] Oral stories that have been written down are always compromised or mediated in several ways. When reduced to a written medium, most performance information is irretrievably lost. As a result some of the meaning of the stories is lost as well. Meanings conveyed by posture, gesture, acting, tone of voice, or voice quality—such as falsetto, monotone, soft voice, and chanting—are gone. Exclamation points, underlining, capitalized words, and bold or italic typeface are anemic orthographic substitutes.[2]

Stories originally learned and told in a Native American language are also mediated by translation into English. Even with the best translation by the most fluent of bilingual speakers, some meaning is inevitably altered or lost. Aspects of expressive style such as wordplay, onomatopoeia, archaic myth names, and the like are also lost in translation. What José Ortega y Gasset said about reading utterances is equally true for translations: "Every utterance [read: translation] is deficient—it says less than it wishes to say. Every utterance is exuberant—it conveys more than it plans" (quoted in Becker 1995:370).

An orally performed story has both a teller and an audience and is always socially, culturally, and historically situated. Its perspective is partial—no two people tell the "same" story the same way—and its performance is motivated. In other words, a story/telling reflects something about the storyteller, something about his or her audience and their reactions to the story/teller, and probably something about the occasion of the telling. Little of the situated meaning of a story survives the transcription process. And few anthropologists working in the Northwest states in the first half of the twentieth century thought to ask questions that might have elicited contextual information.[3]

No text is an island, entire of itself; there are always connections with prior texts—intertextuality. As A. L. Becker explains, contextual relations include "[t]he relations of textual units to other texts, since part of the context of any text is, more or less, all previous texts in a particular culture, especially texts considered to be in the same genre; readable literature is structurally coherent with its own ancestors" (1995:25). Unless you know the entire corpus of an oral tradition, you lack knowledge of the meaningful connections between stories that inform each of the individual stories. The good news is the more stories you read, the more you will begin to see connections among texts. After reading and rereading stories, the texts begin to "talk" among themselves, and if you read enough stories and read them enough times, they will begin to talk to you.

There isn't—nor ever was—a single canonical text; all stories in living oral traditions exist in multiple versions or variants. Change—tempered by the conservative force of tradition—is one of the hallmarks of oral traditions everywhere.

Not only are oral traditions meant to be performed, but they are meant to be performed in front of a knowledgeable audience, one that shares beliefs, values, attitudes, world-view, and sundry associations with the storyteller. Without some knowledge of this shared cultural background, cultural outsiders often find the stories difficult to fathom. As Michael Roemer explains, for Western readers "[w]hen we look back at *Oedipus Rex*, the figures are so clearly bound that the play may seem pointless and irrelevant to us, whereas the figures in our own stories breathe *our* air, hold our assumptions, know what we know, see what we see, do what we do, make our discoveries, and are surprised when we are. We recognize ourselves in them, and since we must believe in our own freedom, we believe in theirs" (1995:34). If we are cultural outsiders, we need to make a special effort to temporarily bracket our European American aesthetic expectations and evaluations. We are going to enter a story world that is quite different from the one most of us are used to. It takes time to learn about and adjust to this unfamiliar world.

Native American myths and tales are *not* children's "Just So" stories, although children did participate in storytelling sessions as auditors. Stories were not bowdlerized, were not altered or "cleaned up" for children's sake. In general everyone in Northwest states Indian cultures heard the same stories.[4]

Stories were told for a variety of reasons: to instruct, to caution or warn, to entertain, to explain, to validate, and to shorten the winter months, among others. Probably each narrative performance had at once multiple purposes.

The highly stylized aspects of these stories, especially ones told in the Native languages, perhaps allowed or encouraged Native audiences to "fill in the spaces" or "identify with" or "project onto" the story in individual ways. Of course, no story in any cultural tradition is ever fully explicit. As auditors we are forced to participate in the story's construction, using our cultural and individual knowledge and opinions to make a story complete.

Stories exhibit many similarities, structural, thematic, and stylistic, throughout the oral traditions of the Northwest states area. Among other things this suggests that we should be cautious about explaining a story's content or themes by the fact that a certain culture told it.[5]

Our attempts to analyze or interpret these stories, especially as cultural outsiders, are always partial and incomplete. Like all great literature, Coquelle Thompson's narratives successfully resist closure. In my experience, though, the attempt to understand and appreciate them is satisfying and well worth the effort involved.

Finally, I would urge the reader of Thompson's stories to be a sympathetic reader, to give the texts a chance to talk to you. As Sigmund Freud once said, "I learnt to restrain speculative tendencies and to follow the unforgotten advice of my master, Charcot: to look at the same things again and again until they themselves begin to speak" (quoted in Malcolm 1987:95). If you listen, with patience, persistence, and humility, they will begin to speak.

Acknowledgments

Many people helped in the making of this book. Foremost among them was Elizabeth Derr Jacobs, known by her friends as Bess. When we first met in the summer of 1975, Bess was still mourning the death of her husband, Melville, and I was in the process of leaving an ill-suited graduate program in linguistics, with no real idea of where I was headed next. Together we each found new directions and purposes in our lives. Our work that summer resulted in a close friendship and intellectual collaboration that lasted until her death in 1983. Without Bess Jacobs, this book wouldn't exist.

A special debt is owed to John P. (Jack) Marr of Fullerton, California, John P. Harrington's field assistant in the late 1930s and early 1940s. Marr has been a faithful correspondent over the years and has generously shared a wealth of reminiscences of working with Coquelle Thompson and other Indian consultants from whom he made phonograph recordings.

As always, my University of Washington, Bothell, writing group, Diane Gillespie and Bruce Kochis, encouraged, stimulated, and challenged my thinking and writing. The UWB is an unusually compatible intellectual environment—due in no small measure to the efforts of Jane Decker, associate dean of academic affairs, and JoLynn Edwards, director of Interdisciplinary Arts and Sciences, my home department. Thanks to the UWB for granting me sabbatical leave for the 2003–4 academic year, during which time I was able to write this book.

Several friends and colleagues read parts or all of a draft of the book and made valuable suggestions: Bob Boyd, Yvonne Hajda, Lionel Youst, Jay Miller, Laurel Sercombe, Dodie Bell, and two reviewers for the University of Nebraska Press. Jim Nason, Amelia Susman Schultz, Victor Golla, the late M. Dale Kinkade, and other friends provided support and encouragement. Susanne J. Young, my good friend of thirty-five years, continues to endure my curmudgeonly ways.

Dodie Bell, Coquelle Thompson's granddaughter, generously provided pho-
tographs of her grandfather for inclusion here. My appreciation to Douglas
Deur, who prepared the map "Principal Ethnolinguistic Groups of the Southern Northwest Coast."

As in the past, thanks are due Gary Lundell and Janet Ness for their always
competent and cheerful archival help with the Melville Jacobs Collection, University of Washington Libraries. Thanks also to Thomas A. Livesay, former
director of the Whatcom Museum of History and Art, Bellingham, Washington,
for granting permission to publish Jacobs's texts. The Jacobs Research Fund of
the Whatcom Museum provided financial support between 1975 and 1978 for
this and related projects.

Thanks to Gary Dunham, acquiring editor for Native studies at the University of Nebraska Press, for his support and help in successfully shepherding my
manuscript through the acquisition process.

Thanks again to my family, especially my sister Cheryl, for their steadfast
support and encouragement.

Abbreviations

APS   American Philosophical Society Library, Philadelphia

JPH   John Peabody Harrington, 1981, *The Papers of John Peabody Harrington in the Smithsonian Institution, 1907–1957*. National Anthropological Archives, Department of Anthropology, National Museum of Natural History, Washington DC. Microfilm edition, part 1: Native American History, Language, and Culture of Alaska/Northwest Coast.

JPH/JM   John P. Harrington–John P. (Jack) Marr correspondence. In John Peabody Harrington, 1991, *The Papers of John Peabody Harrington in the Smithsonian Institution, 1907–1957*. National Anthropological Archives, Department of Anthropology, National Museum of Natural History, Washington DC. Microfilm edition, part 9: Native American Ethnography through Correspondence.

MJC   Melville Jacobs Collection, University of Washington Libraries, Seattle

UC   Elizabeth D. Jacobs's Upper Coquille Athabaskan field notebooks, Melville Jacobs Collection, University of Washington Libraries, Seattle. (UC 1 = nb. 71, box 80; UC 2 = nb. 104, box 84; UC 3 = nb. 116, box 85; UC 4–6 = nbs. 119–21, box 85.)

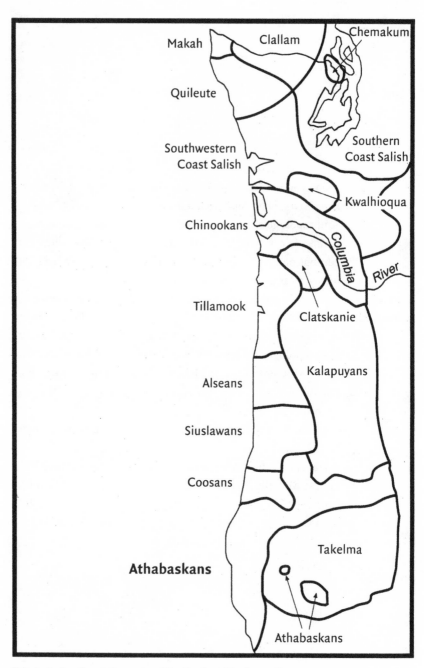

Principal ethnolinguistic groups of the Southern Northwest Coast

1. Introduction

Human beings have been characterized as *homo narrans*—storytellers. Ursula K. Le Guin in *Dancing at the Edge of the World* argues that narrative is such a central, fundamental function of language that "[t]o learn to speak is to learn to tell a story" (1989:39).

Coquelle Thompson, the storyteller whose narratives are reproduced in this volume, knew lots of stories, undoubtedly many more than appear here.[1] He had heard them all his life, beginning as a young boy in his father's sweathouse and later as a resident of the Siletz Reservation for ninety years. Besides his own culture's Upper Coquille Athabaskan stories, he must have heard Applegate Athabaskan stories from his first wife, Annetti. He probably heard stories from Hoxie Simmons, a Galice Creek Athabaskan speaker whose repertoire of stories has yet to be published (M. Jacobs 1935, 1938–39). And certainly he heard stories from the many Tututni Athabaskan speakers on the reservation, such as Depot Charlie, a Joshua storyteller recorded by Livingston Farrand in 1900.

But Thompson's exposure to stories wasn't limited to Athabaskan storytellers. At first through the medium of the regional lingua franca Chinook Jargon and later English, Thompson probably heard and enjoyed narratives from Shasta, Takelma, Alsea, Siuslaw–Lower Umpqua, Coos, and Tillamook de-

Coquelle Thompson Sr., from a picture postcard. Courtesy of Sina Thompson Bell and Dodie Bell.

scendents living at Siletz. As Melville Jacobs (1962, 1967, 1969–70) often lamented, the published collections of Takelma, Alsea, Siuslaw–Lower Umpqua, Coos, and southern Tillamook are meager in size and uneven in quality compared to what could have been recorded and published before it was too late. For the southwestern Oregon Athabaskan cultures, a mere handful of their rich oral traditional texts has previously appeared in print (Farrand and Frachtenberg 1915; M. Jacobs 1968; E. Jacobs 1968, 1977; Whereat 2002; Seaburg 2004). *Pitch Woman and Other Stories*, then, is the first substantial collection of southwestern Oregon Athabaskan stories to be published.

The Storyteller, Coquelle Thompson Sr.

The stories in this collection were all told by Coquelle Thompson Sr., who was born around 1849 in an Upper Coquille Athabaskan village in the Coquille River valley, southwestern Oregon. After the tragic and needless Rogue River Wars of 1855–56, Thompson and his people, as well as many other southwestern Oregon Indian groups, were evicted from their native homelands and

Coquelle Thompson Sr., 1937. Ben Maxwell, photographer; courtesy of the Oregon Historical Society, CNO15067.

resettled about one hundred miles to the north on land that eventually become the Siletz Reservation. Many did not survive this traumatic uprooting or the emotional and physical deprivations of the early years of the reservation, but Thompson did survive, and he lived at Siletz for the remainder of his long life.

Thompson either participated in or witnessed all major events at Siletz from

Coquelle Thompson Sr. and his wife, Agnes Thompson. Courtesy of the Oregon Historical Society, CN015069.

1855 to 1946, including an offshoot of the 1870 Ghost Dance, known at Siletz as the Warm House Dance. He was a well-known singer and dancer of both Native and nativistic songs and dances. He seemed to have known almost everyone on the reservation and their kinship ties to one another. And he had a prodigious memory, as official heirship testimonies and anthropologists' fieldnotes amply demonstrate. He spoke English tolerably well, although he never learned to read or write and signed official documents with an *X* or his thumbprint. He also spoke Chinook Jargon and his native Upper Coquille Athabaskan, a language spoken by only a few others at the time of his death in 1946.[2]

Elizabeth D. Jacobs, circa 1932. Courtesy of William R. Seaburg.

Thompson worked at various times as a farmer, a hunting and fishing guide, a Siletz Agency teamster, a tribal policeman and judge, and a mail carrier. He also served as a cultural and linguistic expert witness for six different anthropologists over a period of nearly sixty years, from 1884 to 1942: J. Owen Dorsey, Cora Du Bois, Philip Drucker, Elizabeth D. Jacobs, John P. Marr, and John P. Harrington.[3] Most of what is known about the Upper Coquille Athabaskan language and culture comes from this cooperative and able consultant. Thompson was a perceptive and intelligent observer. He was also a willing and talented storyteller; both Elizabeth Jacobs and Bureau of American Ethnology (Smithsonian Institution) anthropologist and linguist John P. Harrington recorded hundreds of notebook pages of myth, tale, personal experience, and historical event narratives from him. Thompson seemed to enjoy working with the anthropologists. Jack Marr, who made phonograph recordings with Thompson in 1941, reported that Thompson was always eager to reminisce about the old days—even when the recording machine was turned off (personal communication, 2004).

The Collector, Elizabeth D. Jacobs

On June 23, 1975, I was sitting in the living room of Elizabeth D. (Bess) Jacobs at her home in Seattle, Washington, tape recorder and notebook at hand.[4] I had received a small summer grant from the Melville and Elizabeth Jacobs Research Fund (now the Jacobs Research Fund) and was splitting my time between poring over her fieldnotes in the Melville Jacobs Collection at the University of Washington Libraries and talking with her about her field experiences.[5] It was an exhilarating time for me and, I believe, a time of emotional renewal for her. As the taped interviews show, Bess was mentally sharp and articulate, and she remembered her fieldwork of forty years earlier clearly and in some detail. Her answers to my sometimes sprawling, awkward questions were concise and immediate. Often she began answering my questions before I had quite finished asking them.

Seaburg: OK, on Thursday you mentioned that the Tillamook fieldwork was your first field experience—

Jacobs: Correct.

S: First time in the field. What had been your training up to this point?

J: I was in premed and going to be a psychiatrist.

S: So you were an undergraduate at this time?

J: No, I had graduated.

S: You *had* graduated.

J: Yeah.

S: What was your undergraduate—

J: Literature and drama. And it wasn't until I decided to go into medical school that I went back and took the premed materials.

S: Where did you do your undergraduate—

J: Here.

S: University of Washington?

J: Yeah.

S: How did you get interested in anthropology?

J: By marrying Mel.[6]

S: I see. [laughter] That's a good reason. Had you taken very many anthropology courses before—

J: None whatever—just psychology and psychiatry and a little sociology, including one class with a Professor Stern, who gave us a little anthropological material.[7]

S: So you hadn't taken any formal courses in linguistics or ethnography before you did your fieldwork—

J: I'd had some formal courses in linguistics, but Jones English pronunciation, stage pronunciation.

S: I see. [laughs] I noticed that in the preface to the, the foreword to the *Nehalem Tillamook Tales*, Mel says that he persuaded you to do the work.

J: This is true.

S: I thought that was an interesting verb to use. Did it take much persuasion to get you—

J: I didn't think I would be interested or do well. But he got me to try—and I loved it.

S: I was going to ask if you thought your training in anthropology was adequate, but I guess—since you hadn't had any real training in anthropology—that's not a very good question to ask.

J: Well, the answer would have been "no" except that I had an expert—watching over my shoulder and that's better than most kids get.

S: Um-hm, that's true. Is there anything you wished you would have had, any kind of training you wished you would have had, looking back, before you went into the field?

J: More linguistics.

S: Was that the most difficult part?

J: Yeah, oh sure. Everything else came naturally because they're human beings.

Another excerpt, from a later interview, hints at how we worked together that summer, discussing and analyzing Thompson's stories:

Seaburg: The one story that I made notes on was the "A Man Follows His Wife to the Land of the Dead."

Jacobs: Yes—we read that last night.[8]

S: OK. Do you want to talk about that?

J: If you'd like to.

S: OK. Do you want to start, or do you want me to?

J: No, I want you to—treat me like an informant. And I'll volunteer when I have something to volunteer.

S: Well, this didn't have—I don't know what genre it is. It's obviously—it's not—I don't think it was intended to be a real, a true-life account, I don't know. But it's not really a myth genre either, in one sense. It's a funny kind of in-between stage. I have a feeling—

J: They didn't distinguish that sharply like the Tillamook did.

S: Um-hm.

J: They would call it a true story.

S: Hm, OK. [long pause]

J: Otherwise he'd have never got back with her, you see.

These brief excerpts are from the first of a series of tape-recorded interviews I conducted with Elizabeth that summer, over thirty years ago. They marked the beginning of a close friendship and collaboration between us that lasted until her death in 1983 at the age of eighty. We had set for ourselves two primary goals that summer: publication of her *Nehalem Tillamook: An Ethnography* (2003) and publication of Coquelle Thompson's myth and tale narratives. I am pleased that, with this volume, both tasks are finally completed. Elizabeth would have been pleased as well. Neither of us ever imagined it would have taken this long.

The collector of the narratives published here was Elizabeth Derr Jacobs (1903–83). Working with Thompson for about two or three months in the late fall of 1935 at the Siletz Reservation in western Oregon, Jacobs recorded in longhand myths, tales, personal experience narratives, and historical narratives, as well as extensive linguistic and ethnographic notes. Although Jacobs was not formally trained as an anthropologist, she was a quick study, and she learned phonetic transcription and field methods from her husband while in the field. The Jacobses worked at different field sites, but in the evening hours they would discuss the day's findings, and Melville helped Elizabeth compose the next day's questions.

Elizabeth Jacobs worked on readying her field materials for several years after 1935, her last year of anthropological fieldwork with Native Americans. She prepared a rough draft of her Tillamook ethnography and typed up two different editions of Coquelle Thompson's myths and tales.[9] But her interests began to shift to politics by 1936 and later to psychiatric social work, her eventual profession. The heavy demands of Jacobs's work as a therapist precluded further work on her anthropological fieldnotes. With her husband's help, and after many years' delay at several publishers, her *Nehalem Tillamook Tales*

Sketch of Elizabeth D. Jacobs by her husband, Melville Jacobs, in the early 1930s. Courtesy of William R. Seaburg.

was eventually published in 1959. The plan was for Elizabeth and Melville to work up their unpublished notes after Mel's retirement. But Melville died in 1971, one year short of retirement, and Elizabeth never fully recovered from the loss.

Jacobs's 1935 Fieldwork

Elizabeth Jacobs's fieldwork with Coquelle Thompson was not her first anthropological research. She had recorded ethnographic notes and folklore from her Nehalem Tillamook consultant Clara Pearson at Garibaldi, Oregon, during November and December 1933, with a two-week follow-up visit in September 1934 (E. Jacobs 2003).

In the late fall of 1935 Elizabeth again accompanied her husband to the field. Writing to Boas from Siletz (October 28, 1935, MJC), Melville Jacobs reported on his summer's fieldwork. Regarding Elizabeth's work he says: "My wife

Table 1. Summary of Elizabeth D. Jacobs's 1935 Fieldwork

Number of Notebook Pages[a]	Culture group	Consultants' names
857	Upper Coquille	Coquelle Thompson Sr.
186[b]	Chetco	Billy Metcalf Tom MacDonald (?)
26[c]	Upper Umpqua	John Warren Mrs. Jerden (?)[d] Riggs (?)
11	Galice Creek	Hoxie Simmons Nettie West

[a]Some of Elizabeth Jacobs's linguistic notes were recorded on unbound full and half sheets of unlined paper as well as on (approximately) four-by-six-inch note slips. These are not included in the notebook page count.

[b]Linguistic data from three of Jacobs's notebooks (UC Nbs. 109, 110, and 132) are clearly from a southwest Oregon Athabaskan language, but no language or consultant names are indicated. Some of this material may be Chetco from Billy Metcalf. The 186-page total given here does not include these three notebooks.

[c]Melville and Elizabeth Jacobs's short lexicon of Upper Umpqua apparently was sent to Athabaskanist Harry Hoijer at UCLA and never returned. It is not in the MJC at the University of Washington nor is it among the manuscripts Hoijer deposited at the APS Library. My copy is from Victor Golla, who hand-copied the first four pages of the original manuscript in Hoijer's office and photocopied the remaining six pages.

[d]Mrs. Jerden may refer to Clara C. Jourdan, an Umpqua Indian listed on the 1934 Indian census rolls for the Siletz Reservation.

is obtaining some Upper Coquille folktales in English here, and she is also securing some Chetco texts and miscellaneous grammatical data in various southwest Oregon Nadéné dialects. Her phonetics is not yet perfect, but she already seems to have an excellent preliminary picture of the morphology." Her Chetco informant was Billy Metcalf, from whom she recorded approximately sixteen folktale texts in phonetic transcription with interlinear English translation.[10] She also recorded a few pages of Galice Creek linguistic forms from Hoxie Simmons and Nettie West and a small amount of Upper Umpqua linguistic and ethnographic data from John Warren and (possibly) a Mrs. Jerden and someone named Riggs (Seaburg 1982). Melville worked together with his wife on the Galice Creek and Upper Umpqua linguistics (letter from Jacobs to Boas, January 27, 1936, APS). All of Elizabeth Jacobs's fieldwork expenses were paid from the Jacobses' personal funds. (See table 1 for a brief summary of Elizabeth Jacobs's 1935 fieldwork.)

The bulk of Elizabeth Jacobs's 1935 field time was spent obtaining Upper

Coquille ethnography and folklore, in English, from Coquelle Thompson. She probably began her fieldwork with Thompson by eliciting lexical and grammatical forms in the Upper Coquille language. This data was recorded on unbound sheets of paper of several sizes.

After several days of lexical and grammatical elicitation, she asked for a folktale text in the Upper Coquille Athabaskan language. Twice Thompson began a text dictation in the Upper Coquille language; about halfway through the story he finished telling it in English. He simply did not have the patience for the slow process of phonetic text dictation (Elizabeth Jacobs, personal communication, 1975). The rest of the Upper Coquille folklore was recorded in English, with occasional transcriptions of Native words and phrases.

Elizabeth considered her ethnographic work secondary to her folklore collecting. The bulk of her notes comprise myth and folktale texts. As a sample of the kinds of folklore and ethnographic topics Elizabeth recorded in her notes, table 2 provides an overview of such topics in the order they were written in her second Upper Coquille field notebook.

In this notebook slightly more than half the pages (eighty-nine) comprise folklore dictations, while eighty-two pages cover ethnographic topics. Some of the ethnographic discussions occur in the middle of a folktale dictation. For example, in "Coyote and Wolf" Thompson interrupted the flow of the story to describe a chief's pipe. Elizabeth carefully noted such "digressions."

Throughout Elizabeth Jacobs's notebooks one gets the sense that she is following Coquelle Thompson's lead. The notes have a free associative quality to them. For example, in UC notebook 2, page 47, Thompson briefly discusses the Dream Dance. Perhaps in response to a question, Thompson says that dreaming of a ghost didn't bring anyone a power. This discussion of ghosts evidently reminded Thompson of a story, which Elizabeth wrote down and eventually titled "Ghosts Dance in Empty House."

This text was followed immediately by Thompson's personal experience story about *his* encounter with ghosts, which was followed, again apparently without a break, by Thompson's version of the Orpheus tale, titled by Elizabeth "A Man Followed His Wife to the Land of the Dead." Another text, "A Girl Was Reluctant to Marry an Old Man," grew out of a discussion of co-wives, the bride price, negotiating for a wife, marriage, and marriage with older men. Indeed, with one exception, all the oral traditional texts in this notebook relate to the immediate ethnographic topics under discussion.

Table 2. Ethnographic and Folklore Topics Recorded in Jacobs's Upper
Coquille Field Notebook 2

Topic	Notebook pages
Folktale text: "Coyote and Wolf"	1–30

    chief's pipe
    chief's knife
sweathouses
doctoring
pregnancy and childbirth
    umbilical cord and afterbirth
    naming
    breast-feeding
    twins
    cradle
marriage
    purchasing a wife
baby and infant care

| Folktale text: "How Land Came into Being" .... | 36–42 |

death of a child
    rebirth of infants
childhood
sweathouses
    storytelling
cooking
disciplining of children
lullabies
dream dance
dreaming of ghosts

| Historical text: "Ghosts Dance in Empty House" .... | 48–55 |

| Personal experience text: "Coquelle Thompson's Encounter with Ghosts" ...... | 56–60 |

| Folktale text: "A Man Followed His Wife to the Land of the Dead (Orpheus)"... | 61–73 |

ear-piercing
slavery
co-wives
    bride price
    negotiation for a wife
    marriage
        marriage with older men

Table 2 (*continued*)

Table 2 (*continued*)

Topic	Notebook pages
Historical text: "A Woman Shaman Was Killed for Poisoning"	139–43
sending a doctor's poison back to doctor	
Grizzly Bear power	
Historical text: "A Man Was Able to Kill a Grizzly Bear"	144–51
Snake power	
Singing to fix weather	
Personal experience text: "Coquelle Thompson Was Doctored"	153–55
treatment of person killed or wounded in warfare	
preparing bows, arrows, and arrow points for warfare	
burial of warrior	
burial (in general)	
dentalia indicters on grave	
man's wife's grave	
watching over corpse	
treatment of older people	
burial of money, goods	
house construction	
living quarters for multiple wives	
bride behavior	
kinship terms	
gambling	
women's gambling games	
wrestling	
foot races	
shinny	
tattooing	
Historical text: "They gambled"	166–71[a]
village/dialect names	
Coquelle Thompson genealogical information	
placenames/language names	

[a] This text is continued in UC notebook 3, pp. 15–18.

Despite Jacobs's claims to the contrary, it is evident that she initiated at least some of her investigation of ethnographic topics. We know this because Jacobs preserved some of her ethnographic elicitation questions, and it is possible to match questions with material in the notebooks. The following questions represent one page, front and back, from her elicitation lists.[11]

Ever rub body with fir branches? What for? When does boy begin to smoke? would they try to stop him if started earlier?

Do women have to "train," stay away from husbands before getting roots, berries, etc.?

Did a man who had moon-sick daughter hunt, fish? gamble?

People ever put animals blood on gun to make them luckier in hunting?

On hunting trips when women moved camp did men stay with wives? Where everybody sleep? would moon-sick girl be allowed to go?

Sucker? Power? Story? used for food? Ever eat owl?

When people came home with slaves after fighting did they dance?

Person hurt so bad in war, he sure to die—and too big hurry to pack him, what do with him?

Have to change names that only sound little bit like name of deceased?

People ever carry food to grave when go to visit 1st 5 am.'s

Could a widower go on hunting and fishing parties with other men?

If my child died—do I throw food someplace before I eat? no.

Any woman know how to keep from having babies? drink medic[ine]?

Who decided how much fish each family got? Who cut it up—issued it?

Use urine for anything—scare ghosts—? rub boats with feces? When? like flood time?

Could a woman cook rite away after baby born? tend fire?

Did they ever burn each other to see who could stand most pain—warriors test each other in any manner?

People confess all misdeeds before death?

Women have to do anything special when her husband is hunt-

ing? when at war? Does husband of preg. woman hunt? fish? fight?

Ever put anything in fire to get fire to help? Ever talk to fire? Was fire ever a person? Story? Ever feed it?

Cut off hair of slaves? Mark in any way?

get more fish in trap at nite

Anybody else allowed to tend trap in day time?

Did whole bunch ever move camp to dig roots?—Just women go? For how long?—men help pack? Put roots all together or each woman take home her own?

Any leader of women on root digging or berry picking? Go together or meet at grounds?

Did boy keep hide of first deer? Did people come to his house to eat or was meat carried to other houses? Who cut deer?

All the questions are lined through, indicating that she had gone through all of them with Thompson.

Jacobs seldom commented in her fieldnotes on the fieldwork process itself. She only occasionally indicated that some information was in response to a direct question. Completely absent are editorial assessments of the worth, trustworthiness, or validity of the consultant's words. Jacobs seldom stepped outside the role of faithful amanuensis. There is no evidence of bowdlerization. She did not abbreviate descriptions by the use of "etc." She only infrequently made sketches, for example, of house construction and a paddle for harvesting tarweed seeds.

Jacobs tried to faithfully transcribe her consultant's words verbatim, especially in the narratives. Her notes often reflect the voice, if not always the exact words, of the consultant. Sometimes she employed paraphrasing but not to a great extent. There is no evidence that Jacobs wrote up any of her notes while still in the field.

Sound Recordings

Melville and Elizabeth Jacobs were the first anthropologists to make sound recordings of Coquelle Thompson. Thompson had an extensive repertoire of songs, and the Jacobses wanted to make a collection of music recordings that could one day be studied by an ethnomusicologist.

On December 10, 12, 13, and 14, 1935, Melville Jacobs assisted his wife in the recording of twenty-one RCA Victor pre-grooved 10-inch disc recordings from Coquelle Thompson. The recordings represent a variety of song types: Ghost Dance songs, songs from myth and folktale texts, lullabies, songs from a make-doctor dance, gambling songs, dream-power songs, doctoring songs, a pre-hunting sweathouse song, and a love song. The Jacobses also recorded one folktale text about Pitch Ogress (Seaburg 1982:68–72).

Only partial textual documentation for some of the first six records, all made on the first day of recording, has been found. Notes regarding subsequent recordings, from the field notebooks, are annotated with the following types of information: (1) *the song type*, for example, gamble song; (2) *the words to the song* in the Upper Coquille (or other Indian) language together with an English translation; song vocables are also noted; (3) *information about instrumental accompaniment*, for example, "Uses actual k̓əmá clapper in this record"; (4) *the name of the owner of personal songs*; (5) *informant's comments about a song's owner*, for example, "Jim David's dream—that's ghost song that's how they come. Jim David was a fine actor, good actor (ghost songs)"; (6) *extratextual information about a particular person's song*, for example, "Jim David's first song. When he 1st start dreaming"; (7) *geographical provenance*; (8) *musical performance notations*, for example, "After 1st few bars [Coquelle] changed to lower key"; (9) *the context of a folktale song*, for example, "Coy. don't like [Beaver's song]. Coy. Jim mad, give him dickens. Coy. 'What's the matter with you[.] are you drowning. If I take you cross ocean, oh I be shame. That ain't no song, that's sound of people drowning—so I don't take you, you stay home'"; (10) *performance contextual data*, for example, "(Everybody stand for this song, this dance song.) 3, 4 men coming in to dance from tent in corner—They all got whistles, they come in to front, dance past"; and (11) *notes on the recording process*, for example, "(needle put down [on record] after singer commenced song)."[12]

The ten-inch acetate discs were cut on a portable electric phonograph recorder built for Melville Jacobs in 1934 by Philip A. Jacobsen of the Department of General Engineering at the University of Washington with the help of his assistant, Orin Johnston (M. Jacobs 1939:5). A grant-in-aid of $242.50 from the National Research Council paid for construction of the phonograph.

The sound quality of the Coquelle Thompson recordings is uniformly poor, noticeably inferior to the first records Melville Jacobs made in the summer of

1934 with his Coos informant Annie Miner Peterson. The reasons for the difference in quality are not clear.

The Americanist Text Collecting Tradition

As M. Jacobs (1959c), Leeds-Hurwitz and Nyce (1986), Darnell (1990, 1992), and others have noted, the foundation of the Americanist text tradition was the phonetic recording of texts in the Native language with a close translation into English. Occasionally, as in the case of Boas's early Northwest Coast work, English translations were filtered through the intermediate language of Chinook Jargon. Myths, folktales, and other genres of Native American folklore constituted the bulk of texts recorded in this manner.

It was not always possible to get such texts in the Native language. In some cases anthropologists lacked training or facility with phonetic transcription, and in others consultants were unwilling or unable to dictate texts in their Native language. Indeed, some raconteurs may have felt much more comfortable telling stories in English, having done so for many years prior to the arrival of the anthropologists. This seems to have been the case with Coquelle Thompson, who found Jacobs's phonetic transcribing too slow and tedious to complete even a single story in his native language. Thus investigators sometimes had to content themselves with recording texts in English only.

The ideology of Americanist text production, beginning in the 1870s with the work of Albert S. Gatschet and J. Owen Dorsey at the Bureau of Ethnology, may be summarized as follows:

(1) Collecting traditional texts (myths and tales) is one way of constructing a cultural system or totality (for example, "the culture of the Kwakiutl") because such texts can be seen as communal products. The cultural whole is then employed to interpret the texts themselves, for example, Boas's *Tsimshian Mythology* (1916).

(2) The process of transcribing texts fixes them as unchanging objects of study, akin to museum objects, which can be studied and recontextualized at our leisure (Murray 1991:101). Collected texts lose their contingent nature.

(3) Texts are natural objects—because they're traditional and communal— that exist independently of the ethnographer and the Native storyteller. Their essential nature survives the loss of context, performance features, and the voice of the teller.

(4) Native cultures speak in their own words through these collected texts.

Native-language texts preserve aboriginal patterns of expressive content. They reflect a people's world-view, according to Boas, "as free from the bias of the European observer as is possible" (1935:v).

(5) Texts should be recorded in the Native language and should represent verbatim transcriptions, with nothing added or deleted by the ethnographer.

(6) Texts in the Native language are more valuable than texts in English because they provide Native linguistic and stylistic documentation.

(7) Texts in English are subject to contamination by the expressive style of English discourse and the expressive content of the dominant white culture. English texts are of limited value for serious folklore purposes—except as models of cultural breakdown and acculturation.

Jacobs's Text Collecting and Editing Practices

In Melville Jacobs's text publications, he stressed that he did not solicit particular tale types or ethnographic topics from his Indian consultants. Regarding work with a Klikitat Sahaptin speaker, Joe Hunt, Jacobs remarked, "I have not suggested things or stories to dictate; I have asked him to tell what he wished to tell" (1929:243). In a similar vein Jacobs noted that he recorded from his Clackamas Chinook consultant, Victoria Howard, "solely materials which Mrs. Howard offered in text and translation" (1958:2). Such a nondirective approach reflected the Boasian goal of discovering and documenting the native point of view.

In my interviews with Elizabeth Jacobs (Seaburg 1975), she discussed the advantage of a nondirective approach: "It was our way of letting the informant run the show and showing our respect." She noted, "It was their culture, not something we were supposed to dig out. They were telling us how they lived and how they felt." In her first Upper Coquille field notebook, there is little evidence that she was asking for particular stories; in subsequent notebooks or on elicitation question sheets, Elizabeth carefully noted when she had asked for a tale type or a story about a particular character or motif. For example, a set of elicitation question sheets at the back of Upper Coquille notebook 6 (MJC) includes the following notes:

story of steal baby, put rotten wood in cradle? . . .

story of dead people who purchase bride? no . . .
Story about eagle? Mink? powers? . . .

Chipmunk story? flying squirrel? . . .
story of crow marry girl?
———bluejay?
story of woman made a man of milt?
story of coyote & bees?

Presumably, after Coquelle Thompson had volunteered his repertoire of stories, Elizabeth attempted to elicit more texts by means of direct questioning. Sometimes this technique was successful.

In the field Jacobs adhered to the practice of faithful verbatim transcription. Writing in pencil and sometimes employing abbreviated spelling, Jacobs was able to transcribe English very rapidly. She believed she was getting a verbatim or nearly verbatim transcript of Coquelle Thompson's English, and her assessment seems essentially correct. Evidence includes Jacobs's preservation of Thompson's nonstandard grammar ("But nobody come in house"), pronunciation ("'bout," "doin'," "'cause," "every since White people came in"), and lexical choice ("He just get girl once in while, get her knocked up").

Jacobs sometimes elicited the provenance for a story and its title, if it had one, both in the Native language and in English. She transcribed, identified, and typed up about seventy-five myth, folktale, memorate (or personal experience), and historical event narratives.[13] The present collection contains forty-seven of the myths and tales.

Within a year after her fieldwork, Jacobs had edited her Upper Coquille folklore collection for possible publication. The following texts juxtapose copies of her notebook transcriptions (text 1) to her first edited version (text 2) and to her final edited version (text 3).[14]

Text 1: No title

Once a long time ago, one coq. man going to hunt early in a.m. heavy fog. He saw 1 heavy fog coming—he saw an elk, standing right in snakes belly, there in that fog. He scared, not run home— stay there on trail, snake passed him on his way back to ocean. (Don't give him good luck; [ans. to question]) Then that fellow shot his flint arrow into snake in air—it come down right by side hill. He tell down home, "I shoot big snake, I kill him." "Where?" "Well come on, Everybody get ready to come." Well, they all see it.

One old man, who kno law about snakes told this fello. "Now, you killed that snake, don't go in water for 1 year. Even if you cross a little creek they'll get you. Don't drink water—as soon as you drink water a big snake come up, you can only eat acorn soup. Don't drink water. That's the snake law." If that fello tried to take drink <u>way</u> up on mt.—that water drop, drop, he see big snake coming up, he had to run away. So he had to be careful for whole year, never to drink water, never go near creek. He got well punished.

That tc'ənti awful poison for snake—if bone or stone—it won't kill him—that arrow just break. Only that kind of bullets kill that snake. (MJC, UC nb. 5:42–43)

Text 2: A Man Shot a Large Snake

A long time ago, one Coquille man went early in the morning to hunt. There was a heavy fog. He saw an elk, standing right in the middle of a large snake's belly, in the thick of the fog. He was frightened, but he did not run home; he remained there on the trail. That fog passed him on its way back to the ocean. Then that fellow shot his flint arrow into the snake that hung there in the air. It came down there on the side hill.

Down at home the man told, "I shot a large snake and killed him." "Where?" "Well, come on, I will show you." Every one made ready and went there. They all saw that dead snake.

One old man who knew the law concerning snakes told this fellow, "Now, since you have killed that snake, do not go into the water for one year. If you so much as cross a small creek, they will get you. Do not drink water, as soon as you drink water a large snake will come up; you must have merely acorn soup for your thirst; do not drink water. That is the law concerning snakes." If that man attempted to take a drink, far up on the mountain, that water would drop lower, drop lower, and he would see a large snake arising in it, and had to run away from there. So he was forced to be careful for an entire year, and never to drink water, never to go near a creek during that time. He was well punished.

Elizabeth Jacobs explained to me (personal communication, 1975) that after she had edited and typed up the folktale collection, her husband told her that she had done too much rewriting. He suggested that she reedit the texts, maintaining closer fidelity to the notebook transcription. She completely reedited the texts in compliance with his suggestions. The following text is her final reediting of the story.

Text 3: A Man Shot a Large Snake

Once a long time ago, a Coquille man was going to hunt, early in the morning in a heavy fog. He saw that heavy fog coming. He saw an elk standing in a snake's belly, right there in that fog. He was scared, but he didn't run home. He stayed there on the trail and the snake passed him on its way back to the ocean. Then that fellow shot his flint arrow into the snake in the fog. It fell right down by the side hill.

He told down home, "I shot a big snake. I killed him." "Where?" "Well, come on. Everybody get ready to come." So they all saw it. One old man who knew the law about snakes told this man, "Now, you killed that snake; you mustn't go in the water for one year. Even if you cross a little creek, they'll get you. Don't drink water. As soon as you drink water a big snake will come up. You can only eat acorn soup. Don't drink water. That's the snake law." If that fellow had tried to take a drink way up on the mountain, the water would drop, drop and he would see a big snake coming up. He would have to run away. So he had to be careful for a whole year, never to drink water (and) never go near a creek. He got well punished.

Flint is an awful poison to snakes. If the arrowhead is bone or stone, it won't kill it. The arrow would just break. Only flint will kill that snake.

This final text version illustrates some of Elizabeth's editing practices, which can be summarized as follows: she (1) determined what constituted a text and what the boundaries of that text were; (2) arranged the text into paragraphs; (3) interpreted the text by adding words and phrases to clarify Thompson's sometimes laconic descriptions; (4) edited out or relegated to notes asides or metatextual explanatory comments; for example, in the text presented here she deleted "(Don't give him good luck; [ans. to question])"; (5) added explanatory notes; (6) supplied titles when they were not provided by the consultant;

(7) substituted synonyms for lexical items; (8) edited the consultant's grammar to conform to readers' standard English expectations; (9) completed sentence fragments; (10) often but not consistently edited out Native-language words and phrases; for example, in the quoted text she substituted the English gloss "flint" for the Upper Coquille word; and (11) smoothed over false starts and other anomalies associated with spoken rather than written English.

Two further examples illustrate Elizabeth's editing out of narrator asides and postcontact "intrusions." In many of the Coyote stories, Coquelle Thompson refers to the character as "Coyote Jim." After telling one of the Coyote stories, Thompson explained the usage (MJC, UC nb. 1:69): "Started calling Coyote Jim every since White people came in 'cause White people didn't understand Coyote was person. So they tacked on '*Jim*.' They really just call him Coyote." Despite the narrator's explanation, Jacobs deleted "Jim."

In a passage from the folktale "Panther and Deer Woman" (MJC, UC nb. 5:88), Thompson says, "Then Panther told that Sunday Brother Wildcat . . . he told him 'What you doin' layin' round house all day?'" In the middle of this sentence, Elizabeth wrote in parentheses, "Sunday Man is epithet for ugly person. Indians call government or disliked person 'Sunday Man.'" In the edited text she kept the phrase "Sunday Brother" but again excised the narrator's explanation.[15]

Ideological concerns clearly motivated some of Elizabeth Jacobs's editorial decisions. She wanted the texts to be accorded the same respect given to written literature. William Clements's explanation of Henry Schoolcraft's editing practice can also be applied to Jacobs's work: if "Native American oral performances were indeed literature, they should evince the qualities of literature—even if some of those qualities had to be added by the textmaker" (1990:186). When I asked Elizabeth during an interview in 1975 why she had changed Thompson's grammar, she replied that she didn't want readers' negative responses to nonstandard English to influence their judgment of the stories' worth.

John P. Harrington's Text-Collecting Practices

Another anthropologist recorded stories in longhand from Coquelle Thompson: John Peabody Harrington. To provide a context for evaluating Jacobs's text production practices, it is useful to compare briefly her texts with those Harrington recorded in longhand from Thompson in 1942.

In December 1939 John P. Harrington visited Melville and Elizabeth Jacobs in Seattle (Mills 1981:81). He made extensive notes based on his conversations with the Jacobses (JPH, reel 030). It was probably during these conversations that Harrington learned the names and locations of many of the Indian consultants he and his assistant, John P. Marr, worked with between 1940 and 1943.

Like Jacobs, Harrington also recorded texts from Coquelle Thompson in English. There is no evidence in the notes that he attempted to write out the texts phonetically. Harrington recorded approximately thirty-five stories, less than half the size of Jacobs's edited corpus. A number of versions of Harrington's texts were also recorded earlier by Jacobs, providing us with excellent data for a comparative study.

Harrington's corpus of texts presents the same kinds of challenges as any collection of unedited fieldnotes: problems of legibility, meanings of shorthand abbreviations and symbols, consecutive sequencing of the notes, and so on. When working with Harrington's linguistic notes, I have seldom had difficulties with his handwriting—especially compared with the handwriting of Franz Boas or Edward Sapir. But Harrington was clearly writing these stories down rapidly, and this resulted in a number of undecipherable forms. In this respect Harrington's texts present more difficulties than Jacobs's texts do. The more one works with Harrington's texts, the clearer his abbreviations become, for example, "upr" for "upriver" and "dr" for "downriver," and the like. Harrington's pagination is not always to be trusted—as the editor realized when arranging the papers for microfilming—and some of the pages may be out of order.

One of the questions that arises in working with Harrington's (and Jacobs's) text collections is that of voice. Whose voice is represented in Harrington's textual notes, Harrington's or Coquelle Thompson's or some combination of both? Whose voice dominates? Is there any principled way one can separate the voice of the anthropologist from the voice of the narrator? Of what value are Harrington's texts for purposes of stylistic analysis?

Harrington's voice is particularly evident in lexical choice, in certain syntactic constructions, and in the relative lack of nonstandard grammar. Coquelle Thompson's voice is manifest also in lexical and phrasal selections, and in recurring similes, in descriptive precision, and narrative strategies. I will examine Harrington first and then Thompson.

In comparing Harrington's with Jacobs's text transcriptions from Coquelle

Thompson, we find lexical differences. For example, Harrington's texts include words, underlined in the following examples, that do not occur in Jacobs's transcriptions:

(1) "'What is he packing, what is he packing?' _ejaculated_ people of the big town as they passed through" (JPH reel 027, frame 0247).[16]

(2) "The two girls told their father, 'We were _scrutinized_ and the woman took in that we were wearing camas'" (JPH, reel 027, frame 0243).

(3) "The one who hollered was running _hitherward_" (JPH, reel 027, frame 0231).

(4) "The corpses they placed together _preparatory_ to carrying them home" (JPH, reel 027, frame 0232).

(5) "The man went out and _bethought_ himself and came back quick" (JPH, reel 027, frame 0352).

(6) "And all the people were _congregating_ outside" (JPH, reel 027, frame 0298).

We also find complex syntactic constructions in the Harrington texts that are not apparent in Jacobs's transcriptions. They are difficult to describe, but here are a few examples:

(7) "These were poor girls and they fixed themselves up with camas having three or four of these, tail up, hanging on upper lip from nose _septum_ and more in their hair" (JPH, reel 027, frame 0243). (Note also the use of the word _septum_—undoubtedly a Harrington lexical choice.)

(8) "That woman cut the little devil's head off, her first, then each of the brothers in turn—she was a _doctress_" (JPH, reel 027, frame 0435). (Again, note a Harrington word: _doctress._)

(9) "They fixed up to fight, for the devil girl had told that the man had at the beginning of a month he had threatened to kill all the bears including father and mother—and that was why the devil-girl had been afraid to tattle for a month" (JPH, reel 027, frame 0435).

(10) "The man thought he would get in a boat that came across

from the land of the dead (Japan) and the man was bailing its
water out with a big abalone-shell, which shell he admired"
(JPH, reel 027, frame 0305).

(*11*) *"There were two flying men who in the war jump 50 yards*
when the enemy set fire to the sweathouse out through the
burning door and jumped into the middle of the river" (JPH,
reel 027, frame 0296).

Finally, compared with Jacobs, Harrington records fewer instances of non-standard grammatical forms such as:

(*12*) *"Everything was stout in them days" (JPH, reel 027, frame*
0288).

(*13*) *"'My spear, you won't kill nobody; people will use you to*
make a living'" (JPH, reel 027, frame 0289).

The Voice of Thompson

On the other hand, Harrington's texts also include words and phrases that often recur in Jacobs's transcriptions and certainly represent Thompson's voice. For example,

(*1*) *"Little Man told him how he was a good hand to run on the*
ocean" (JPH, reel 027, frame 0035).

(*2*) *"Now he studied: 'What am I going to do?'" (JPH, reel 027,*
frame 0042). (The word studied is also used to describe a char-
acter who is ritually preparing for a spirit-power encounter.)

(*3*) *"Those that caught hold of him were not stout enough" (JPH,*
reel 027, frame 0232).

(*4*) *"The two old father and mother chewed up human bones like*
carrots" (JPH, reel 027, frame 0435). (This is typical of the kinds
of similes also used by Thompson in Jacobs's texts.)

The "Oh" interjection is a frequently occurring initial word in both the Jacobs and the Harrington texts, for example,

(*5*) *"'Oh, I want to pay you.' 'Oh, I don't want you to pay me.*
I just want to help you.' Oh, she was glad" (JPH, reel 027, frame
0292).

One of the stylistic characteristics in Thompson's dictations to Jacobs—also found in Harrington's texts—is descriptive precision with regard to numbers, time, and measurement. For example,

(6) *"Then that man packed in deer meat at about <u>10 o'clock"</u>* (JPH, reel 027, frame 0433).

(7) *"That woman was pretty good for about <u>six months</u>"* (JPH, reel 027, frame 0436).

(8) *"'You will get away. You will run by here where I am, only <u>four feet</u> ahead of her'"* (JPH, reel 027, frame 0438).

Yet another example of Thompson's voice can be seen in the extensive use of dialogue in the stories—a narrative strategy found in both text collections. It is in such "reported speech" that I believe Harrington is most faithfully recording Coquelle Thompson's speech. To aid in comparing their text-making practices, first Jacobs's, then Harrington's version of the same text are reproduced verbatim in appendix I.

Some of the differences between Jacobs's and Harrington's text collections reflect more than the stylistic differences of the recorders. Some are undoubtedly the result of different dynamics between the consultant and the investigators. There is evidence that Coquelle Thompson may have been telling a story in a certain way to Harrington because he was a man. In a text recorded by Jacobs titled "Big Head (Cannibal)," Thompson says: "His face and head were all right (not eaten) but everything below his neck the flesh was all gone, just bones. (I don't know about his guts, it doesn't say.)" In the Harrington-recorded rendition, Thompson says: "Then he, already nothing but bones on his legs and arms but only his snake, I guess he could not eat his snake somehow, and his head, a big head."

In Harrington's "Wren and His Grandmother" story, Thompson has the people saying that Wren *fucked* his grandmother, while in the Jacobs version Thompson says, "Someone upriver has been staying with his grandma" (UC nb. 4:96). In another text Harrington reports that Grizzly Woman's little sister "eats only shit," while in the Jacobs version she eats guts, and so on.

Some of the differences between the two text collections probably reflect a certain permissible flexibility in story form: Harrington reports that "[t]he titles of myths are as variable in exact wording as the texts themselves are" (JPH, reel 027, frame 0211).

On the whole Harrington's versions are not as long or probably as well told as Jacobs's versions of the same stories transcribed seven years earlier. Some of the Harrington texts are somewhat confused and difficult to follow in places. They are, nonetheless, a very valuable collection and deserve to be published for several reasons.

First, Harrington recorded a few texts that Jacobs did not get. Second, Harrington's texts are quite useful for sorting out the *voices* of the storyteller as well as of the recorder by providing a basis of comparison with the Jacobs collection. Third, Harrington's texts vis-à-vis Jacobs's illustrate changes in the same story told on different occasions by the same consultant. This situation is rare for our collections of oral traditions from western Oregon. Also, after a story's telling, Harrington sometimes asked for clarification or more details about some aspect of the story, providing a Native perspective or exegesis that Jacobs did not often get. Consider the following example:

> *I ask details about Little Man on ocean. He plays shinny—with shinny stick. He played on the ocean, no one played against him. Thompson asked his father in sweathouse this story, and whom he played against. The ocean waves come quick and mean, and Little Man with a stick played against them.*
>
> *"My father said Little Man is alive yet, he knows the ocean. We don't." (JPH, reel 027, frames 0362–63)*

Although neither collection is *ideal* for a study of Coquelle Thompson's oral narrative style in English, Harrington's valuable collection certainly helps in sorting out the dancer from the dance.

Seaburg's Editing Practices

Editing Jacobs's transcriptions of Coquelle Thompson's stories for publication was more of a challenge than I had anticipated. I had originally planned merely to lightly edit Jacobs's second transcript of the texts, described earlier. As I began to compare her typescript with the notebook originals, however, I decided to restore the texts closer to the original transcriptions, with the goal of preserving as much of Thompson's voice as possible. By "voice" I mean his nonstandard English grammar, pronunciation, lexical choices, and syntax; Native-language words and phrases; explanatory asides; and the like. I had hoped to intrude on the stories as little as possible, but I eventually realized that it was impossible *not* to intrude on the texts. Every editorial decision is an act of interpretation just as much as every listening to or reading of a story is an act of interpretation—and unavoidably so.

One format I experimented with was versification, arranging the text into lines and groups of lines similar—but not identical—to the format Dell Hymes (2003) has done much to popularize. Two of the stories in this collection are arranged in lines: "Panther and Deer Woman" and "Moon." I kept the texts very close to the way Jacobs wrote them in her field notebook, adding punctuation and several words in square brackets for clarification, translating the Native-language words, and in the "Moon" text moving them to endnotes. None of Thompson's words was deleted.

My division into lines and groups of lines is somewhat impressionistic. Each sentence gets a separate line. Some sentences are broken into phrases or clauses, and each phrase/clause is indented. Various discourse markers, such as changes of scene, the introduction of a new character, and transitional terms ("Now," "Then," "After that," and the like) are used to group lines into units. This format has advantages: it highlights features of discourse such as parallelism and repetition; it draws attention away from nonstandard grammar; and it slows the reader down and encourages her to read the text aloud. Some readers, though, have remarked that the texts sound like a pidgin English that does not rise to the level of literature. Of more importance for my purposes, the line format requires twice as much space to print without clearly offering a more accurate reflection of actual oral performance.

Thus, I ended up using a modified prose format for most of the stories. Each change of speaker begins a new paragraph. The beginnings of other paragraphs are signaled by discourse markers, changes of scene, introduction of new characters, and so on. Words and phrases enclosed in square brackets in the texts presented here indicate where Native words have been translated into English and the original phonetic transcription moved to an endnote; where words have been added to turn a sentence fragment into a complete sentence (although to avoid a distracting proliferation of brackets, not every *a*, *of*, or *the* is so indicated); and where assumed cultural knowledge or explanations of potentially confusing or ambiguous phrasing have been added. Verb tenses have been made consistent. Except in a very few necessary cases, none of Thompson's words has been deleted from the texts.

My choice of formatting represents a space somewhere between presenting

Thompson's voice exactly as transcribed by Jacobs at the one extreme and silently creating a Standard English text at the other. Different kinds of formatting require different editorial choices, and every choice is a matter of interpretation. There is no one right way to represent oral traditions in writing. This format creates a readable story accessible to a wide range of readers/listeners while also capturing a feel for Thompson's narrative voice and style.[17]

2. An Upper Coquille Athabaskan Cultural Sketch

Two vexing questions that confront the cultural outsider when reading or listening to another culture's oral literature are How do these stories relate to or represent the culture of the people who once told them or continue to tell them? How do the events that occur in the tale world—the world created within the stories themselves—relate to the world of the storytellers, their life world? In some cases the stories reflect well what we know about the culture independent of the stories: certain social relationships, cultural values, behaviors, and feelings. Clearly, not all aspects of a people's culture find their way into the oral traditions, but many do. The primary goal of this chapter, then, is to introduce the reader to some of the principal features of Upper Coquille Athabaskan life, customs, and beliefs, indicating in the process selected texts where these features seem to be reflected.[1] I will postpone discussing follow-up questions such as why some things are represented and others omitted or distorted until chapter 4.

The following sketch of Upper Coquille Athabaskan culture is based primarily on Elizabeth Jacobs (1935) and Philip Drucker (1937), to a lesser extent on Cora Du Bois (1939), and on my own extrapolations from the oral traditions. Coquelle Thompson was the primary expert witness for each of these investigators during their research on the Siletz Reservation. Drucker also worked for about one week with one other Upper Coquille consultant, Nellie Lane. While Du Bois was conducting ethnohistory with a number of individuals, Jacobs and Drucker were engaged in salvage or memory ethnography and were necessarily dependent on the experiences and memory of one elderly man. Much of the material that Thompson provided these investigators fits regional cultural patterns reported for other culture groups in the southwestern Oregon–northwestern California area (Barnett 1937, Drucker 1937). Some of Thompson's observations do not fit. One wonders if such differences represent aboriginal cultural differences, historical changes resulting from the disruptive influx of non-Indians into southwestern Oregon from about 1850 on, or the specific life experiences of an individual consultant. We may never know. What *is* clear is that without the ethnographic notes and oral traditions that Thompson so willingly provided the visiting anthropologists, our knowledge of Upper Coquille Athabaskan culture would be virtually nil.

The Upper Coquille Athabaskan language, formerly spoken in southwestern Oregon, belongs to the Pacific branch of the geographically widespread Athabaskan-Eyak-Tlingit family and is related to Athabaskan languages once, in some cases still, spoken in Canada, Alaska, Washington, Oregon, California, and the American Southwest (Mithun 1999).

Subsistence and Division of Labor

As throughout the Northwest Coast culture area, there was a general sexual division of labor among the Upper Coquille people. Women dug several different varieties of camas bulbs, returning to the same locations year after year. They also dug Indian carrots, fern roots, and other root vegetables. They picked salmonberries, strawberries, and other varieties of berries and harvested acorns, tarweed seeds (tɬ'u·dɛ), and hazelnuts. Acorns and camas are mentioned frequently in the stories, suggesting that they were staple foods. Women cut and smoke-dried fish, deer, and elk meat and processed these and other preservable foods for winter storage. On a daily basis they gathered firewood for the cookhouse, carried water, cooked meals, and looked after small children. They also wove a variety of utility baskets and mats (E. Jacobs 1935).

Men hunted deer and elk, employing a variety of hunting methods, including snares and pitfalls on deer and elk runways. With the help of specially trained and highly prized dogs, they drove deer or elk into water, where they were shot or clubbed from canoes. Game animals were also stalked with bow and arrow.

Men used weirs, nets, basket traps, and harpoons to fish for Chinook and Coho salmon, trout, and lamprey. They cured hides, made nets and other fishing equipment, and built canoes, cookhouses, and sweathouses.[2] Men burned berry patches in the fall. Every so often brush was burned out of hunting places and hazelnut areas (E. Jacobs 1935; see "Coyote" text). They grew Native tobacco on specially prepared and fenced-in grounds, gathered firewood for the sweathouse, and looked after and trained older boys (E. Jacobs 1935). In the tale world of "A Man Grows a Snake in a Bucket," a headman demonstrates the ritual use of tobacco in his pursuit of whales. The ritual predawn gathering of wood for the sweathouse is mentioned in several stories, for example, "Pitch Woman."

Food anxieties and fears about famine are projected onto a number of stories in this collection, including "Panther and Deer Woman," "A Man Grows a Snake in a Bucket," "Skunk," and "Coyote Jim." The importance of sharing food resources with others, especially during lean times, is a cultural value demonstrated in "A Man Grows a Snake in a Bucket," "Coyote Jim and His Neighbor Crane," and several other texts.

Structures and Transportation

Paralleling the sexual division of labor were gender distinct residences. Men and boys slept together in small, semisubterranean, earth-covered sweathouses. Larger villages might have two or more sweathouses. Here the men sweated morning and evening, then swam in a nearby stream. In the morning boys had to get up, go for a swim, then sit on top of the sweathouse while the men sweated inside. An older man built the sweathouse fire; he was the "boss," supervising the gathering and drying of the firewood and the sweating itself (E. Jacobs 1935). The sweathouse was a site for telling stories, instructing the young boys, and ritually preparing for long life, acquiring wealth, and good luck in hunting, gambling, and other efforts whose outcomes were uncertain. Ritualized smoking/speaking in the sweathouse is emphasized in such stories as "A Man Grows a Snake in a Bucket." Sweathouses are also the scenes of attacks and warfare in several stories, such as "Mean Warrior."

Women, infants, and young children lived and slept in the living or cookhouse, cedar plank–constructed dwellings that served as a center for food preparation, consumption, preservation, and storage and as a general work area for men and women. When a man wanted to sleep with his wife, he slept with her in the cookhouse; the sweathouse was strictly off limits to women. The plank living house consisted of "rectangular gabled structures over a shallow pit, with roof and walls of cedar planks. The space between the double front wall was, as usual [in the region], used as a woodshed. The outer doorway was closed by a sliding door; . . . Houses of grass thatch were used at summer fishing camps" (Drucker 1937:279). Some of the larger cookhouses may have been twenty by thirty feet in size.

Two types of canoe were employed: the Yurok-Tolowa-Rogue River "blunt-ended dugout" and a "double-pointed dugout" made either by the Upper Co-quilles themselves or traded from the Coosans (Drucker 1937:279–80).

Social Organization

Upper Coquille social stratification was more flexible than among the more northerly Northwest Coast groups. Each Upper Coquille village had a headman or chief and his immediate family, "the well-to-do, the poor, and a small num-ber of captured or purchased slaves" and their offspring (M. Jacobs 1959d:16). The responsibilities of a headman included organizing work teams, negotiating with strangers, conducting "slave and punitive" raids on other villages, arbi-trating inter- and intravillage disputes, levying fines for various social infrac-tions, and generally overseeing "the lives of everyone in his settlement" (M. Jacobs 1959d:17). The headmen of "A Man Grows a Snake in a Bucket" and "Panther and Deer Woman" model exemplary upper-class behavior by sharing their recent acquisition of food resources with neighboring villages during a time of famine.

The position of headman was inherited through the father's line, "subject to village consensus on the wealth reserves and personality of the heir" (Miller and Seaburg 1990:583). As elsewhere on the Northwest Coast, wealth was the key to a headman's lineage: it allowed him to have more than one wife and to purchase slaves. Indeed, the "hallmark of a chief seems to have been that he was involved in all financial transactions as the donor of treasure, as an arbitra-tor, and as the recipient in a division of any acquired wealth" (Miller and Sea-burg 1990:583). In several stories in this collection (e.g., "Little Man," "Snake and Money," "Gambler and Snake"), when a man becomes wealthy through a wealth-supernatural encounter, invariably the first thing he does is to share his newly found wealth with his headman.

Wealth items included dentalium shells, flints, and red-headed woodpecker scalps. Different sizes of dentalia were named; the larger the shell, the more valuable it was. Shells were also strung in strands of ten and valued according to the length of the strand (Drucker 1937:280, 273). Thompson noted in an aside in the "Snake and Money" text: "Each length [of shell] had to be exactly matched. [Ones] a little shorter in one pile, [ones] a little longer in one pile—lots of work." A persistent theme in Upper Coquille oral traditions is the acquisition of wealth-giving powers, especially the ability to be successful in gambling, either through ritual preparation or by means of a wealth encounter experience.

Women had lower status in Upper Coquille culture as evidenced by the bride price in marriage transactions, the institution of being half-married, and the confinement of "females . . . to rather narrowly domestic" activities until after menopause (M. Jacobs 1959d:16–17). Indeed, the stories reflect an overwhelmingly androcentric perspective on Upper Coquille Athabaskan life.

Life Cycle

A midwife or female shaman attended a baby's birth. "The midwife took the baby, cut the [umbilical] cord with an heirloom flint knife, and washed the baby using a deer tail and warm water. The afterbirth was put into a split sapling. . . . [A] man pierced the nasal septum and each ear in three places when the baby was a week old" (Miller and Seaburg 1990:584).

Babies received a nickname after five days and a "good name" at ten years of age. This latter name had belonged to a "paternal relative of the same sex" who had been deceased for at least a year. A boy's first kill was distributed to each household in the village. Similarly, a girl distributed to everyone the first acorns and berries she had gathered (Miller and Seaburg 1990:584).

There were no puberty rites for adolescent boys. In contrast, "[a]t puberty a girl was secluded . . . 10 days on her bed platform. She wore her finery, used moss menstrual pads, a shell scratcher attached to her wrist to avoid touching her hair and skin, and ate only dry food for a year afterward. She swam early and late each day. Her father could not gamble, hunt, or fish at this time" (Miller and Seaburg 1990:585).

Marriage was an arrangement between families that encouraged alliances and served to preserve or enhance their prestige and make claims to offspring. Although marriage was not primarily an economic transaction, "to be respectable a woman had to be purchased in marriage." If their mother had not been paid for, children were considered illegitimate. Ideally the parents of the bride and the groom arranged the marriage.

> *If the parents, the chief, and a man "who knew dentalia" approved, the bride with her family and chief went to the groom's village after five days, gave half the bride price to the groom's father, and held a feast with acorn soup. The bride gave her mother-in-law a fine buckskin dress decorated with shell beads. The bride slept in the home and the groom in the sweathouse. Both sets of parents exchanged gifts and foods. The male members of the families of the groom and bride exchanged their weapons and clothes. The next night the bride and groom slept together in a corner bed platform of the house on a bearskin. (Miller and Seaburg 1990:585)*

A man could have as many wives as he could afford to pay the bride price for and support. Polygynous households are valorized in the oral traditions as signs of wealth and high social status, with myth and tale actors acquiring five or ten wives—undoubtedly a case of pattern number and wish-fulfillment trumping social reality. In only one or two texts are the drawbacks of polygynous households revealed, for example, spousal jealousy in the myths "Frog Woman" and "Brown Bear and Grizzly Bear."

Marriage variations included the levirate, where a woman married her deceased husband's brother; the sororate, where a widower married his deceased wife's sister; and the half-marriage, involving "a rich couple purchasing a husband to live with their daughter in her own home village" (Miller and Seaburg 1990:585). That such half-marriages were stigmatized is clearly demonstrated in the story "Raccoon."

An Upper Coquille man confessed his wrongdoings to his wife or son before dying. As a result of his confession, if he didn't die right away, his family was obliged to make a settlement payment. When a person died, a nonrelative washed the face; women tended women, men tended men. Before the corpse was lowered into the grave, an old man "who knew how," perhaps a formulist, would quietly talk in the dead person's ear. After he talked, the attendants lowered and raised the corpse five times, then placed it in the ground. A man's treasures were buried with him. The deceased's soul remained in the grave for five days before it crossed the ocean (E. Jacobs 1935). An oral traditional basis for this last belief is the story "A Man Followed His Wife to the Land of the Dead (Orpheus)."

Shamans

Perhaps the second most powerful individual in Upper Coquille society, after the headman, was the shaman or Indian doctor. Although both men and women could become shamans, women could doctor only after menopause, as was true for female shamans throughout the Northwest Coast. Many Upper Coquille shamans were women. "The object of their medical treatment was the removal of a 'pain': a tiny living object sharply pointed at both ends and holding in its midsection the blood it had sucked from the patient" (Miller and Seaburg 1990:583). Shamans were paid for their services. Interestingly, compared to headmen, shamans play only a small role in the oral traditions from Coquelle Thompson. Two myth texts with shamans as minor actors include "Raccoon and His Grandmother" and "Panther and the Grizzly Bears."

Spirit powers came to individuals in dreams, and a shaman's powers included "Eel, Big Snake, Dog, Knife, Bullet, Otter, or birds (Hawk, Flicker, Hummingbird). Coyote was the best power and Grizzly Bear the most dangerous. A person might have shamanistic powers for years before they finally made him ill" (Miller and Seaburg 1990:584). The only cure for this spiritual illness was the public acknowledgment of his or her powers in an initiation ceremony known as the Make-Doctor Dance.

Other people who were "gifted with specific shamanistic abilities" by their spirit powers included those with the ability to cure dog and rattlesnake bites, to "talk to medicines and herbs for remedies and love-charming," to cure war wounds, and to call forth South Wind. Other spiritual specialists included those with "the power of the spoken word or spell, sometimes called a formulist" or a ritualist. An important function of a ritualist was to conduct the cleansing rite of gravediggers and those who had handled the corpse in preparation for burial. Spell power normally was inherited but could also be purchased (Miller and Seaburg 1990:584). Formulists or ritualists do not play a role, even as minor actors, in the oral traditions in this collection.[3]

Games and Ceremonials

Women—and most likely also men—played a popular stick-and-ball game known as shinny. Women also played a game using four long, split sticks that were shot like dice. People also enjoyed foot races and a javelin-like pole-throwing game (E. Jacobs 1935). The most prestigious game was the stick (guessing) game, played by men only. Upper Coquille oral traditions suggest that considerable time and care went into ritual preparation for luck in these stick game gambling contests, which could continue for several days.

The number five and its multiples were the dominant pattern or ritual numbers for the Upper Coquille as for other groups in the Southwest Oregon–Northwest California area. Aboriginal rites included the ritual eating of the first five or ten Chinook salmon and a Lamprey Dance celebrating the catching of the first lampreys. After the killing of a bear, "a feast had to be given. All the meat was cooked at once, and had to be eaten then and there. It must never be dried. The skull was not saved, however, and the hide was dressed for use as a robe, etc." (Drucker 1937:281). Rituals also included feasts and gift giving at the birth of a child, the child's naming, a boy's first animal kill, a girl's puberty, war, and death, and in the "celebration of the Make-Doctor Dance for new shamans" (Miller and Seaburg 1990:585). These ritualized events seldom appear in Upper Coquille Athabaskan myths and tales.

When a person dreamed something repeatedly (e.g., of dead people), he had to sing what he dreamed "in front of all the people" in what was referred to as a Dream Dance. "If the song [was] good enough, the people dance[d] with it for five nights." If someone tried to conceal the fact of his dreaming, he became sick, and a shaman was called in to find out what was wrong. The shaman "told the sick man he was hiding a song and he had better give a dance the next night. After the dance, the sick man felt better. Dreamers of songs had no curing power" (Du Bois 1939:34–35). Anyone could hold a Dream Dance. Every month or so there might be one (E. Jacobs 1935). Although Dream Dances apparently predated reservation times, they seem to have been used "as a vehicle not only for the Ghost Dance doctrine but also for its subsequent outgrowths," such as the Feather Dance (Du Bois 1939:34).

The importance of dreaming as a source of knowledge and power can be seen in stories such as "A Man Grows a Snake in a Bucket," "Panther and Deer Woman," and "Pitch Woman."

Warfare

Wars between neighboring groups were precipitated primarily by feuds or by the need to settle uncompensated injuries or to avenge murder or wrongful deaths by shamans. Some men might prepare for fighting by dodging headless arrows shot at them by fellow villagers. "If you are a good dodger, no arrow, nothing touches you" (E. Jacobs 1935). Tactics such as ambushes and surprise attacks on sweathouses, as reported for the Tututni (Drucker 1937:274), were probably employed by the Upper Coquille people as well. Fighting and warfare occur repeatedly in Thompson's stories, for example, "Moon," "Mean Warrior," "Panther and the Grizzly Bears," and "Wren and His Grandmother."

Warriors performed a war dance before going to war and when they returned home, and people remained vigilant against a possible counterattack. To settle the fighting each group hired negotiators—preferably "good speakers" who were not related to either party in the dispute—to meet with both sides and mediate a settlement payment. "If the claimants were not satisfied with the settlement, one of them kicked the fire to signal the start of a fight between the sides. They fought until the arbitrators stopped it and negotiated the amount of treasure each side had to supply" (Miller and Seaburg 1990:586).

Cosmology and World-View

Only portions or aspects of Upper Coquille Athabaskan cosmology are explicitly expressed in the oral traditions.[4] Occasionally anthropologists' ethnographic notations supplement such data. The creation of land and women and the peopling of this world are described in "How Land Came into Being." A catastrophic flooding of the world and its gradual repopulation when the flooding recedes constitutes the main expressive content of "The Flood." "Moon" describes Coyote's successful battle against the Moon people in order to shorten the number of months in the year to twelve. Sun is a man who packs dead people in his daily travels across the sky. His home is underground at night. "Star" explains the creation of several stars and constellations. Several stories describe the transformation of dangerous myth-era actors into harmless flora, fauna, and tools utilized by today's people.

The land of the dead is described in unusual detail in Thompson's "A Man Followed His Wife to the Land of the Dead (Orpheus)," with briefer references to the dead and their abode found in several other texts. In an ethnographic note Thompson alludes to the land from which babies came. Besides the land of the dead and the land of babies, there is a land across the ocean. In "Coyote and God" Coyote and his followers travel across the ocean to the land of God and succeed in securing fire, fish, and berries for the world of the animal people and for future human beings.[5] Apparently if one travels far enough across the ocean, one ends up in Sky Country, as shown in the "Star" and the "Moon" texts. The Sky Country sometimes seems conflated with the land of the dead ("Star") and sometimes with a Christian (?) notion of heaven ("Coyote Jim"). Thompson's stories lacked the "arrow chain ladder to the Sky Country" motif, widely distributed elsewhere in Northwest Indian oral traditions.

Apparently the Upper Coquille Athabaskan language had only one word, ts'əsda, "story," to refer either to myths or to tales set in more recent times.[6] Some of the stories in this collection take place in a time that clearly pre-dates the advent of Indian people; in these stories the actors are predominantly animals, plants, or objects with human or humanlike characteristics and oc-casional human beings who are not identified as flora, fauna, or objects. Other stories involve humans—that is, Indian people—but may also involve nonhu-man people, such as Pitch Women. One is tempted to call the former texts myths and the latter tales. However, it is uncertain how the Upper Coquille Athabaskans categorized their stories into genres.

Along with the more familiar animal people, such as Coyote, Panther, Griz-zly Bear, Frog, and Raccoon, this collection introduces perhaps less familiar nonhuman people, such as Pitch Woman, Little Person, Mountain People, Sea Wolves, and the interesting unicorn-like animal, Hollering-like-a-Person.[7] No doubt such nonhuman people were as real as deer or elk to the southwestern Oregon Athabaskans.[8]

The following comments by Melville Jacobs on Clackamas world-view de-scribe well my understanding of a general southwestern Oregon Athabaskan world-view pattern. Jacobs argues that more important than origin myths, cos-mology, or so-called trickster-transformer figures for comprehending Clacka-mas world-view

> was the ideology of relationships of people and kin, major arti-facts, foods, and spirit-powers. These linked like a chain welded by intense feelings of mutual belonging. People, artifacts, foods, and animistic supernaturals needed, wanted, and upon occasion effected helpful relationships with each other. But the role of in-dividual people—their initiative, courage, potential for maturity, and cleanliness—was the decisive factor in bringing about such relationships. Self-identity and props to feeling of personal worth and security were not located in cosmology, least of all in a deity or pantheon of great supernaturals.

The Clackamas—like the southwestern Oregon Athabaskans—lived in "a concrete world of kin, kin in the broadest sense, in a big chain or pattern" (M. Jacobs 1959b:197).

Value Ideals

Values can be defined as "beliefs about the desirability or quality of . . . things" (Thomas 2001:137). As Melville Jacobs (1959b:187) found in his analysis of the Clackamas Chinook oral literature corpus from Victoria Howard, values or ethical principles are also "not often explicit in the stories" told by Coquelle Thompson. Two noticeable exceptions are "Coyote Gives the Law on Death" and "Coyote Jim Gives the Law on Gambling." When ethical precepts are made explicit in Thompson's stories, it is usually done so by Coyote or by Thompson himself in an evaluative comment on a character's actions, which will be discussed in more detail in the next chapter.

The following discussion of Upper Coquille value ideals, though not a thorough systematic analysis of the stories together with the available ethnographic literature, nonetheless offers striking evidence of how consonant are the value ideals outlined here with those sketched by Jacobs for the Clackamas Chinooks (1959b:187–95). Personal values or qualities are presented first, followed by a discussion of social, then aesthetic values.

Personal Values

The proper care and treatment of children is a minor but important theme in the stories "How Land Came into Being" and "Pitch Woman." Parents or their substitutes were expected to model and assist children to become competent adults. For boys early maturation of exceptional competence at hunting can be seen in "Rabbit's Son and the Grizzly Bears" and "Wind Woman" (Seaburg 2004; also in this volume), where a young man only needs one arrow in his quiver because he never misses his quarry.

Basket making and food preservation are mentioned in the oral traditions; relatively little is said about women's plant and shellfish harvesting. Except when women were performing as shamans, their work was not as prestigious or celebrated as men's work. Wind Woman represents an exemplary female role model.

Incompetence was generally negatively valued and was probably a source of amusement; witness Coyote's bungling attempts in several stories and Little

Man's incompetence at hunting in the "Little Man" text. Acceptable incompetence included that of older people who were no longer able to hunt and forage. Providing for such folks was a positive social value. We know little about attitudes toward the incompetence of the physically and mentally impaired, although there is some evidence in the ethnographic notes (E. Jacobs 1935) that erratic behavior might be attributed to the demands of one's spirit power.

Physical prowess, strength (usually described by Thompson as being "stout"), and endurance were valued ("Little Man (2)," "Wind Woman," and "Hollering-like-a-Person").

Acquisition of spirit powers or kin was highly valued, especially powers that led to success in gambling. Usually associated with a wealth encounter power was the acquisition of highly valued wealth items, such as dentalium shells ("Snake and Money"). Hunting powers were also highly valued, particularly the ability to "control" whales ("A Man Grows a Snake in a Bucket"). Several stories mention hunters who *always* returned from a hunting trip with game animals. The ethnographic notes (E. Jacobs 1935) suggest that acquisition of shamanic powers was probably both highly valued and feared. Sometimes shamans lost control of especially dangerous powers, such as Grizzly Bear, and might use them against fellow villagers—with dire consequences.

Obeying parents ("A Man Grows a Snake in a Bucket") and competent leaders ("Panther and Deer Woman") was valued. People, especially headmen and other high-class worthies, were expected to be judicious in their use of language. As demonstrated in "Weasel and His Older Brother," loquacity, inquisitiveness, inattention, and impulsiveness were disvalued traits.

Remembering and applying what had been previously learned was a positive value ("Little Man (2)" and "A Man Followed His Wife to the Land of the Dead [Orpheus]"). Resourcefulness in overcoming obstacles, bravery in warfare, and ability as a fighter were all valued traits ("Mean Warrior"). Trickery, especially for a just cause, also appears to be valued in these southwestern Oregon Athabaskan cultures ("Coyote and God" and "Panther and the Grizzly Bears").

Social Values

High social status was both admired and desired. Such status, particularly of headmen or leaders, was displayed by the wearing in public of wealth items such as dentalium shells, having multiple wives from well-to-do families, sharing surplus food and wealth with those less fortunate, and being respected and treated with deference ("A Man Grows a Snake in a Bucket" and "Snake and Money"; many other texts could be cited here). "Raccoon" and other texts indicate that poor people, though pitiable, were not to be ridiculed or treated badly. Indeed, as we see in "Snake and Money," a worthy headman was expected to help the poor: "'Now, I have money for you, chief. You have helped me [for] a long time. All the time I have been poor, you have helped me. You are to get that big basket piled full of Indian money.'"

Marrying without paying a bride price was ridiculed, in private if not publicly ("Raccoon"). Missing from this collection are stories of high-class young women who refuse to marry—a popular motif in the oral traditions of more northerly Northwest Coast groups.

Solidarity with immediate kinfolk and commitment to the community, especially the village headman, were positive cultural values. Several texts indicate close bonding between brothers ("Coyote and God" and "Little Man") and also between brothers and sisters ("Wind Woman" and "Big Head [Cannibal]"). Wives in a polygynous household were expected to get along ("Brown Bear and Grizzly Bear" and "Frog Woman"). There was ambivalence toward in-laws because it was not always clear where their loyalties stood, with blood kin or with kin-by-marriage ("Panther and Deer Woman" and "Rabbit's Son and the Grizzly Bears"). "Coyote Jim and His Neighbor Crane" focuses on the importance of sharing food. Stealing food from kinfolk was punished ("Raccoon and His Grandmother").

Aesthetic Values

Aesthetic values are difficult to infer from the stories. Physical attractiveness of both men and women is not described in the texts. Women may be said to be "pretty" and men "good-looking" or "handsome," but with very few exceptions, no anatomical features are singled out for remark or description. Only unusual or nonpreferred physical characteristics are noted in the stories, for example, Little Man's hairy butt, the bigness of Pitch Women, the diminutive size of the Mountain People, and Coyote's magically expanding penis. In one text, "Coyote and God," Coyote dislikes his youngest son because he is "a small fellow" who is "too small" and "can't do anything." Consequently, Coyote won't believe his oldest son's report that this youngest and smallest son is the best hunter of all ten of Coyote's sons.

There are no descriptive references to nature unless the plot requires such, for example, a "stony trail," a "sunshiny day," a "silvery salmon." Nor are there ever rhapsodies regarding the beauty of sunsets, rainbows, cloud formations, waterfalls, meadows, landscapes, grand vistas, and the like. Melville Jacobs (1972) argues that such descriptive omissions were required stylistically for proper Northwest states Indian oral tradition recitals. Max Lüthi (1986) notes similar omissions from the European oral folktales he investigated.

Jacobs's final thoughts on the value ideals he found reflected in Clacka-mas Chinook oral literature seem an appropriate summary of values among the southwestern Oregon Athabaskans, living some two hundred miles to the south. According to Jacobs's analysis, "literary indications" of "important values and aspirations" included "high social status, wealth, absence of hu-miliations or slights, and need for the utmost feeling of security in ties with kin, foods, and animistic supernaturals. Emphases seem to have been also on maturity, intelligence, shrewdness, and courage. The opposite of the good was to be poor, stupid, immature, humiliated, and lacking in the ties indicated" (1959b:194).

Humor

Trying to determine what conditions or events were thought to be amusing and why in another culture's stories "seems to be among the more difficult aspects of culture for outsiders to understand, because catching the point of a . . . [hu-morous text] so often requires cultural information that's been left unstated. If people are to be amused, they must fill in the unstated information from a store of knowledge they share with fellow members of their society" (Thomas 2001:175). What follows is merely a sampling of the humor situations deduced from the oral traditions that might have elicited smiles or laughter in a south-western Oregon Athabaskan audience. Filling in culturally taken-for-granted information is necessarily a matter of interpretive speculation, and I have made no attempt to posit a system of psychological dynamics to explain why some situations are considered funny and others not.

Some aspects or techniques of humor may be widespread in the world's cultures. Melville Jacobs (1964:245) lists twenty-five such "worldwide fac-tors" that generate humor.[9] Arthur Berger (1996:73) lists "the forty-five basic techniques of humor."[10] Undoubtedly, many more factors are culturally condi-tioned. What seems clear is that most humorous situations or events represent a constellation of factors, all working together to generate the humorous response. I will illustrate with several examples.

The first example is from "Coyote and Wolf." Coyote is pursuing Wolf and his sons to retrieve the magical resuscitating medicine they have stolen from Coyote's sons. After a journey of many days, Coyote has just about caught up with them and decides to consult his spirit powers for advice:

> He lay down. "I'll get ready tomorrow morning." The next morning he got up. [The] sun's way up now. "Oh, I forgot something. It's about my boys. I'll have to ask what I'm going to do." He sat down [squatted] a little ways away [off the trail] and defecated a little.[11] He stood up. "Now my [shit], you must tell me what to do, what's the best way I can do?"[12] It didn't answer. "You going to answer?" It didn't answer at all. "Now you tell me quick. I'll mash you if you don't tell me." It never answered. Now he cussed it, jumped on it, and mashed it. "All right, I'll kill you if you can't talk." He sat down again. A long time he pulled [strained]. Finally there came a little tiny bit. Now he got up. "Well, [are] you going to tell me what I'm going to do? What's the best way for me to do it? That's what I want to know."
>
> Well, that feces answered. She said, "All right, I'll tell you. You can be chief. Those folks are bound to call you chief. Don't go straight down here but go around and come up to them from tatc'tdən way."

Upper Coquille men were up before dawn to sweat bathe and start their daily round of activities. When Coyote finally arises, "[the] sun's way up now." A southwestern Oregon Athabaskan audience would probably have laughed at Coyote's lazy behavior. "Oh," Coyote says to himself, "I forgot something. It's about my boys. I'll have to ask what I'm going to do." Forgetful behavior is probably a universal source of amusement but funnier still is that only now, on the eve of his important encounter with the Wolves, does Coyote decide to make plans about what he's going to do.

It is appropriate that Coyote consult his spirit powers for advice, but of all the myth and tale actors in this collection, only Coyote has feces for his advisers, a loathsome albeit powerful ally. Certainly no southwestern Oregon Athabaskan would have had feces as his or her supernatural advisers.[13] Such a thought would have produced gales of defensive laughter. In only one other non-Coyote story from Thompson is defecation mentioned ("Crow Eats Feces, Marries a Woman"). But Coyote's summoning forth his feces advisers is a recurring motif in the Coyote stories, as it is in Coyote stories throughout the Northwest states—and he usually defecates just "a little," adding to the amusement. The next humor factor, heightening the amusement and the tension of the scene, is his power's nonresponse. " 'Now you tell me quick. I'll mash you if you don't tell me.' It never answered." Coyote's appeals to his spirit power and its failure to respond surely triggered humor-inducing anxiety in these cultures. But a southwestern Oregon Athabaskan wouldn't think of threatening his or her power—one was trained to do his or her power's bidding, not the other way around. To insult or disobey one's power was to risk losing it. In such ways Coyote often makes the unthinkable thinkable.

Finally Coyote's impatience and impulsiveness get the better of him, and "he cussed it, jumped on it, and mashed it." Once again, defensive laughter from the audience must have greeted such outrageous behavior. Not only has he badly mistreated his advisers, but he has also stepped on them, indeed mashed them with his feet—a repulsive hence very funny action. The scene winds down with repetition as a humor factor: "He sat down again. A long time he pulled [strained]. Finally there came a little tiny bit." The suggestion of constipation and the meager result of great effort caps this very humorous episode.[14] The tension is broken when his advisers finally answer him.

A second example comes from two episodes that comprise a short text Jacobs called "Coyote Becomes a Steelhead":

> *Two young women were digging camas. They got [their] baskets full [and] came back [about] two, three o'clock. [It was a] warm, hot day. They came right in the creek. They saw one steelhead right there, in low water, about a foot deep. [It was] just a little hole there where salmon played.*
>
> *"Put your pack down. We'll get him!" one said. They put their packs down [and] took [their] dresses off. One sat at each end [of the pool]. [They] put [their] hands out to try to catch his tail. He swam back and forth. He rubbed one's vulva with his nose, the other with his tail. They kept him there. They liked it. They played half an hour or more. After a while he jumped out. He ran off. It was Coyote.*

"Yoo-hooh, you girls catch salmon!" he called [mockingly].[15]
Those two girls could hardly walk. [They were] getting big bel-
lies right there. They stepped on each other's bellies. That stuff
[seminal fluid] all came out. [It was] half water. Then they were
all right.

Coyote went [on]. He saw lots of women digging camas. [There
was a] little mountain between [Coyote and the women]. He came
up on the hill. He shit a little.

"What can I do, my shit? I want to get that woman over there."

"Run your thing [penis] along the ground. It can stick up where
she's stooped and straddled, digging." They dug in a row. He did
that. He put [his] thing on the ground. He sat down. He watched
that woman, that woman digging camas. Pretty soon she saw
something rising up off the ground. She pretended she didn't no-
tice. Suddenly she just chopped right down hard on it. Now Coyote
fell over dead. When he began to stink, something bit him [and]
he got right up. They killed him lots of places, but he always came
alive again.

Multiple threads of humor bind the first scene together. One of the defining characteristics of Coyote's personality in Coyote stories throughout the western United States is his unrestrained libido—Coyote the lecher (Bright 1993). Coyote wants—and often gets—sex but without the social responsibility of marriage and in-law relations. That is considered funny, perhaps especially so in cultures where adolescent girls were carefully chaperoned until marriage, as in southwestern Oregon Athabaskan cultures, and adultery was a serious offense. But traducing the forbidden and getting away with it is probably funny everywhere in the world.

Another thread of humor is the trickery Coyote resorts to, his transformation from Coyote to Steelhead to deceive the girls. Yet another thread is the young women's obvious enjoyment of Coyote/Steelhead's sexual attention, while oblivious to the consequences. "They put their hands out to try to catch his tail. He swam back and forth. He rubbed one's vulva with his nose, the other with his tail. They kept him there. They liked it. They played half an hour or more." At least two more humorous threads tie up this scene. First is Coyote's mocking words and tone of voice as he runs away from the scene of the crime.

Second is the girls' pregnancies and smiles of relief at their quick release from this potentially humiliating situation. In effect all three parties have had their fun without suffering real-world consequences—humor combined with wish fulfillment.

Repetition leads off the humor factors as scene 2 finds Coyote randy as ever. Elizabeth Jacobs's (1935) ethnographic notes suggest that unrestrained sexuality was considered animalistic, as were multiple births and large families. Also a man's successful acquisition of supernatural powers depended in part on strict sexual abstinence. Coyote, then, exploits and helps relieve the presumed psychological tensions around sexual restrictions and taboos.

The humor of Coyote's feces advisers has been explored earlier. In this scene his advisers answer without intimidation, providing Coyote with an expandable penis that can traverse the distance between a small mountain and the woman he desires. The incredibly expanding penis—whether his own or a borrowed one—is a motif closely associated with Coyote and other trickster figures in Pacific Northwest Indian oral traditions. Exaggeration and unusual sexual prowess are the dominant humor factors here.

The scene concludes with a bundle of humor factors: reversal—the trickster is himself tricked ("Pretty soon she saw something rising up off the ground. She pretended she didn't notice"), slapstick ("Suddenly she just chopped right down hard on it"), exaggeration once again ("Now Coyote fell over dead"), and his miraculous resuscitation, even after putrefaction sets in, by being bitten by something. Smiles surely accompanied the storyteller's concluding announcement that "[t]hey killed him lots of places, but he always came alive again."

The third and final example of humor comes from the story "Raccoon and His Grandmother." Like the previous story this one is divided into several recognizable episodes. In the first episode Raccoon, who lives with his grandmother, steals fish from her, then lies about it when she confronts him. After he confesses,

> *[t]he old lady whipped him for his mischief. Oh, he cried! She kept*
> *on whipping, slap, slap. He ran out, ran down to the river, crying:*
> *"She whipped me,*
> *She whipped me,*
> *She whipped me,*
> *My grandma."*[16]

Now he went along crying. He wouldn't go back to his grandma
anymore.

I suspect people laughed at Raccoon's greediness and foolishness—why steal
food from one's own family? Also funny is the song he sang—a pathetic attempt to generate sympathy—and the immaturity of his overreaction to the de-
served punishment, running away from home. Raccoon's exaggerated self-pity
must have brought smiles to an audience.

In the second episode, things seem to go from bad to worse as Raccoon
foolishly wanders into an empty house—one that happens to belong to Grizzly
Bears. The first of five Grizzly Bears arrives home, eyeing Raccoon as "a pretty
good breakfast," but is easily distracted by "the black streaks on Coon's eyes,
from his weeping," streaks that Grizzly naively assumes to be black paint.

"Oh, where did you get that black paint to fix your eyes up like that?
Have you got any?"
"Yes, I got some."
"Will you paint me like you are painted?"
"Yes, but you'll have to shut your eyes and lay down here."
"All right." Maybe that Bear wanted to hurry lest another Bear
come back too soon. He wanted to eat Coon himself.
"Shut your eyes good. Don't try to look. If tears get on it, it will
make it no good."
"All right." Grizzly Bear lay down, shutting his eyes. Now Coon
took out his sharp rock.
"You ready?" he called. He didn't want to miss.
"Yes, ready." Coon cut right through his eyes. Grizzly Bear never
moved, never squealed at all. He [Coon] pulled him outside and
threw him down the hill.

Fun factors include the naiveté, vanity, and gullibility of Grizzly Bear, as well
as Raccoon's quick-thinking cleverness in so easily dispatching such a dangerous foe. The same basic scene is repeated three more times as four of the five
Grizzly siblings meet a similar doom. Repetition to the point of saturation is
probably a universal feature of humor at play here. The fifth, the Grizzlies' sister and a shaman, uses her shamanic powers to escape her siblings' fate. More
humor follows as Raccoon eludes Grizzly Woman's pursuit.

The reader can expect to find many more examples of humorous scenes in the stories in this collection, scenes involving predictable violations of prohibitions or injunctions, sexually insatiable older women, the faking of illness to kill unsuspecting victims, Coyote's ability to dismember his body to escape entrapment and to reassemble it—but missing an important body part—Pitch Woman's desperate attempts to secure a husband, and on and on.

Missing from the transcriptions is humor lost in translation, such as Native-language wordplay, vocal mannerisms such as humorous ways of talking, tones of voice, or singing styles, and funny facial movements and gestures.

3. Features of Style and Performance
in Coquelle Thompson's Storytelling

Expressive Style

There have been relatively few studies of the expressive style of Pacific Northwest Indian oral traditions. According to Melville Jacobs's (1959c) thorough review, Franz Boas's contribution to the analysis of folklore style was meager. Boas "did not explicitly differentiate between content and formal features," and in all his writings Boas "enumerated few specific characteristics of style. The list includes vocal mannerisms or special speech forms, consonant changes as in Chinook, rhythmic repetition or pattern number, repetition to provide emphasis, simile, metaphor, omissions of certain features of nature and prescribed citations of others, notations of literary forms . . . and a few others" (1959c:134). It was evident to Jacobs that Boas never intensively studied style in any oral tradition.

Gladys Reichard's (1947) stylistic analysis of Coeur d'Alene and Melville Jacobs's (1959b) and Dell Hymes's (1981, 2003) work on Chinookan expressive style, as well as Jacobs's (1972) important areal survey of the Northwest states, are all based on texts originally recorded in the Native language. One important exception is Dell Skeels's (1949) dissertation, "Style in the Unwritten Literature of the Nez Perce Indians," based on texts recorded in English, many of which were transcribed from wire recordings.[1] Other than Skeels's early work, little has been written on style in Northwest Native texts either transcribed by hand or mechanically recorded directly in English.

Some of the broad questions of expressive style that interest me are What kinds of recurring stylistic features characterize Coquelle Thompson's English-language texts? How do these features compare with those found in comparable English-based texts? And how do stylistic features in Native-language texts compare with those in English-based texts? Here I will restrict myself to a stylistic survey of Thompson's English narratives, with comparative notes to stylistic elements in Native-language texts. My sources for the latter are chapters 17 and 18 of Jacobs's *Content and Style of an Oral Literature* (1959b) and his 1972 article, "Areal Spread of Indian Oral Genre Features in the Northwest States," in which he proposes "twenty-one contrastive classes of stylistic features."

In analytically separating expressive content from style, Jacobs cautions that "[n]o hard and fast line separates content and style because most classes of features of oral literature style constituted repetitive or other manipulations of items of expressive content" (1964:332).[2] For example, in Thompson's story "Raccoon and His Grandmother," Raccoon encounters a succession of five Grizzly Bears, the first four of whom are dispatched by Raccoon in nearly identical fashion. Five is the predominant frame or pattern number in southwestern Oregon Athabaskan cultures. The progression of five encounters between Raccoon and the Grizzlies, then, is an example of the repetition of content for stylistic purposes.

A set of linguistic devices commonly found in Native-language oral traditional narratives in the Pacific Northwest area serve a stylistic function in Coquelle Thompson's narratives.

Rhetorical lengthening involves the drawing out of a consonant or vowel sound, such as the lengthening of the *a* in this English example, "He went waaaaay over there," to emphasize a great distance. Rhetorical lengthening is usually indicated orthographically by repeating the consonant or vowel symbol or by a series of raised dots, that is, wa······y. The following examples are from Thompson's texts:

> (1) "One day about eleven o'clock someone hollered on that
> mountain, 'Wooooo.' That fool, he answered [the hollering]."

(2) *"He put [an] arrow in his bow, pulled slooooow. Plop, [it was] just like somebody [had] cut [the] string."*

(3) *"So [the] Snake got ready, made two or three times that kind of noise, like a big winnnnnnd."*

Onomatopoeia refers to words that by means of cultural convention are thought to sound like their referents, for example, *bam, zoom, quack-quack,* and the like in English. Examples from Thompson's stories include

(1) *"Coyote blew a little, "P——f, p——f, I wish she'd go to sleep."*

(2) *"[But her] fire wouldn't go, just 'ts-s-s-s-s'—it made a noise that way. She couldn't figure out what had happened."*

(3) *"Those old Wolf women would pick up sticks on the trail, and then a deer would come, z-z-z."*

(4) *"The man came and asked the old women, 'Did you holler this morning?'*
One old lady said, 'I hollered bɛ· bɛ· bɛ· bɛ·.'
'Oh,' said the Grizzly Bear, 'it didn't sound like that.'"

(5) *"Pretty soon he heard someone coming, dút, dút, dút, and [heard him] drop one big piece of [his] firewood load."*

(6) *"It was like tch tch tch where the arrows hit his coat but didn't go through."*

Lexical reduplication is the third technique. Unlike most of the Indian languages in the Northwest, the Upper Coquille language lacks grammatical reduplication, but Thompson uses lexical repetition without the use of conjunctions in his English versions for rhetorical effect:

(1) *"'Lú·q, lú·q is what those people will say who come to marry you. That will mean he wants water,' Coyote had told his daughters." (This is apparently an imitation of someone speaking the Klamath River [i.e., the Yurok] language.)*

(2) *"One day Skunk claimed he got sick, sick. His belly got big, big."*

(3) *"[They] killed [deer] every day, every day."*

(4) *"That fellow [the son-in-law] talked, talked, [and] talked."*

Thompson's repertoire also evidences a set of rhetorical devices that functioned stylistically. This set includes *free direct speech*, where dialogue/speech is represented "without the accompanying reporting clause or tag, characteristic of direct speech (Wales 1989:189). For example,

> *"Oh, your name [is] [Up-from-the-Ocean]. All right. Well, what can you do for me? You'll have to pay me before I can let you go."*
>
> *"Well, it's nearly daylight now. I'd like to go. What do you want?"*
>
> *"You give me my eyes back. I want good eyes."*
>
> *"What kind of eye do you want?"*
>
> *"Oh, I want good eyes, like stars I want."*
>
> *"All right, you shut your eyes."* He rubbed on them. *"Now look at me."*
>
> *"You aren't fooling me?"*
>
> *"No, you've already got me. I have to help you. I wouldn't fool you."* Now the man looked. Oh, he had fine eyes. He saw that it was nearly daylight.

Many of Thompson's stories exhibit extensive use of *dialogue*, both without reporting tags, as in the preceding excerpt, and with reporting tags, as in the following:

> *Their sister, an old lady, told them, "They'll fix you fellows for this. You never will beat him, Coyote Jim."*
>
> *They said, "We'll have to go [to the] Klamath River, run to tatc'ɛ·. He can't go there. He can't go that far."*
>
> *"All right," she said, "I won't say anymore." She kind of held for [sympathized with] Coyote. They had no business to kill those innocent people. Now they were four or five days getting ready. Old Wolf visited Coyote.*
>
> *Coyote said, "How does it happen that they killed only my boys? They didn't kill a one of your boys?"*
>
> *Old Wolf says, "I don't know."*
>
> *Coyote, "That's all right. They killed my boys, that's all right."*

Unlike Native-language texts in the Pacific Northwest, Thompson's narratives frequently employ a stock of *similes*. For example:

(*1*) *"Just like a little cat she grabbed them and cut their necks off,
       each one as they came."*

(*2*) *"They saw dead people lying around there just like cut
       brush."*

(*3*) *"One Pitch Woman's power came through, like a bullet shoot-
       ing by, zoom!"*

(*4*) *"Then that fellow got up; he shook his war coat—it made a
       noise like thunder."*

(*5*) *"I want a good pipe, a good long sack, a chief's sack, packed
       like a camera."*

(*6*) *"Oh! [There was] lots of meat. [A] chuck-full house, piled
       up like bacon."*

(*7*) *"It went just like an automobile."*

(*8*) *"[The snake was] dripping water like rain."*

(*9*) *"That whale went just like a streak right out to [the] ocean."*

(*10*) *"Jay Bird was scratching his sore. It came down, just like
        snow, scabs."*

(*11*) *"People who had been won had to stay in one place, just like
        prisoners."*

(*12*) *"Woodpecker chopped just like a sharp ax."*

Parallelism, or repetition of the same structural pattern, is another rhetorical figure utilized by Thompson in his stories. It is easier to notice when the text is formatted in lines. Both examples are from "Panther and Deer Woman."

> *The rest of the people go back in house,*
> *No bones,*
>   *no hide,*
>   *no meat,*
>   *<u>nothing</u>,*
>   *everything cleaned up.*

> *Everything went,*
> *<u>bones</u> go,*
>   *dry meat go,*
>   *everything go.*

Another rhetorical structure Thompson uses on occasion is *chiamus*:

(1) "My dog, don't get mad," she said. "Don't get mad, my dog."
(2) Lots work,
> *cut Deer all day,*
>> *all next day they cut Deer,*
>>> *they dry lots Deer.*

Thompson also occasionally employs the rhetorical strategy called *prolepsis* (or *anticipation*), defined by Katie Wales (1989:378) as "[t]he narration of an event at a point earlier than its strict chronological place." In "Coyote and Wolf," Thompson anticipates a fight to come later in the story by saying, "There'd be a big fight, you know, *bound* to be a big fight."

Melville Jacobs (1972) recognized several stylistic classes of items that express location or distance and "depictive allusion" to nature, movement, and travel. Each of these classes is characterized by spare inventories of highly stylized items in Native-language-based texts. In rather sharp contrast, Coquelle Thompson seems to have delighted in descriptive precision with regard to numbers, time, and measurement. In Thompson's stories an actor's age might be indicated (e.g., "That little girl about seventeen, she's worst of all") or participants enumerated (e.g., "At home everyone, fifteen or twenty men, were hunting all over the mountain for him"). Events take place "about ten a.m." or "[a]bout six months later." People travel "not so far, two, three miles," or "[t]hen the people went back, they had followed him four or five miles". Objects are located "about twenty feet" away. A vine maple branch is described as "about ten foot long." With reference to numbers, Thompson often hedges the amount with "about," and he usually supplies a sequence of two or three numbers, for example, "two, three" or "four or five." Thompson's texts are as rich in such depictive details as the Native-language texts Jacobs consulted for his 1972 survey were lacking in them.

Jacobs's areal survey also found that "[t]he class of references to moods and feelings were . . . almost nil. Sentiments were deduced from plot action. They were not put into morphemes or words" (1972:15).[3] In Thompson's stories, on the other hand, *moods*, *sentiments*, and *feelings* are not infrequently made explicit, occasionally by, but more often for, the actors. For example:

(1) "Oh, her brothers got crazy [to] hear their sister had [a] man."

(2) *"Only nine came up, one's gone. Oh! He felt bad."*

(3) *"Oh, that woman was glad."*

(4) *"Oh, it tickled him. He hollered."*

(5) *"He hated to go there, but he had to go there."*

Actors' *motives* and *thoughts* are also frequently spelled out in Thompson's texts:

(1) *"So he didn't believe what he dreamed, but he had to do it. He had to go there."*

(2) *"She thought he had gone [to the] sweathouse."*

(3) *"He tried to get in where [the] fish played. He knew if he could get some of that water the fish would follow him."*

(4) *"He had decided the best thing he could do was jump into Whale's mouth. He could not get out [of his predicament] any other way."*

(5) *"He wondered what to do."*

In Native-language texts in the Northwest states, we are seldom allowed into the heads of the characters; they do not have an overt psychological dimension. As Max Lüthi observes about the European oral folktale, its characters are figures "without inner life"; they lack "psychological depth" (1986:11–12). As these and many other examples in this volume demonstrate, Thompson often gives his characters a psychological dimension.

Another prominent aspect of Coquelle Thompson's narrative style is abundant *evaluative* or *explanatory comments*, sometimes attributed to the actors, sometimes to the narrator himself. Elizabeth Jacobs often enclosed these within parentheses in the notebook transcriptions to separate them from the "real" story as she perceived it. I agree with Robert Georges (1981) that such comments "are all integral aspects of narrating" and ought not to be bracketed or dismissed as asides or digressions or, worse, eliminated from the published record.

(1) *"Ha ha, [she's a] smart devil, you know."*

(2) *"Coyote Jim [was] already in bed. He's glad now, [a] young woman [was] coming to bed with him. He ought [to] be hanged."*

(3) *"Coyote Jim said, 'I've killed everything, but one thing I've*

never killed, that's a white deer.' He's lying, ha! ha! He never
killed anything. He never hunted."

(4)   "He answered his sister, 'What do you think I am? I'm not a
coward. I'm no coward.' By that he meant he had his power.
He's got a power to get away from any place."

(5)   "'Don't open your eyes, or I'll drop you. I have no power to
pack a man who looks around everywhere. I have no power for
that.'"

(6)   "He [Coon] pulled him outside and threw him down the hill.
Coon was stout. Maybe something helped him, you can't tell."

Sometimes the explanatory material is ethnographic in content, for example,

(7)   "She sat turned the other way, making a basket. [With their]
back to [the] fire, women always sat that way to get light for
basket making."

(8)   "In olden times you [were] not supposed to bring up some-
thing said [in the past]. [It] made no difference if [you were]
alone or not. Especially in hard times it [was] bad to bring it
up."

In Native-language-based texts, actors rarely justify their actions; consultants'
overt evaluative metacommentary is similarly rare.[4]

Other stylistic features found in Thompson's stories include titles, songs
sung by an actor, the pattern number five and its multiples, etiological elements (e.g., "Now [Pitch Woman] was dead, and the people all got off. There's
a mountain there where she lay down," and "They [Panther and Grizzly Bear]
said, 'We'll never quit fighting, we never will, we'll be fighting in the moon and
people will see us.' When you see something in the moon, that's them. They're
fighting"), and many nonetiological motifs. A brief sampling of *motifs* follows,
many of which are widely distributed throughout the Northwest region:

A wife becomes pregnant by swallowing one of her husband's head
lice.
A daughter-in-law is tested.
A hunter only needs one arrow because he never misses his target.
Coyote transforms into Steelhead, then back to Coyote again.
Coyote's feces act as his advisers.

Children grow at a miraculously rapid rate.

Dead people can smell live people in the land of the dead.

An actor dismembers its body, then magically reassembles its parts into a whole being again.

An actor is swallowed, for example, by a whale or a snake, then kills the animal by cutting its heart out.

The origin of death is described.

Coyote creates land on which to cross the ocean by throwing sand in front of him.

Mice gnaw through the enemy's bowstrings, rendering them useless.

Crane extends his leg as a bridge for fugitives crossing a river or stream.

The youngest of a group of age-graded actors is the smartest/cleverest.

River Mussels are transformed from men killers into harmless edible mussels.

Killer Rocks are transformed into edible camas.

A magic sack of medicine can revive the dead.

An impersonator is disguised by wearing the skin of his flayed victim.

The origin of land is described.

A flood occurs that destroys most of the world's population.

Coyote scratches his head and wishes for something, and right away it magically appears.

A man shoots an arrow into the sky, and it falls on his head, splitting him into two people.

A boat moves as directed by the owner's thoughts.

According to John P. Harrington, "The titles of myths are as variable in exact wording as the texts themselves are. A story was largely never labeled at all or was referred to by various shortcut descriptions to which some did not catch on" (JPH, reel 027, frame 0211). Most of Harrington's texts are untitled. All of Elizabeth Jacobs's texts are titled, at least in their edited versions, and she seems to have provided the majority of the titles herself.

Several actors in Thompson's myth and tale dramas sing songs in the course of the play's action. Although songs express both content and style, some songs seem to function predominantly in a stylistic way, as entertainment or comic relief. A nice example is Raccoon's crying lament in "Raccoon and His Grandmother," which Thompson sang for the Jacobses on RCA record 14711 (Seaburg 1982:69).

Another example of song as comic entertainment occurs in "Coyote and God," where Coyote forbids Raccoon, Red Squirrel, and Beaver to accompany him to the land of God because their power songs are no good. Coyote especially disliked Beaver's song: "What is the matter with you? Are you drowning? If I were to take you across the ocean, I should certainly be ashamed of you. That is no song at all; that is merely the sound of people drowning. So indeed I shall not take you. You will stay home." The words to Beaver's song follow:

> í· ' íx̣ 'í· 'íx̣
> í· ' íx̣ 'í· 'íx̣

According to Jacobs's notations, Beaver's song "is a fine example of native humor resulting from the aesthetically grotesque. Coquelle considered this song hilariously funny; only with difficulty did he restrain his laughter long enough to record it."[5]

Performance

We have only fragments of information about the performance of these stories in the men's sweathouse. Thompson told Elizabeth Jacobs that they told stories in the fall and the winter, not in the summertime.[6] The men and boys would be lying down in the dark in the sweathouse. Thompson told John P. Harrington that "[t]he teller of these stories was always seated in the middle of the sweathouse and told long story [stories] in the dark." He recalls, "I would then fall asleep, to awake in the morning sweating, since the fire had been built up. My father would wake me up. I would go outside and seat myself above the sweathouse door, where warmth came up. It was nice in the sweathouse but cold outside with nothing on you" (JPH, reel 027, frame 0210).

At the end of the version of "Rabbit's Son and the Grizzly Bears" that Thompson told to Harrington, Coquelle says, "The Rattlesnake Woman had the line on the man—but here I fell asleep" (JPH, reel 027, frame 0439), suggesting that he never learned the end of the story. He did, however, provide an ending for the version he told Jacobs several years earlier.

John P. (Jack) Marr, 1942. Courtesy of John P. Marr.

We know next to nothing about the performance etiquette required of the storyteller or the audience. Were audience members required to respond periodically with certain stylized phrases, as was the case in other parts of the Northwest states? Were there culturally required postures for children or adults or both during storytelling recitals? Did storytellers ever physically act out certain scenes? Were some storytellers known for different storytelling techniques? We may never know.

There is evidence in both Jacobs's and Harrington's texts that Thompson used hand gestures while telling a story. It isn't known, though, how assiduously the investigators noted such gestures. In two examples from "Panther and Deer Woman," Jacobs writes: "He did that again, just before twelve, they all jump up, just that quick [clap of hand]." Another example is "One had big long knife, arm length," where it seems fairly certain Thompson indicated the length by pointing to the length of his arm. A final example from Jacobs's texts: "That other person lay there in [the] boat, like this [with his arm over his eyes]." Harrington also notes hand gestures: "Now it was that the people had to clean up that house, no fire, and opening the roof of the house (gestures to indicate roof opened to the sky 4 feet wide), and no fire" (JPH, reel 027, frame 0266); "Big snake now, he curled up, curled up (gestures to show snake was all curled up in the house)" (JPH, reel 027, 0266).

Performance on Sound Recordings

Harrington employed a young field assistant, John P. (Jack) Marr. Sometimes accompanying Harrington, sometimes alone, Jack Marr was sent to "48 different tribes in California, New Mexico, Arizona, Washington, and Alaska. At Harrington's command, Jack got into his old car and went off for months at a time, using hand-drawn maps to search out people in the remotest areas, carrying a 150 pound 'portable' aluminum disc recording machine over mountains and across rope bridges" (Hinton 1992–93:9).

In the late winter–early spring of 1941, Marr traveled from California to Oregon, seeking out the Indians Harrington had met on earlier research trips or whom Harrington had heard about from researchers familiar with western Oregon, such as Melville and Elizabeth Jacobs. Marr's excursions were not without problems, primarily monetary and mechanical. The following letter poignantly illustrates the former (JPH/JM, reel 007, frame 0491):

> *March 12, 1941*
> *Dear John,*
>   *Its a funny situation that I am in right now. I have only 22c in my pocket and your telegram just came saying to have mail from Burnt Ranch forwarded to here. This means I will be waiting two days on 22c. I talked a hotel man into taking my top coat as security for two days rent and I have taken a room, also I have put the car on a safe parking lot and told them I would pay for parking my car there in two days.*

I thought you would wire money to me so I had the garage go ahead and rewire my car as it had to be done. I also bought a used tire, a good bargain and after sending night letters to you it left me with only 22c so here I am in a pickle. About the only thing I can do is to go over to the library and study. I have smuggled some pork and beans and crackers up to my room so at least I have something to eat.

My legs still ache from the long walk back into where Martha lived. But in spite of all this trivial luck I really like this work a lot.

Its really a shame that these old Indians are dying so fast and I realize this work is far to [sic] important to let a little tough luck stand in our way.

Write to me at Siletz.

Jack

Marr's job was to make phonograph recordings of stories, songs, and word lists in the Native Indian languages, and the eighteen-year-old assistant made thirty-eight 18-inch aluminum records from Coquelle Thompson, recording stories in the Upper Coquille Athabaskan language and in English.[7] Apparently the recording equipment was beginning to wear out by 1941, and Marr's work suffered from several machine failures. Around March 20, 1941, Marr wrote to Harrington (JPH/JM, reel 007, frame 0497):

Bad news! The recorder has gone haywire, just won't run at all, and I was getting perfect work done with Hoxie too. damn *the* luck!

Portland is about 100 miles from here and I'm sure there is someplace or person there who can fix it. So without sending you telegrams or anything I am going into Portland and have it fixed, I think it is in one of the transmitters or something has burnt out. I'm sure nothing serious is wrong with it!

On March 25, 1941, several days after the recorder was repaired, Marr again wrote to Harrington (JPH/JM, reel 007, frame 0520):

I am so mad that I could swear for a year! The recorder has broken down again.

It has been running perfect for the last few days and then all of the [sic] sudden this morning it started acting queer. Making a funny noise. I noticed on the records that I was making with old Kokel [Coquelle] this morning that the sound vibration waves weren't cutting in spots. And then it quit cutting sound on the records altogether. I am taking it to the people in Portland right away in order not to waste any time as I want to get old Lucy *quick.*

According to Marr's memory (personal communication, 2004),

We recorded in his [Coquelle Thompson's] front room, me on the floor with the recording machine and him sitting in a chair, other people coming and going and closing doors, thus the door noise [on the recording].

He was always willing to talk of his childhood days, tell stories and even when the recording [machine] wasn't running he would talk of many things, i.e. fishing, hunting, going to the seashore, catching big fish and even how they took whales.

He and his wife were always gracious and hosted me fine—even fed me once or twice at lunch. As I recall we had beans, squash, and melons—possibly venison, I can't recall, but there was some kind of meat. I shared my canned corn beef, which was a Harrington staple. He bought it by the case and it was always in the car along with chili beans, hardtack crackers, and strawberry soda pop. This latter soda was enjoyed by all Indians as a favorite soda, even warm.

Although Marr enjoyed warm and cordial relations with the Thompsons, he was viewed with suspicion by some of the whites in town:

The postman and general store manager were always curious as to why I was there working with Coquelle and others. They spoke ill of them and called them worthless. When I wouldn't tell the postmaster what I was doing there in Siletz he would give me a hard time. He even refused to give me jph's [John P. Harrington's] letters a couple of times until I did admit I was "working for the government." He—the postmaster—asked me if I was an FBI *agent. With* JPH's *swearing me to secrecy constantly I was sometimes at a loss to tell anyone what my mission was or why I was in that area.*

The Recordings

Listening to Jack Marr's records of Coquelle Thompson is both a treat and an exercise in patience and frustration. The task is frustrating because many of the records are very difficult or impossible to understand. One factor contributing to the poor quality was machine malfunctioning, as described in Marr's correspondence with Harrington. A second factor may have been either that Thompson wasn't positioned close enough to the microphone or that he may have turned away from the microphone from time to time. A third factor is Thompson's Indian English pronunciation and his tendency to soften his voice at the end of sentences. Transcribing the three and one-half minutes of recording time reproduced here took between three and fours hours of repeated listening to my tape-recorded, unenhanced copy of the original aluminum recording.

Some records are relatively easier to work with than others, and listening to them provides a rare and valuable opportunity to hear Thompson's performance as a storyteller. First, one notices the background sounds—the noise of the recording machine, the scratch of the needle on the record. For anyone who has made field recordings under less than ideal circumstances, the following ambient noises will not come as a surprise: a rooster's loud crowing; hens cackling—sometimes contentedly, sometimes excitedly; a screen door opening and banging shut; someone's footsteps on a wooden floor. Other noises are more intimate: sneezing, clearings of the throat, and belching.

Next, one notices the kinds of linguistic or paralinguistic phenomena that tend to be elided when oral traditions are written down: false starts, hesitations, abrupt word endings followed by new starts. Also one notices intonation contours and word stress, pitch, and loudness, dialect pronunciation of lexical items, for example, k'rɪk' rather than k'rik', for "creek," slɪp' rather than slip' for "sleep," and so on. Often what looks on paper like instances of patterned repetition, for example, "Well, he went down, he went down, he went down, got the ocean" or "He feel, he feel, he feel, . . . He feel—a road come down that way," sounds like hesitation repetitions as Thompson thinks of what to say next.

The following is my transcription of approximately three and a half minutes of the second half of the "Little Man" text as recorded by Marr (1941). Elizabeth Jacobs's version of the same story is presented and analyzed in chapter 4. I have provided some paralinguistic information in this transcription, sometimes indicated orthographically (roman type for emphasis, raised dot[s] for lengthening, long dash [—] for pauses, short dash [–] for the abrupt breaking off of a word, etc.) and sometimes inserted like a stage direction in curly braces, { }, following the form being described. Words enclosed in square brackets, [ ], indicate my best guess as to the word. Bracketed ellipses, [. . .], indicate parts of the text I can't understand well enough even to make a guess.

> *Well, he went down, he went down, he went down, got the ocean where [the] water come, water splashing there, right there was [. . .]*
>
> *"I know where the– I know where the creek come down, I know." Just [. . .] he listen [to] himself, he told about himself.*[8]
>
> *"I know where that creek come down, not too far." [. . .]*
>
> *We·· ll, just keep on beach, right along the beach. O·· h [. . .] ca·me. Lo·· ng ways he go then—before water come down.*
>
> *"All right, now that, that's the place, that creek all right." He wanted that creek. He went up, went up, went up where the creek coming. Oh, sometime—sometime go a little farther, dip, dip, dip, sometimes go halfway [i.e., up] his body. And he* keep *on that way. Go·····, I don't know how many—*days *he traveled, nobody know. He's travel, keep on traveling. Sometime he rest, sit down [. . .]*
>
> *Well,* he went *to* where *a creek come, where a creek come up from ground, creek come up from ground, a little ditch come, a little ditch come.*
>
> *Well, it seem like* he *knew where to go, he* know *it. He knew the* place *anyway.*
>
> *Well, now come, right here, right there big lake right left-hand side, when you go up, left-hand side {sound of shoes walking on the wooden floor}, right-hand side. Big lake there. He know where big lake is. He wanna go* there.
>
> *Well, he just [dodge?] down that way, right-hand side. He knew the way. He walked down maybe—couple hundred yards somewhere. He feel, he feel, he feel, [. . .] He feel—a road come down that way.*
>
> *"Yes, {almost whispered} [. . .] this is trail. I know it." He went down this way, he feel oh maybe twenty feet, thirty feet he go. He*

came back again [. . .] where he come back. Where he come up then he's standing right there. Just [right in] road. Here's someone coming from the north, someone coming from the north, keep coming north.

"Zzzzzt zzzzt," making noise that way, that fellow come [. . .]

He say, "Hello."

"Hei."

"Hæ."

He feel it, he catch it. He catch [that one?]

"That's me," he says. He [was?] feeling around. Yes.

"What's your—[are you?] Indian?"

"No. I come from the ocean," he says.

"What's [. . .] the name? What name, your name, what'd, what'd they call your name?"

"Oh, my name's sınčındɛʔ sınčındɛʔ sınčındɛʔ"

"O·· h, I know. I hear about you," he says. "You better help me. I want you. That's all I care. I want you." [. . .]

"Why, what I gonna do?"

"Well, you done wrong," he says. "You don't have no right to do that." [. . .] cut your eye off [. . .] do that [. . .]

"That's what I do that for [. . .] What I say, I bet my eye. If they win my eye, he had to cut. People don't want to cut that way, no, no, but I make them cut, I make them cut. You have to do it because I bet, 'cause they win. Well, can you help me now?"

"Oh, yes. I guess I have to. You not do that anymore. Put your eye down, move down this way, don't look [. . .]. Just move down, kinda slo·· w, kinda [. . .]" He heal him. [. . .]

"Well, now you done now?"

"Yes, I'm done now. Well, you look right at me. [He look . . .]. You see me?"

"Yes, yes. Just what I wanted," he says. "Ju–, that's what I wanted. You wanna get your pay?" {Chickens cackling in the background throughout this whole section.}

"Oh no, no. No, no. I don't have to get paid. Just have– help you. You ask for help, I help you. I do best I can."

This transcript resembles Jacobs's handwritten notes more closely than Harrington's and reinforces my faith in the basic fidelity of Jacobs's transcriptions. (Compare the verbatim transcriptions of the same text by Jacobs and Harrington reproduced in appendix I.) What is probably missing from Jacobs's notes are Thompson's rather frequent—at least in this short sample—hesitation repetitions, noted earlier, that allowed time for Thompson to think about what to say next. Omitting these hesitantly repeated words and phrases would have made the recording process easier, assuming that Jacobs was always a phrase or two behind Thompson's utterances as she wrote them down. Perhaps with future advances in technology it will be possible to enhance the sound quality of Marr's records and better appreciate the performance aspects of Coquelle Thompson's storytelling.

4. Analyses of Four Stories

I have selected four of Coquelle Thompson's stories to analyze in this chapter. For each text I have provided an outline of the plot structure of the narrative, an analysis of features of sociocultural content and style, bibliographic citations of known regional cognate texts, then the story itself. Elizabeth Jacobs's analytical voice joins mine in the analysis of the third story, "A Man Grows a Snake in a Bucket," and her thoughts dominate in the analysis of the last text, "Panther and Deer Woman."[1]

Anyone familiar with Melville Jacobs's pioneering content-and-style analyses of Clackamas Chinook oral literature (1959b, 1960) will recognize his influence on the text analyses in this chapter. Jacobs suggests that the myths and tales of Northwest states peoples more closely "resemble the theater of Western civilization . . . than its short story or novel" (1959b:211). I agree with Jacobs and describe the plot structure (or "gross architectural structure," in Jacobs's terminology) in terms of acts and scenes and actors.

Jacobs's content-and-style analyses offer a running commentary on the text under discussion, from introduction to ending, in a fairly linear fashion, usually discussing stylistic elements and features of sociocultural content together. I also prefer this style of analysis but do not summarize the plot along the way as frequently as does Jacobs.

In lieu of Native peoples to consult and question—the last knowledgeable Clackamas storyteller died in 1930—Jacobs drew on different resources for his interpretations: his knowledge of Clackamas Chinook culture as described by Victoria Howard, the storyteller; his knowledge of comparative folklore and the ethnography of other Northwest states Native peoples; a detailed study of *all* the texts in Howard's repertoire, which he then used to inform individual texts—a necessary circularity given the paucity of ethnographic data; and application of psychological theory, usually psychodynamic in nature, occasionally psychoanalytic.

In a similar fashion I draw on the southwestern Oregon Athabaskan ethnographic notes of Philip Drucker, Elizabeth Jacobs, and John P. Harrington as well as my study—albeit neither an exhaustive nor a systematic one—of the content and style of the stories dictated by Coquelle Thompson. I also access the published ethnographies and oral traditions of non-Athabaskan Native groups of southwestern Oregon–northwestern California and appeal to a psychodynamic psychological theory, though less often than Jacobs does. Like Jacobs's analyses, mine are studded with hedges such as "I suppose," "I believe," and "no doubt." These analyses are interpretations—as are, of course, the stories themselves—always subject to rethinking, revision, and retelling.

Sometimes the actors' behavior seems to accurately reflect aboriginal cultural reality as best we can know it (see chapter 2). Other times their behavior refers to the "pre-cultural" times (as Jacobs calls it) or to special circumstances of the long-ago myth world, for instance, the story's actors lack knowledge of how to cook food or are vulnerable to the sexual seductions of the killer River Mussels.[2] Whether in myths or tales, though, I would agree with Jacobs that the overwhelming emphasis in story content is on actors in their social relationships (M. Jacobs 1959b:127). Why is this so? Jacobs argues that the oral traditions emphasized elements that represent aspects of social life that caused anxieties and tensions "for which the society had not provided public outlets" (M. Jacobs 1959b:130). One of the major functions of oral literature, then, is to project these unresolved (and perhaps unresolvable) societal tensions onto the myth and tale stage, where they can receive expressive outlet if not resolution.

Analysis of "Pitch Woman"

Gross Architectural Structure

One way to conceptualize the structure of myths and tales, a method preferred by folklorist Melville Jacobs in his analysis of Clackamas Chinook and other oral literatures in the Pacific Northwest (1959b,d), is to see them as play structures, composed of acts, scenes, and *entr'actes*. The following is an outline of the play structure of "Pitch Woman":

Prologue	*The characteristics and habits of Pitch Women are described.*
Act 1	
Scene 1	*The son of a wealthy headman is kidnapped by a Pitch Woman.*
Scene 2	*The captured young man refuses to play the role of husband despite Pitch Woman's enticing behavior.*
Scene 3	*The man's father ritually mourns and receives a spirit power dream that enables him to rescue his son. The Pitch Women are burned up.*

Features of Sociocultural Content and Style

"Pitch Woman" is the first of four different Pitch Women stories that Coquelle Thompson narrated for Elizabeth Jacobs in 1935. Prior to beginning the story proper, Thompson introduces his audience to the personality and habits of Pitch Women in a lengthy scene-setting prologue. Pitch Women often travel in pairs at night, and they sleep during the day. They steal children—sometimes men—and feed them disgusting things such as snakes and frogs. They live in a "big stone mountain with a stone door," and it is difficult to escape from them. Because the text was dictated early in their fieldwork together, perhaps Thompson thought Jacobs needed this cultural background to properly understand the story. It surely would have been stylistically inadmissible in a Native-language rendition.

In the first scene of this one-act, three-scene drama, the "last son" of a wealthy old man is out before daylight gathering wood for the sweathouse.

We know the old man is rich because his son wears quantities of strung dentalium shells around his neck, a visible sign of his wealth and upper-class status. Women could gather fuel for the cookhouse, but only men gathered wood
for the sweathouse, an exclusively male domain. Doing so was probably part
of a man's ritual training for acquiring luck, as it was among the Yuroks of
northwestern California, and the best time for gathering such firewood was
before sunrise. The young man is kidnapped by Pitch Woman and carried to
her mountain stronghold in her pitch-lined pack basket.

Scene 2, which takes place in the Pitch Women's home, combines the pathos of the well-to-do man's imprisonment with the humor of Pitch Woman's
antics. What she wants is a husband, but the captured young man won't coop-
erate—he won't even look at her. She lays herself at his feet and "roll[s] around
[there]," which is apparently intended as an enticing gesture. Her "husband"
continues to ignore her. Three inversions mark this scene. In this tale world
a woman seeks and finds a husband on her own and without regard to his
wishes—an action probably unheard of in the life world of the southwestern
Oregon Athabaskans. Second, by traveling all night and sleeping during the
day, Pitch Women invert the natural order of work and sleep, enhancing their
repulsiveness. Finally, the human children are given culturally unnatural things
to eat. Thompson also mentions that the Pitch Women snored as they slept. I
suspect that southwest Oregon Athabaskans may have found this detail funny.

Scene 3 shifts our attention to the young man's village, where his father
stays in the sweathouse, mourning his son's disappearance. He cries for two
days and nights; perhaps a mixture of real tears and ritualized crying is involved here. On the third day he falls asleep and dreams a spirit power dream.
Such dreams often came to people on whom spirit powers took pity. The man
in the father's dream tells him that his son is alive and where he can be found.
Although the old man doesn't believe what he has dreamed, he feels compelled
to check it out. This suggests that it was not always clear when a dream was
merely a dream and when it represented a message from a spirit power helper.
As happens in this story, we would expect a village headman to be a wise leader
who would correctly choose to investigate his dream and act accordingly. We
would also expect fellow villagers to accompany the headman or chief and assist him in rescuing his son as well as the stolen children who could be saved.

Following the dramatic rescue, the fiery demise of the two Pitch Women is accompanied by some comic relief. Before setting the soundly sleeping ogresses'

pitch dresses afire, the erstwhile captive ties their long hair together. When the Pitch Women wake up, they accuse each other of pulling their hair. They fight and eventually "[b]oth [are] burned up there." Like ogres and ogresses elsewhere in the Pacific Northwest, such creatures—while supernaturally endowed—are not too bright. Note that the only sure way to kill such dangerous beings is by burning them up, another areal motif featured in this text.

Pitch Woman

The story presented here is taken from Jacobs's Upper Coquille Athabaskan field notebook 1 (pp. 19–26). According to Thompson, tł'əsɛ·tc'u, "Pitch Woman," was a big, tall woman who carried a big pack basket, ate frogs and snakes, and stole children. Elsewhere Thompson indicated that the frogs and snakes were intended as food for the captive children. For cognate texts, see the Miluk Coos story "He eats human children" (M. Jacobs 1939:56–58) and the Hanis Coos "The Giant Woman" (Frachtenberg 1913:7– 77). A character similar to Pitch Woman, often referred to collectively as the Basket Ogress, occurs throughout the Northwest states cultures. Besides Pitch Woman and Giant Woman, she is known by various other names translated, for example, as Wild Woman among the Tillamooks (E. Jacobs [1959] 1990), Basket Ogress among the Clackamas Chinooks (M. Jacobs 1959b) and the Lushootseed (Hilbert 1985; Ballard 1929), Soft Basket Woman among the Cowlitz and the Upper Cowlitz (M. Jacobs 1934), and Owl Cannibal Woman among the southern Okanagons (Spier 1938).

One girl—Pitch Woman stole her. They [Pitch Women] picked them up through [the] smoke hole, picked up a child with [their cooking tongs].[3] That girl sat right by [the] door. She cried. Everyone [else] slept. Pitch Woman was sitting up there. She took that child and put her in her basket. When the people awoke, the girl was gone. They looked everywhere in all the houses. No one knew where the girl was. They thought Pitch Woman had done it. That Pitch Woman would go to all [the] different tribes and pick up children, sometimes a boy.

There were two Pitch Women who stole children, sometimes men. Pretty soon they had lots of children, big boys and girls. They lived in a big stone mountain with a stone door, right over [the] water. Pitch Women traveled at nighttime. They had good meat but fed [their] prisoners only snakes and frogs.

They were all getting big bellies from eating that. They [Pitch Women] carried snakes and frogs stuck to the pitch in their baskets.

At daytime they [Pitch Women] slept. They traveled only at night. Day—sleep. I don't know what the boys and girls did for a toilet, but no one could get out the door when the Pitch Women left, although they [Pitch Women] could open and close it easily—a wall door of rock. They had good grub. They'd eat at night. Pitch Women wanted husbands—don't know why they stole girls. Sometimes Pitch Women would stand on [the] mountain, and people would see pitch dropping just like light. No one could get away from them. They could get you in just one step.

People lived not so far from there, like a house away. [The] mountain came down to [the] water. People lived near [the] water. One old man had one son, his last son. He [the son] had lots of money around his neck.[4] One morning he went before daylight to get [wood for the] sweathouse. He passed that Pitch Woman, about twenty feet [to] one side. He never noticed her—was just watching his path. He'd break wood, break wood. [There] came [along] a big branch—about ten feet long—of vine maple wood. He got [it] ready, tied it in two places, [and] lifted [it] up [to] pack right on the top of [his] head. He never noticed Pitch Woman standing there. Pretty soon someone lifted up that wood on his head, threw it away, [and] picked him up and put him in [her] basket. He can't do anything—he's stuck on that pitch.

Now the Pitch Woman had what she wanted. She went home. She wanted to marry. She took him, opened that door, shut that door, put [the] basket down, and picked the man up. They sat by [the] fire that was burning. He saw lots of kids sitting by the fire there.

"Well," she said, "My man, my husband, you are my husband." She lay down and rolled around [there].

"Now you come on, lay down here on my arm," she said. That fellow never noticed. He held his head down [and] never looked at her. She got up again [and] walked around [the] house. Pretty soon [the] door opened again. Her partner had come back with snakes and crab and so on to feed the children. So they fed them.

She [the second Pitch Woman] said, "Oh, you got a man now, huh?"

"Yes, this [is] my man now. I think so much of him."

"Let's lay down," [they] both said. They were sleepy [from] traveling all night. They snored right away.

[The] fellow looked around, tried to get out but no—nothing but a stone wall he felt everywhere. He sat down. He couldn't cut their throats. He had no knife. He studied.

At home everyone, fifteen or twenty men, were hunting all over the mountain for him. His father was in [the] sweathouse. He cried [and] cried. [He] cried all day long, all night. He never slept, just cried. [He] wouldn't eat.

"I'm going to lie here," he said, "and think about my son." He cried [for] two nights and two days, never lying down, never resting. On [at] daylight [the] third day, he slept. Soon as he slept, he heard a man come in. He saw a man come in.

"What are you crying about, old man? Why cry so hard? Your boy is not dead. He's not far from here. He's sitting down in one place. He never sleeps either since they got him. Soon as you wake up, you go. You know where it is, where that fern bunch is right at [the] top of [the] mountain. You pull up that bunch of ferns, very easy, not violently, and you'll see your boy. The Pitch Women got him. You'll see him there."

So the old man came in [the] house and got ready.

His wife asked, "Where're you going? Where're you going?"

He said, "Keep still; I'll be back soon. I'm just going [a] little ways. I'll come back pretty quick." So he didn't believe what he dreamed, but he had to do it. He had to go there. So he went there. Everything was just like that dream, [what the] man had told him. He found that not-so-big bunch of ferns. He lifted it. Oh, [it was] loose! He put it to one side. He looked down in there. Then he saw his son sitting down with his head in his arms. He must hurry. He threw a little stick down on his son's arm. His son looked up, [and] there he saw his father way up [above], twenty feet.

So the old man ran back to fix a net and rope. The old man [was the] chief. He fixed it. They all go. They took a big thick board. They got there. He picked up [the] ferns again. They all saw the children, saw the man, all sitting there. The Pitch Women slept with their heads [crowns] together. So the men put a rope on [the] net and dropped it down for [the] man, telling him to put the not-so-bad [sick] boys and girls in [the] net. [The] bad ones with great big bellies, who couldn't get better, they left. Well, they pulled out about a half dozen, two at a time.

Then they told him, "You tie together Pitch Women's long hair." He tied it good. They slept sound. Then they told him to light their pitch dresses, and they pulled the man up. Then they watched them burn to be sure they did not get away. The Pitch Women woke up.

"What are you pulling my hair for? Why do you want to pull my hair?" they said. They got mad.

"You pull my hair too," they said. Pretty soon they fought. Pretty soon [there was a] big fire now. About two hours it took to burn them, then the fire quieted down. Both burned up there.

Two men stood on that board, which they had placed over the hole, waiting to see if a power would come through. One Pitch Woman's power came through, like a bullet shooting by, zoom! Now everyone was quiet. Those men went home happy.

Analysis of "Little Man"

Gross Architectural Structure

The following is an outline of the two-part play structure of "Little Man":

> *Part 1*
>
> > *Act 1*   *An unnamed actor meets Little Man, his supernatural, and acquires a wife.*
> >
> > *Act 2*
> >
> > > *Scene 1*   *Little Man's powers are presented and his gambling habits revealed.*
> > >
> > > *Scene 2*   *Little Man goes undetected to his brother-in-law's house and reports back that his people mourn for him.*
> > >
> > > *Scene 3*   *The amusing traits of Little Man are set forth.*
> >
> > *Act 3*   *The actor goes home to visit his people and gives his supernatural's gifts—money and gambling pieces—to his village's gambling team.*
> >
> > *Act 4*   *The home team wins valuables from other villages in several gambling scenes.*
>
> *Part 2*
>
> > *Act 5*   *A new unnamed actor comes on stage. He bets and loses his money, his wife, and his eyes.*

Act 6

Scene 1   *The new actor encounters a supernatural and re-*
gains his sight.

Scene 2   *The new actor goes to a lake and speaks to a magi-*
cal tree, which grants him five wishes.

Scene 3   *The new actor returns home just in time to save*
his brother from suicide. They gamble, using the
magic dentalia the new actor has obtained, and be-
come wealthy. The new actor and his brother each
obtain five wives.

Features of Sociocultural Content and Style

This recital of how two men acquire gambling supernaturals would have been thrilling to a Coquille male audience.[5] Foremost in their wishes was the acquisition of wealth and women. They were avid gamblers.

"Little Man" is an amalgamation of two separate plays sharing the same theme. The first play can be divided into four acts. Act 1 begins with an unnamed actor who is training to be a gambler. Because it was bad luck to reveal the nature of one's training regimen for acquiring a power—at least until one was an old man—this story, along with others in the collection, suggests only that frequent swimming or bathing was one feature of successful ritual preparation.

The particular hypnotic power over the person that his supernatural possessed is explicitly enunciated in this account. "The man couldn't stand it. He had to go, just like a fish, to that place. . . . He had to get into that boat." His supernatural immediately addresses him with a kinship term. These lines underscore two aspects of world-view or ideology, originally posited for the Clackamas Chinooks by Melville Jacobs (1955) but equally relevant to the southwestern Oregon Athabaskans. First, spirit powers often need and want relationships with people, just as people need and want relationships with powers. Second, people may have seen their powers as a special kind of kin and the symbiotic relationship between power and person as similar to a kin relationship. Little Man has been looking for a husband for his sister, and our gambler-in-training seems pleased to oblige his power. Thus they share an in-law as well as a person-supernatural relationship.

The motifs of a thought-propelled boat or canoe directed by Little Man's thoughts and his ability to "travel unseen among people" both reflect his powers and represent a nice bit of wish fulfillment for the audience. Ethnographic asides, such as women always sitting with their backs to the fire to ensure sufficient light for basket making, are a stylistic characteristic of Thompson's storytelling.

The personality delineation of the supernatural, as set forth in act 2, may come as a surprise to someone of European American cultural background. Little Man often did not tell the truth. He gambled away boats belonging to other people. Besides lying and stealing, he was somewhat foolish and immature. He called mice his deer, but was afraid of them, and was terrorized by the real deer meat and antlers his brother-in-law brought home. He dismembered his body as a practical joke. This is reminiscent of Coyote, who is the only other myth actor in the collection who can accomplish this feat. The Coquille people did not require that supernaturals be moral, ethical, or even intelligent. The one important requirement of a supernatural was that it be powerful and able to confer that power. Undoubtedly Little Man's antics were sources of amusement to the Native audience.

Planning to defer action "until tomorrow," as the leading actor does when he sees the deer and the mice, serves as a promise to the audience that there is more to look forward to regarding both animals. This stylistic feature of deferment of important action until the next day can be found throughout the Northwest states Indian oral traditions. Jacobs (1959b:231) notes that "when preparing to take action or go on a trip" actors "almost always departed 'the next day.'"

Act 3 foregrounds social relationships. First, consider marital and in-law relations. In southwestern Oregon Athabaskan cultures, patrilocal residence was the rule. A man living with his *wife*'s relations implied that he was working for his father-in-law because either his family or he couldn't afford the requisite bride price. But in "Little Man" the protagonist inverts the usual residence pattern with no apparent opprobrium. In Native culture a husband and his wife would periodically visit the wife's family, bringing gifts and renewing the interfamily ties. This is mirrored in our story when the man's wife sends her husband home for a visit, "to see his mother and father and tell them he's not dead," although she does not accompany him, perhaps because of her supernatural nature. He does, however, bring extraordinary gifts provided by his brother-in-law.

Thompson's description of the return of the gambler to his home village is revealing: "He just opened [the] door—now he was on [a] different earth. He was all right. He was just a little ways from home." Apparently Little Man and his sister lived in a different realm, a realm to which the gambler would return forever after visiting his natal family for a short while. His passing from one realm or "earth" to another was made instantaneous by Little Man's power.

Parent-child and person-community relationships are also reflected in the text. Little Man has visited his brother-in-law's people, reporting back that they miss him, feel bad about his disappearance, and continue to search for him. When the man returns home, he first visits his parents, asking them not to cry and reassuring them that he has not died, that he has a wife and is living in another place. The whole community turns out to welcome him home, including the headman or chief. Notice how circumspect the man is in describing his new circumstances: "He told everyone, 'Come in a little while, I can tell a few things.'" Appropriately he reveals little about his spirit power.

Also reflecting person-community relationships, the man makes the gifts from his power—quantities of Indian money and gambling equipment—available to his chief and to the gamblers in his village. And what impressive gifts he has given them: as long as they bet Little Man's money, they can't lose.

Act 4 quickly sets forth several gambling scenes in which the man's community wins every game they play. Such wish fulfillment is reminiscent of Thompson's story "Gambler and Snake" (Seaburg 2004; also in this volume). At this point in the narrative, the protagonist and Little Man leave the stage as Thompson seamlessly segues into part 2 of this two-part drama.

The second play is composed of two acts, beginning with act 5, in which another unnamed man and his brother invite the unbeatable gamblers to come to their village to try their luck at gambling. True to form, the visiting gamblers win all of his money. He bets his wife and loses her as well. In desperation, perhaps compulsion, he bets his eyes. Although the visiting gamblers don't want to accept such wagers, they feel compelled to.[6] There was an etiquette system or set of rules regarding gambling; apparently a person could not refuse to gamble if invited to do so. The hapless gambler loses his eyes, and the visiting team returns home. The fact that he had both won and lost his wife in gambling reflects the patriarchal nature of southwestern Oregon Athabaskan cultures.

In the first scene of act 6 our sightless protagonist lays in the cookhouse studying how to escape his desperate plight. The word "study" here seems to connote mental ritual preparation. The action in this part of the recital is swift, stark, and—until his eyes are restored—grim. The nature of the blind man's encounter with Up-from-the-Ocean differs from the first man's encounter with Little Man. People related to different powers in different ways. Here the protagonist holds on to Up-from-the-Ocean until he grants him a wish, a motif also employed in another Little Man story in the collection. With his successful power encounter and new pair of eyes, the mood of the story lightens considerably.

In scene 2 of this act, our newly sighted gambler finds the magic lake with its wish-granting tree stump, a delightful fantasy. He is careful to follow each of his power's instructions—failure to do so would jeopardize the success of his quest as well as his power relationship. First, he breaks off a piece of the stump as a talisman for luck in gambling; then he asks the big tree stump six requests: to be a chief, to never lose at gaming, to never be sick, to have ten wives, to be born ten times, and to live to be very old. The tree grants five of these wishes. It does not answer the absurd request to be born ten times, no doubt a source of amusement to the audience.

The number five (and its multiples) is stylistically significant, the dominant pattern number for the southwestern Oregon Athabaskans. Note also Thompson's especially effective use of dialogue, both as the gambler relates what his power has told him and as he interacts with the stump.

Two themes dominate the third and final scene of the act and the drama. Other than the special relation to one's supernatural, the major reference to relationships is brotherly love. In a depiction as full of pathos as any in the entire story, we see the newly powerful gambler return home just in time to save his weeping and despondent brother from killing himself: "He was digging a hole on [the] other side of his house. He was going to die right there because he felt so badly over his blind brother." The second theme reflects pure masculine wish fulfillment for southwestern Oregon Athabaskans: wealth, multiple wives, and the prestige that accompanied both. "Before one year was up, both had five wives. They went everywhere, won money, money, money. They never lost a game anymore. So they got rich, both of them."

Little Man

The story presented here is taken from Jacobs's Upper Coquille
Athabaskan field notebook 3 (pp. 72–89). Harrington recorded a

version of this text from Thompson in 1942 (JPH, reel 027, frames 0355–63). An unpublished Chetco text, "Gambling," recorded by Elizabeth Jacobs in 1935 is cognate with the second half of this two-part text.[7]

One man was training to be a gambler. Every night he went out to [the] river, swam, [and] came back before daylight. One night about ten o'clock [when] he got to [the] river, he heard someone drowning right near him.

"Nh" nhγ" nh", I'm drowning," that person said.

The man couldn't stand it. He had to go, just like a fish, right to that place. Just that quick he got to the middle of the river. He touched something, a boat. He had to get into that boat. That other person lay there in [the] boat, like this [with his arm over his eyes].

He said, "Hello, brother-in-law.[8] I'll take you home pretty soon to my sister. She wanted me to get a good man. She wants to marry you."

He just lay there, [the] boat just hanging there, I don't know how. He had pretty good power. Just wherever he thought he wanted the boat to be, it would go there. Presently that boat went to shore. He got out [and] tied the boat.

"Come on," he said, "let's go."[9] They went. That man followed where he was going. They got in [the] house.

"Sister, I have brought one man," he said.[10]

She never answered. She sat turned the other way, making a basket. [With their] back to [the] fire, women always sat that way to get light for basket making.

"Come on, let's go in [the] house," he said then and brought [the] man in. Then the sister believed him. Lots [of] times he didn't tell [the] truth. Now she put her basket down and made a place for the man to sit down.

"Sit down right there, brother-in-law," the man told him.

The woman began to cook—acorns and everything. They had good grub. That Little Man was traveling all the time. He's [a] good gambler.

He asked his brother-in-law, "What were you training for when I got you?"

"Yes, I was training because we lose games all the time, we never win."

"Oh, that's nothing, I gamble alone, all over, everywhere."

That fellow had noticed [in] the Little Man's boat, cards, shinny equipment, everything.[11]

"I went to gamble right in [the] middle [of the] ocean. Sometimes I lost a game. Of course, I didn't bet money, but they bet money to me. I bet anybody's boat along the river, whatever kind of boat I wanted to bet, I just bet that boat."

When [it was] kind of high water and people lost [their] boats, that was because that fellow had gambled the boat. He untied the ropes and let it go. People just thought the water had taken them. That fellow was on the river all the time.

Now that man's people were searching everywhere for him. They believed he had been drowned somewhere. Now, that Little Man could travel unseen among people. He went to his brother-in-law's place.

When he got back, he reported, "Your people miss you over at your home. They all feel bad about you. They think you drowned.[12] They hunt for you.[13] They look for you."[14]

They slept [in the] sweathouse together, came back [at] breakfast time.

One morning he told his brother-in-law, "If you aren't doing anything, go to the end of that prairie, look in the holes I have for catching deer. Maybe there's some in there."

"All right."

Then that Little Man went back to the sweathouse. His brother-in-law went to look at the holes. He looked all around. He never saw any holes, but oh, he saw lots of deer, thick like rabbits. They weren't scared [of him], just looked at him. Oh, lots of deer.

He thought, "I'll kill some tomorrow." Then he came back. His wife was home, working at something.

She asked, "Where have you been?"

"Why, your brother told me to look at those deer holes. I went all around that big prairie." Oh, that woman laughed.

"Don't you believe that. You look right here in [the] corner of the house," she told him. "He's got two little holes for mice, that's all." She laughed. He went there; he saw two little mice there in that hole.

He thought, "Oh, let it stay there till tomorrow sometime." He fixed a bow, arrow. His brother-in-law had all kinds [of] good bows and arrows.

He told his wife, "I think I'll kill a deer."

"Oh my, sure. I like meat," she told him.

"How about your brother? Does he like meat?"

"Oh, he eats those mice. He calls those mice, deer. But I never notice what he does with it. Maybe he eats those mice, I don't know. He believes so strong. But he's hardly ever home, he's gone all the time, so I don't know."

That Little Man was in [the] sweathouse. Now his brother-in-law went to [the] sweathouse. Right by [the] sweathouse door lay his brother-in-law's hat, one arm. He was all cut to pieces. Oh, he got scared, he ran in the house.

"Your brother got killed!" he told his wife.

"Killed?"

"Yes, his body was lying scattered all around, head [here], arm there." She kind of got ready, slow. She laughed a little.

He wondered, "What's the matter? Why does my wife laugh?"

"All right, we'll go now," she said. They went, they got there, his head lay right in front of the sweathouse.

"Oh," she scolded, "what are you doing, what you *doing*! Why did you scare your brother-in-law for? Are you crazy?"

"Huh' huh' huh'." He rolled around, his body came together, he stood up.

"Let's sweat, brother-in-law," he said. His sister went back.

They sweated together. Everything went fine. They talked about his [Little Man's] gambling.

"Not here [but] way out in the ocean, there's lots of people there," he said. They went back for supper. They ate supper. It was getting dark; that little fellow went back to [the] sweathouse, and, of course, the man stayed in the house with his wife. He didn't tell his brother-in-law, "I'm going to hunt tomorrow." But he was busy getting arrows ready.

Early [the] next morning, just [at] daybreak, he went. He just killed one, packed it home. Oh, that woman was glad. She helped her man cut it. They put the meat right on the horns, fixed it. Now her brother came in—he had never seen any deer. He went and got the Little Man.

"Come on to breakfast."

"All right." He got to the house, he saw that deer, it paralyzed [him] with fright.

"What is it?" he yelled, falling down.

"That's deer, deer meat!" his sister told him. He got up, he saw those horns, he fell down paralyzed again. He fell backwards.

"What is it?" He kept on that way.

Finally his sister got after him. "Don't do that," she said. "Eat, you have to eat some meat." They sat down and ate and ate. He kept watching that pile of deer meat. He ate.

"That's good meat, sister," he said. Her husband went out to the corner of the house to get those mice.

Her brother asked, "Where's he gone?"

"Oh, he went out to look where you told him to hunt deer." Now he came in holding those two mice by the tail.

"Here's your deer." Oh, that little fellow [was] paralyzed.

"You're the stoutest man in the world; put them outside."[15] He [was] afraid of [a] *mouse*—it isn't going [to] hurt him. Now he went out and tried to throw them away.

"I don't want that kind anymore." He couldn't pull them so his brother-in-law picked them up and slung them down [the] hill.

"Oh! Stout man." Now that little fellow ate meat after that.

His wife asked him, "Would you like to go home for [a] little while? I'll let you go home for [a] little while."

"Yes, I'd like to go."

"You go [to the] sweathouse and get my brother." He went [to the] sweathouse.

"You here, brother-in-law?"

"Yes, I'm here, brother-in-law."

"Well, your sister wants to see you."

"All right." He came to the house.

His sister said, "I'm going to send my man back home for [a] little while."

"All right, he's yours, but do you think he'll come back?"

"Oh, he'll come back all right. But he has to see his mother and father and tell them he's not dead."

That Little Man said, "When you gamble, call my name, I'll play your cards." So he gave him lots of money. "You'll gamble and you will win," he told him.

He just opened [the] door—now he was on [a] different earth. He was all right. He was just a little ways from home. He went; people saw him coming. Oh, everybody ran out. He stood right by his father's door.

He told everyone, "Come in a little while, I can tell a few things." He told [the] old folks, "Don't cry! I'm not dead, I'm a man, I'm a [live] person." The old folks quieted then.

Now everyone came in. The chief came in and all the people. They told him,

"We missed you. That's why we were lonesome. We didn't know but what you were drowned."

"Oh no, I'm not dead. I'm married. I have a wife now. But one thing, you folks can't see me anymore, after I go back. I'll stay with you a little while, then I'll go back. Now I want to tell you people. While I was training for cards, I got into a different place. Now I brought cards back, I brought money back. You folks have to bet that money. [The] chief has to bet that money."

Then he asked [the] chief, "What tribe do you want to play? You have to decide it."

"All right, I'll send word already to be there tomorrow. I had guessed what you got." He knew that man wouldn't come back with nothing when he had been gone that long.

Down at the next village people were cleaning house good, getting ready. The next morning they got ready and went. Those people were kind of scared. They weren't sure of his power, [and] they had to bet big money. They all got ready; they started to gamble. This fellow never played. He didn't have to as long as they bet that little fellow's money. He knew they wouldn't lose it. They played cards all one day, all night, and the next day. They bet big money. They won. They won again, each time the other side making good every time in [the] old-fashioned way.

[The] next day about ten o'clock those other people's money had run out. They couldn't bet anymore. They had to quit. They had taken the game. They got home.

One or two days after, they were sleeping good, early in [the] morning they heard different people coming up the river. They came to gamble. They wanted to see how that new gambler played. But he never played because as long as they bet that Little Man's money it was all right. They played only one night and one day, and those strangers' money had run out. They lost everything.

Now the chief got word from another place to come gamble. They wanted to see that fellow play cards. This fellow that sent for them had only one brother. His brother had two wives and children. They two had a big house. He had won [his] wife. They won everything from him.

"Well, I haven't any more money. I'll have to bet my wife," he said. So he lost his wife.[16] They took that game.

"Well, I haven't any money now. I'll have to bet my eye," he said.

"What can we do with your eyes? We don't need them."

"Well, you have to cut them, that's all. I *mean* it. I'm going to bet my eyes, *both* of them."

They thought, "Why, we don't want to do that. We don't want his wife, his eyes, and such things."

But he insisted. "You have to win my eyes before you fellows can go home. You got my wife, my money."

"Well, we hate to do that, but we have to," they said. Well, [the] next night they won his eyes.

"Take my wife along. I don't want her. I *bet*. I lost," he said.

"What [are] we going [to] do with your wife?"

"Take her, take her!" They had to take his wife. Now they went back.

That man's brother didn't say anything. He was out in [the] sweathouse. That man lay down in [the] house and studied, studied. He knew where there was a small creek. He studied about that.

He said, "If I get there, I have to follow that creek." He studied that. His brother [was in the] sweathouse. His brother [was] waiting, worrying about how he would get to the sweathouse, with no eyes.

This fellow went, he took [a] cane, he got on [the] beach [and] felt along. He found that little creek.

"That's the creek I want," he said. He followed that creek. He waded up it, right in the middle. Some places [there] were holes up to his armpits. He didn't know if it was day or not. He just kept going. Finally he got up to the head of that creek. Now he felt no more water was running down. He felt around. He had heard that there was a lake up there; that's where he wanted to go.

Now he found a little trail. He had heard there was a lake up above the head of that creek. He followed that trail, picking around with his cane. It was along a side hill he felt himself going. He heard something coming, making a big noise. He stood right in [the] trail, [and] he grabbed that fellow. It was an ocean person who had been to that lake.

"You'll have to pay me before I let you go." That man he held never answered. "Who are you? What's your name?"

Then that man answered, "My name is Up-from-the-Ocean."[17] This man had heard in [a] story that name. He had heard to treat him good.

"Oh, your name [is] [Up-from-the-Ocean]. All right. Well, what can you do for me? You'll have to pay me before I can let you go."

"Well, it's nearly daylight now. I'd like to go. What do you want?"

"You give me my eyes back. I want good eyes."

"What kind of eye do you want?"

"Oh, I want good eyes, like stars I want."

"All right, you shut your eyes." He rubbed on them. "Now look at me."

"You aren't fooling me?"

"No, you've *already* got *me*. I have to help you. I wouldn't fool you." Now the man looked. Oh, he had fine eyes. He saw that it was nearly daylight.

"All right, I'll let you go."

"All right, sometime I'll meet you again," [Up-from-the-Ocean] said. He went, like wind, back to the ocean.

Now that man went to the lake. Oh, he saw everything drifting around. He saw dead otter, dead woodpeckers. This water had given it to him because he had beat the best man.

But [Up-from-the-Ocean] had told him, "Don't touch a thing, just go look at it, but don't touch anything." So the man didn't touch anything. One big stump went straight up and down in [the] water. The man decided to swim there. [There were a] whole lot of big snakes right under[water], big deep water, five or ten acres of water.

The fellow had told him, "You swim. If you can get out to that stump and break just one little stick off the top, that'll be an ace, a good luck for cards."[18] That water was rough now, like [the] ocean. He didn't care. He knew it wouldn't drown him because that [Up-from-the-Ocean] had promised to help. That big stump stood in the middle [of the lake]. He saw that big stump. He saw that brush on top.

Now [Up-from-the-Ocean] had told him, "You talk to that tree; you tell it you want to be rich, that you want to win games, and every time you talk to it that tree can answer you." Now that was all he wanted.

He swam, just like [a] fish. He had to hurry because if he was in too long, the water would get mad,

[As] soon as he caught hold of that tree, he said, "I want to be a chief."

The tree said, "Hooooooooo."

"I want to beat everybody's game."

"Heiiiiiii," the tree answered.

"I don't want to be sick."

"Huuuuuuu."

"Ten wives I want."

"Heiiiiiii," it answered.

"I want to be born ten times!" [There was] no answer. No answer.

"I want to live to be very old."

"Heiiiiiii." It answered that.

Now he broke one little stick. The water was rising now; he just swam like a fish. He got to [the] shore all right, no trouble. He stayed there all day; he never touched any otter or anything drifting around there.

Now he went home, near evening. That brother was feeling badly for him. He feared he [the brother] had killed himself. He was looking all over for him. But now he came back in [the] house, built a fire, wondered where his brother was. He heard someone making noise, half crying. Then he heard no more. Then every once in a while he'd hear that noise like crying. He went out. It was his brother. He was digging a hole on [the] other side of his house. He was going to die right there because he felt so badly over his blind brother.

He went. He said, "Come on, get up, brother. I'm all right now. I've got eyes now." Now they went in [the] house, cleaned it up, had supper. They wanted to talk right away, where to go to gamble.

His brother said, "It ought to be a big town, with a big crowd, where you can get lots of money." They had these long Indian money [beads]. They went to a big town and gambled there. They won everything. They won women. Now both had two wives. They won everything. They went [to] different places that way. He never bought any women. He won young girls all [the] time.

Before one year was up, both had five wives. They went everywhere, won money, money, money. They never lost a game anymore. So they got rich, both of them.[19]

Analysis of "A Man Grows a Snake in a Bucket"

Gross Architectural Structure

	Act I	
Scene 1	An old man ritually prepares for acquiring a super- natural power.
Scene 2	He acquires his power, which grows into a very large Snake, eventually taking over an entire house.
Scene 3	The Snake power is sent to the ocean to hunt for whales, and it returns with one.

Scene 4	*Boys torment the Snake, which swallows them and returns to the ocean.*
Act 2	
Scene 1	*The old man's village is experiencing a famine; he and his son visit the man's daughter and son-in-law, hoping to be fed.*
Scene 2	*The son-in-law insults his father-in-law and brother-in-law, who leave without eating. By means of the old man's power, his son-in-law's entire village is soon starving as well.*
Act 3	
Scene 1	*The father prepares his unmarried son to visit the old man's Snake-power mountain abode with instructions on how to enter the Snakes' sweathouse and what to do there.*
Scene 2	*Aided by his father's power, the young man succeeds in his mission and is returned home.*
Scene 3	*The Snakes send five whales to the old man's village, ending the famine.*
Scene 4	*The watcher man who helped the young man in the Snakes' sweathouse is sent a woman for his efforts.*
Act 4	
Scene 1	*The old man's married daughter visits her natal family and is fed.*
Scene 2	*She returns to her husband, brings him back with her, and they are given the Snake's abandoned house.*
Act 5	
Scene 1	*The old man's unmarried son and daughter visit upriver villages looking for famine survivors. They find one woman alive at the first village.*
Scene 2	*At the second village the son encounters a man who has become a cannibal and barely escapes his clutches.*

Scene 3   *At the third village they find two women and one*
man still alive. The survivors of the first and third
villages are brought back to the old man's village
on the return trip downriver.

Scene 4   *People come from all over to get whale meat. The*
three surviving upriver women become the wives of
the unmarried man who rescued them.

Features of Sociocultural Content and Style

The story begins, as many Northwest states Indian oral traditions do, by in-
troducing the principal actor. He has purchased a wife for his son, a positive
cultural value, and is "studying something," intimating mental ritual preparation for acquisition of a supernatural, another highly valued endeavor in southwestern Oregon Athabaskan cultures. Appropriately, "[n]obody knew what he
wished" for: seeking a supernatural kin was a private affair, although the successful acquisition of a power could have enormous public consequences, as
can be seen in this text.

Women seldom play leading roles in Thompson's dramas, perhaps reflecting women's lower social status in these cultures. The daughter-in-law, for instance, is a stylistic device to get the action under way. She does not participate
beyond the first scene. Traditionally it was the chore of a daughter-in-law to
bring water. That she is here repeatedly requested to do so signifies that something unusual is afoot.

The old man's Snake power exhibits miraculous growth—a motif—growing so large that it takes over the entire house. The Snake's huge size indexes
the enormous strength of the man's power. It is important to note that while
the people of the village are grateful for the whale the Snake provides them,
they are also afraid of the Snake. "Every so often he made a noise, just like a
big wind came in [from] his mouth. They didn't let children play near there.
They [were] afraid [that the] Snake [might] get mad and just swallow [them]
all." Supernaturals are not unambiguously good. As happens in scene 4, when
provoked, when mistreated, one's power is capable of doing harm. Act 1 ends
with the Snake's return to the ocean.

Act 2 opens with the village experiencing a famine. It is tempting to speculate on a causal relationship between the Snake's abandoning the village and

returning to the ocean and the onset of "hungry time." Such a connection, though, is not made explicit in the text.

The old man's visit to the daughter and son-in-law during the beginning of the famine adds to the tension of the drama. The garrulous son-in-law is portrayed as uncouth. One didn't rattle on before making courteous inquiry about the well-being of others. When it is time to eat, the son-in-law refers to the joking earlier exchanged between him and his brother-in-law, which is in bad taste. In general, one didn't make fun of, joke about, or otherwise abuse—figuratively or literally—food animals or plants in Pacific Northwest Indian cultures, especially not during a famine. The son-in-law manipulates the metonymy of the jest so that it becomes an overt insult, and the visitors leave without eating. The wife's ensuing scolding is an unusual occurrence in this literature. Women did not criticize men. This instance perhaps not only demonstrates the enormity of the son-in-law's misconduct but also may imply that the wife comes from a more affluent, hence higher-class lineage than her husband. Although the old man's "wishing" his son-in-law's village into a state of famine might strike a European American audience as a draconian response, his action strongly suggests that insults and social gaffes were important matters in southwestern Oregon Athabaskan cultures.

The drama gets under way speedily from this point. The old man discusses his supernatural with his adolescent son. The unmarried youth is chosen for the potentially dangerous job because he is "clean," that is untainted by sexual contact with a woman. The old man explains his supernatural's habits in some detail as well as how the boy is to proceed and what he can expect to encounter. The father learned about his Snake power's ways "because he had dreamed it that way." Earlier in the story Thompson says, "If a man raises that Snake, he can get help from [the] ocean anywhere, if he knows how to sing." The old man would have learned the appropriate songs from his power dreams. His final instruction to the lad is to jump off the cliff backward—facing away from the ocean. This is similar to the advice in another Thompson story, "A Dead Person's Nose Mucus Is Money," where a boy is told to walk backward toward the ghost.[20] One must know the proper method of approaching dangerous and powerful beings. The boy's fear of jumping from the cliff is not openly stated. The raconteur says simply, "He stood there a little while." Then he decides that he cannot fool his father and jumps.

The compactness of the episode in the Snake's sweathouse adds to the impression of urgent haste. The speed with which the boy's mission is carried out is again stressed when the recitalist says that the old man thought that he must have turned back from the cliff because he returned so quickly.

Now that the famine is alleviated, there is room for humor. When the boy calls his father at daybreak to see the whales, the old man says, "Oh! You should have told me early this morning." Coquelle Thompson laughed and to make sure that the irony was not missed added, "It was just barely daylight."

The young man and his sister get ready to visit upriver villages on the following day. Frequently "getting ready to leave on the following day" is a stylistic scene marker or transition to another episode, as it is here. The scene shifts to the daughter and son-in-law up on the mountain.

The two short scenes comprising act 4 highlight the personality of the old man. The daughter asks her husband to visit her father. He refuses out of shame for his earlier behavior. She goes alone, although she is much weakened by hunger. We are not told directly that her father feeds her immediately, but we have the information from his words to her: "Take it easy; don't eat too much, just a little bit at a time." The action is frequently implied in direct discourse in this literature.

Then with a forgiveness and generosity that befits a noble man, he sends his daughter with food for his son-in-law and orders her to "bring him down." Later these personality traits in the village elder are again singled out for attention when he gives his son-in-law the former Snake house.

Act 5 begins with the unmarried boy and his younger sister traveling upriver with food. Fear of a cannibal remaining at a starved-out village is introduced at their first stop. Contrast the brevity of conversation between the young man and the first woman he rescues ("Well, are you alive, yet?" "Yes.") with the garrulousness of the son-in-law cited earlier. This simple question and answer is in accord with customary polite exchange. With beautiful economy of style, the audience learns that she will become his wife. The raconteur says he brings a large chunk of meat from the boat and cuts a slice for her and one for himself. To eat with her is symbolic of their future relationship.

At the next stop, scene 2, the cannibal for whom we have been prepared is encountered and eluded. The young boy peeks through a crack in the cannibal's house and sees a man eating a boy's arm and hand. The cannibal notices a shadow. He moves and shouts, "I eat now!" The young boy answers and runs. He barely gets into the boat in time to escape from the pursuing cannibal. A few macabre details emphasize the horror of this encounter. "He had eaten [the] last people; he ate his own baby; maybe [he] ate his wife."

At the third village smoke from two houses provides relief from anxiety about confronting another cannibal. In the first house of this village, the boy sees a woman sitting there "with her head down." This descriptive stroke suggests both the debility and the despair of the starving woman. He finds a youth sitting in the second house with a young woman seated across the fire from him. Thus the storyteller reveals that the young people are not married to each other, for a man and wife occupied the same side of the fire. From the terse comment, "That's as far up[river] as [there] were people," we know that the major action is finished.

The moving of the rescued people downriver is briefly cited, and the boy's asking his mother to cook meat and soup for the people. In what appears as a flashback to act 2, scene 2, the recitalist comments: "When they [first] fed that brother-in-law, they said, 'You eat what [the] Snake spits on [i.e., whale].' He ate. He didn't care; he liked to live." Thompson apparently simply forgot to include this item earlier in his recital and put it in at the end because the performance was incomplete without it.

Thompson then rounds out the drama with a pleasant account of the many people from "all around" who come for a month to share the whales and with the romantic restatement that the young man now had three wives: "Those three he saved all [became] his wives. [The] first one he found, that's [his] first wife."

The central interests in this tale recital are food anxiety and great supernatural power. Next in importance are references to traits of personality and in-law relationships. The old man with great power is the epitome of a fine village headman. His elder son and the son-in-law represent ordinary villagers whose everyday capabilities contrast with the extraordinary capacities of the village elder and the youth. The four women are not characterized by citing special traits. They are mainly plot expediters. The daughter-in-law brings the water with the Snake in it. The daughter up on the mountain provides the excuse for the visit and underscores the son-in-law's odious conduct by scolding him. The mother in the household is not depicted. She is merely asked to cook. The younger sister is not described. She only accompanies her hero brother upriver.

Touches of humor provide contrast and relief from the general horror of cannibalism, regard for the awesomeness of great power, tension arising in in-law relationships exacerbated by conditions of famine, and the culture's apparent disregard for older females.

The cannibal person in this play is an actual victim of starvation who is so fixated on eating that all controls are off. He will eat anything edible, including next of kin.[21] The cannibalistic Grizzly Woman of other regional literatures, such as the Clackamas Chinook, represents an angry, orally sadistic person, not a terribly hungry one.

The narrative also exemplifies this culture's preference for circumlocution of reference to the use of personal names. Kinship terms are used throughout in identifying the actors: the watcher man calls up-above people "uncle." In addressing a Snake in the Snake's sweathouse, the young man refers to it as "my nephew." And the use of "what the Snake spits on" for "whale" and "what the dog barks at" for "deer" indicates the extension of this preference to major food animals. The Snake is called "raised-by-people" or "ten white stripes circle it." The old man calls it his dog.[22]

A Man Grows a Snake in a Bucket

The story presented here is taken from Jacobs's Upper Coquelle Athabaskan field notebook 5 (pp. 23–41, 43). Jacobs supplied the title. Harrington recorded a similar version from Thompson in 1942 (JPH, reel 027, frames 0262–82). For cognate and analogous versions, see the Yurok story "Long One Was His Pet" (Kroeber 1976:165–67), the Karuk "The Long Snake at Saʔváɽi" (Harrington 1932:7–9), and the Hanis Coos "The Girl and Her Pet" (Frachtenberg 1913:85–91).

A man had one son. He bought a woman for his son. They [her people] brought her. That old man was studying something. He came in, [in the] evening. His daughter-in-law [was] cooking. His son came home.

He said, "I'd like a drink of water, if my daughter-in-law gets water." She heard. She took a bucket and left, in [the] evening. She brought water, gave her mother-in-law [some], gave her husband [some].

Now the old man was fixing a pitch flare. He held it over [the] water [and] looked into it, like [he was] looking for something.

He told her, "Take the water away." He didn't drink. He would do that all the time. Every evening he would do that: put light over [the] water [and] look around [in it]. He never drank. He [was] probably trying [to] get what he wished. Nobody knew what he wished. [The] same way he'd do, [and] the same way he'd do. One evening he did that again.

He came in. "If my *daughter*-in-law gets water, I'd drink." She heard. She had to go get water. She brought water, gave [her] mother-in-law a drink, [and] brought it to him. He already had that torch ready.[23] He looked in. This time he saw something. [It was,] oh, like a fine hair. "That's what I wanted, my daughter-in-law," he said. He took that bucket [and] put [the] whole thing on a storage bench [and] covered it over.

They left the water there. Nobody bothered it. [The] next evening he came back [at] suppertime. He didn't say he wanted water to drink. His daughter-in-law got water. He said, "I'm going to drink now, all right." After supper he drank that water. He drank it, [the] fresh water. When that put-away water [was] about a week old, he looked. That thing was bigger than a hair now. He gave it fresh water and put it away again. He tended to it. No one else touched it.

Well, maybe three, four weeks later, someone [his son] saw a big Snake in that bucket, just circling around. It nearly filled that bucket. He [the old man] took a great big bucket, put [the] Snake in fresh water, [and] put it away again. [It was] getting [to be] three, four yards long, now. That Snake was fine. Every two or three inches, white stripes ringed it. That Snake grew all right. It grew pretty fast. In a month that big bucket was full.

Now the old man decided, "We'll have to give it *this* house anyhow. Make a bigger smokestack hole, clean [the] house all up good, [and] take everything out." They moved away from that house. They gave the house to the Snake. These people had had no whale last year or [the] year before. The old man called the Snake his dog. He talked to his dog. He told him, "You go hunt, now. I want something to eat, whale!" That Snake got ready. Every so often he made a noise, just like a big wind came in [from] his mouth. They didn't let children play near there. They [were] afraid [that the] Snake [might] get mad and just swallow [them] all. So [the] Snake got ready, made two or three times that kind of noise, like a big winnnnnd. They saw him get out at [through the] roof and go to [the] ocean. He was going to hunt, now.

[The] next day, about one o'clock, he came back. He had one whale right in his mouth. He threw [it] right on [the] beach there and came back in [his] house. Oh, he made a big noise x········h·· [a hissing sound]. Everybody [was] scared. Maybe about an hour after, he was still. Now [the] people all went after that whale. Oh, [they] cut and cut. [They] didn't wait for anybody. Everybody just cut [to] put away the meat for "hungry time."[24] He [the Snake] made noise once in a while. [He] pretty near took [the] whole house in his mouth. He [was] getting kind of mean, now. One half of him lay outside [the house].

Some little boys came around, picking at his eyes with sticks. They wouldn't stay away. [The] people were gone getting mussels. Those bigger boys went there and bothered that Snake. That Snake got mad and swallowed every one of them. From there he went. He knew he had done wrong. He went—he went back to [the] ocean. He knew he'd done wrong [even though] they had no business to bother him. That was all settled then. That thing was gone. He killed a half dozen children and took them with him.[25]

If a man raises that Snake, he can get help from [the] ocean anywhere, if he knows how to sing. One day that Snake man sat there on [a] big rock going to [reaching into the] ocean. He saw lots of Snakes, each one bringing one whale. [There were] five of them. They went to their house on [the] mountain. They've got a sweathouse [there].

It's hungry time now. [The] mussels [were] no good, and that year everything [was] no good. [They] couldn't catch any fish. [They] couldn't get any deer, elk, [or] seal. Everything [was] quiet on [the] ocean. All over [the] mountain, nothing [i.e., there was no game]. He [the Snake man] sat on a big cliff straight over [the] ocean. He saw Snakes go into [the] mountain, right under [the] mountain. They called that Snake "raised-by-people" and "ten-white-stripes-around-him."[26]

He just watched to see where [the Snakes'] house was. That's why he sat there, because he had dreamed it that way. Those Snakes [each] use one whale for their pillow in [their] sweathouse, people claimed. That's what the man found out in his dream. This [was] hungry time. [The] mussels [were] poison. People hunted [but] couldn't get any deer. People were dying. [For] six months [they had] nothing to eat.

One day the old man came in. He smoked. He blew out smoke. "I don't want to die. I want to be saved," he said. All the time he talked that way, one line [with] each puff [of smoke]. His son got mad.

He thought, "He doesn't need to talk that way."

The old man said, "We'll have to go see my daughter. Maybe they have [had] good luck. Maybe [they] have something to eat."

The old man's son had joked with his brother-in-law one time when [they were] hunting and said, "A dog eats feces, but I want to eat what he barks at [deer]."

Then the other fellow said, "How about Snake's slime? I wouldn't want to eat that." He meant whale, because Snake's slime got on it [whale]. They were joshing. That was way before hungry time.

Now they went, he [the old man] and his boy. That son-in-law was just getting back, packing meat. Oh, [it was a] good time. They ate. That fellow [the son-in-law] talked, talked, [and] talked. Finally he inquired, "How is it up that way?"

"Oh, nearly everybody [has] died up there—nothing to eat," they told him. They [the daughter and son-in-law] made dinner ready, boiled meat, and put deer [meat] right in front of them on a plate.

"Now, brother-in-law, you eat. You can eat feces, go ahead, bark at it." He wouldn't eat. The old man didn't eat, either. He smoked. [The] sister cried. [The] old man and [his] son went back [home]. She scolded her husband.

He said, "I never thought anything [of it]. A long time ago we joked like that."

"Well, you have no right to say that. You know very well a gentleman [a good upper-class person] wouldn't eat after that." In olden times you [were] not supposed to bring up something said [in the past]. [It] made no difference if [you were] alone or not. Especially in hard times it [was] bad to bring it up. His wife said, "I have a notion to leave you." In about two or three weeks, that son-in-law was getting nothing.

That old man had been wishing, "I hope you can't get anything. I hope you can't get anything." Now all the people at that place [the son-in-law's village] were starving. Their mussels [were] poisoned. [They] couldn't get anything.

In the evening about five o'clock, the old man said to [his] younger son, "My boy, your brother is a married man, but you are clean. I'll tell you what we are going to do. Now, if I send you to a dangerous place, you are *bound* [certain] to come back. You won't have bad luck there, dying. Now I want to send you down here, where you look on [the] ocean." His son never answered him. The old man continued, "I hold [the] ocean in my hands, just like that [cupped palms up]. I know it. [When] I sing, I can make it be quiet. I'll be here, but I'll send my voice over there where [the] Snake house is. Now, I have it ready for you to take down there. I have made you five little sacks of tobacco to take with you. [As] soon as you get in that sweathouse, you smoke. They'll have a man there to watch out for you. Two big Snakes lay right by [the] sweathouse door, but he'll watch over you. They won't do anything. I'll be singing here. I have to send five little plates [the size of a palm], but you won't take them. My power will take them there, [placing them] in front of each Snake, one little plate. [There are] five of them. You'll have to take these five little sacks of tobacco and be quick about raising each Snake's head and putting the tobacco under it on that whale pillow. While the Snake's head is up, cut a two-inch strip of whale meat. You will get five little pieces of whale meat. You hurry about it. Now [as] soon as you get there, my power will get there."

[As] soon as he gets in [the] sweathouse, he has to smoke. When he gets to those two lying right inside by [the] door and they open their mouths to swallow [him], he [that watcher] hits them and says, "My uncle is here. You keep still." Now the old man [had] told him all about it there in [the] sweathouse. Then he began to sing. I don't know how he sang. They [raconteurs] never mocked [imitated] that song. He brought a big belt and tied up his boy. He put those little bags of tobacco around in his belt.

He told his boy, "When you get ready to jump off that cliff, don't jump facing it [the ocean]. Turn around and jump off backwards."

Finally that boy got ready to go.[27] "All right, I'm going," he said.

"All right," the old man answered and continued singing. That boy went out and stood on [the] cliff. The ocean was roaring. He stood there a little while.

Finally he said, "I can't fool the old man." He turned around, he couldn't see [down below], he jumped. As soon as he jumped, his feet lit on [the] sweathouse door. Those two Snakes roared up at him.

That watcher man hit each one with a club, calling out, "Keep still. My uncle is here." He [that watcher] called the up-above people "uncle." [He was] some kind of bird, I think.[28] He belonged right there on [the] ocean.

Now he went in [the] sweathouse, that watcher with him. Oh, he saw those five Snakes lying there. He hurried; he made a big smoke so everyone [would] kind [of] be paralyzed. Then he went to a Snake, [and] he said, "Raise your head, my nephew." That Snake raised his head. He put his tobacco in there and cut a little whale [and] put [it] back in [his] belt. He did that to each one. As he did it, he saw a [basketry] pan come sliding along through the draught hole and come over in front of [the] Snake, just like [his] old man had said. Now he was ready, he had to hurry.

[The watcher] said, "Uncle, I want a woman. You send down a woman to me."[29]

The young man said, "All right."

[The watcher] said, "Now, go."

That young man shut his eyes [and] jumped out. [The] ocean carried him right up on [the] beach, not far from [his] house. Now he got up, [and] about forty feet apart, he buried his pieces of whale meat. Now he went back [to the] sweathouse. [The] old man was singing, singing. Of course his older brother was in the house with his wife. Now he came back. [He went in the sweathouse.]

"Hei⋯. My boy came back." The old man thought he [the boy] must have turned back, [because] he got back so quick. Pretty soon, "Son, did you turn back?" He never answered, so the old man didn't ask him anymore. [The] boy just lay down. He slept. [The] old man never slept. [The] young man got up [at] daybreak [and] went to [the] sweathouse door. He saw on the beach five whales lying there.

Then he called his father, "Come see. What is that over there?" [The] old man got lively. [He] came, [and] he looked.

"Oh! You should have told me early this morning." Ha! Ha! It was just barely daylight.

They sent for everybody to cut [whale] for breakfast. [The] young man just slept in [the] sweathouse. He didn't say anything. Now that day they had to make ready an old lady—maybe [it was] his grandmother. She wasn't going to die: she [was] going [to] be a young girl over there. She [was] not afraid— maybe she didn't know [what would happen]. [They] didn't dress her up. They took a basket [and] put her in [it with] her head sticking out, tied it up good. They turned her around like he [the boy] had done [not facing the ocean], then let it go. They thought she might come up in [the] water. She didn't come up. She just went right in that sweathouse door, I guess. Her man [was] there, ready. He [the young man] took her all by himself. [He] made [the] old lady walk from [the] house, then fixed her right there [on the cliff].

Now he went back home now. He went in [the] house [and] told his mother, "Boil whale good, maybe a hundred pounds or so, so I can take it upriver." He figured some people might be alive up there, yet. [The] old man and [the] old lady worked [and] cooked a big basket full [of whale meat]. [The] old man told his daughter to go with her brother. They got ready to go tomorrow. Everybody living there [was] busy cutting whale. [They] packed [and] packed.

That [other] daughter up on [the] mountain, she told her man, "Go down there. See how my father is doing." No! He wouldn't go. He's ashamed [of] himself. So she had to go, herself. She's starving [and] didn't know what to do. She got ready. She went. She [was] so weak she [could] hardly make it in [the] door.

[The] old man told her, "Take it easy; don't eat too much, just a little bit at a time. Where's your man?"

"Oh, he's home over there. He might be dead by now, starved."

[The] old man told her, "You better go back and take a little bit of whale, already cooked. But you bring him! You bring him! If he's alive, you bring him. Walk slow."

She ate. She started out. It must [have] been not so far. That fellow was sitting by [the] fire when his wife came back.

"Hello," he said. "You came back? Anything?"

"Oh, lots of grub, lots of whale. My brother went and got it [five whales]. You eat now. We've got to go, pack [our] blankets. My father told me to bring you down. We've got to work." So they got ready. They went. They got there late in [the] evening. He could hardly eat. Well, they [the in-laws] cleaned up that house where [the] Snake [had] lived, cleaned it up good. They gave him that house. He got lively; he's a man now.

Now that young son and his sister went upriver. They went by boat, taking grub. They got to one village where lots of people had lived. He saw smoke in only one house. He saw tracks down by [the] water where people had got water. His sister stayed in [the] boat. He [was] afraid maybe [there would be] only a cannibal left. People go crazy and eat other people in bad times. The sister had to keep [the] boat out a little ways from shore.

He said, "If anyone runs after me, I'll have to jump in [the] boat quick." He went. He went slow towards [the house with] that smoke. He peeked in a crack. He saw one good-looking woman sitting there. He opened [the] door, [and] he said, "Well, are you alive, yet?"

She said, "Yes." Now he went back and got one big piece of grub. He cut a slice for her [and] one for him.

He told her, "Don't eat too much. Eat a piece, lay down, then eat again. When I come back, I'll take you down." Then he asked her, "Has anyone come this way from upriver?"

She said, "No. Nobody [has] come around."

"Well, I'll go that way," he said. He went. It didn't take long, maybe only four, five miles to another town. He went there. He saw one smoke, oh, a big smoke from that one house. He got ashore. He saw tracks. It looked like a man's tracks, where someone had come to get water. He's kind of afraid. They always thought about that cannibal thing. He went and looked in a crack. He saw a man sitting there, eating a boy's arm and hand. That eater person saw a shadow. He moved around.

He yelled, "I eat now!"

The boy answered, "All right, you can eat now." He turned and ran fast, jumped in [the] boat and pushed [the] boat out. He knew that fellow [had] opened [the] door and run after him. Just as he got in [the] boat that man [was] right there trying to catch the boat rope. He missed it. He stood there [like] he [was] dead. He smelled grub. He had eaten [the] last people; he ate his own baby. Maybe [he] ate his wife.

Now that boy went on up to [the] next town. There he saw two smokes.

"Well, some people are alive yet, all right," he thought. He went ashore, he got ready. He got out quick; he had to be lively. He looked in a crack, saw one woman sitting there, holding her head down. "Well, I know she's alive." He opened the door. That woman looked at him; he went in. "You all right?"

"Yes, I'm all right." He ran down to [the] river, got grub, [and] brought it up for her. She ate.

"Don't eat too much. Take a little at a time." He went to [the] other house. He looked in a crack. He saw one young man sitting there. Across the fire sat a young girl, sixteen or seventeen years old. He went in [the] house. "You folks all right?"

"Yes, we're all right." He ran down for grub, gave them each a little piece. That's as far up[river] as [there] were people.

He said, "Come with me. We'll go down home now." They took blankets [and] tied up a few things.

He had three women and one man. That's all they found. When they got to that first woman, she [was] stout [strong] now, walking around good. They all got in [the] boat, [and] they went. They got home late. [They] had to go about a half a mile on shore. They pulled [the] boat way up [on the shore]. That young man had to pack that basket back up [home]. They got in [the] old lady's house. [He] told his mother to boil whale meat. Soup [was] good for people.

When they [first] fed that brother-in-law, they said, "You eat what [the] Snake spits on!"[30] He ate. He didn't care; he liked to live.

For a month people were coming, coming. Stout boys and others came to get whale. Oh! [There was] lots of meat! [A] chuck-full house, piled up like bacon. Some stayed two days [and] got stout, [before they] packed grub back to those living at home. That young man had three wives now. Those three he saved all [became] his wives. [The] first one he found, that's [his] first wife.

They didn't give [watcher] a young woman, because as soon as that old woman got there, she became a young woman.[31] Every so often [watcher] [would] send them a whale. That's how [watcher] bought her with whales, an old lady.

The old man sent those five little sacks of tobacco to the Snakes so [the] Snakes would send [them] whales. Those little plates carried his power and his songs, words, from the old man to the Snakes' place. That was a great power that old man had.

Analysis of "Panther and Deer Woman"

Gross Architectural Structure

Act 1

Scene 1   Panther has poor luck hunting, while his younger brother Wildcat stays at home doing nothing.

Scene 2   Panther observes his wife, Deer Woman, defecate in her camas basket and cover it with camas roots.

Scene 3   Deer Woman serves her brother-in-law the real camas and her husband the feces.

Scene 4   Confronted with her deceit, Deer Woman steals Panther's pancreas, runs away, and gives it to the congregated Deer to play with.

Scene 5   People are starving, and the disabled Panther urges Wildcat to try to hunt.

Act 2

Scene 1   Wildcat successfully kills a Deer, but two men take it from him.

Scene 2	*Wildcat kills a second Deer and has it similarly taken away.*
Scene 3	*Wildcat kills a third Deer only to have it also taken away.*
Scene 4	*Panther accompanies his hapless brother and recovers the meat and hides.*
Act 3	
Scene 1	*Wildcat dreams of the whereabouts of Panther's stolen pancreas, confirms the truth of his dream, and is sent to retrieve it.*
Scene 2	*Wildcat successfully retrieves the pancreas and puts it back inside Panther, who recovers.*
Act 4	
Scene 1	*Panther and Wildcat hunt without success, and the people are starving.*
Scene 2	*Wildcat dreams of the whereabouts of the Deer and how to capture their heart, ensuring a steady and easy supply of Deer.*
Scene 3	*Wildcat goes where the Deer are, captures their heart, and sneaks away with it.*
Act 5	
Scene 1	*Possessing the Deer's heart makes it easy to get Deer without hunting.*
Scene 2	*Panther orders the people to take food to other starving villages.*
Scene 3	*In Panther's absence, Coyote, unprepared, foolishly hollers for the Deer to come, and the Deer recapture their heart.*
Scene 4	*The Deer flee to their home across the ocean, all except the last one, whom Panther captures and kills.*

Scene 5   *Panther plants hairs from that last Deer all over the*
                country, and the land is replenished with lots of
                Deer.

The format of this story is lines and groups of lines, instead of paragraphs, giving it an appearance of poetry. Such a "poetic" arrangement emphasizes certain features of Coquelle Thompson's *oral* style of storytelling, such as repetition or syntactic parallelism. For example, when the Deer people retrieve their heart, Thompson's parallel structure emphasizes the dramatic result:

> *The rest of the people go back in house,*
>   *No bones,*
>   *no hide,*
>   *no meat,*
>   nothing,
>   *everything cleaned up*

This type of verse format also encourages the reader to read the story more slowly than a paragraph format might and to focus less on Coquelle's nonstandard English and more on the structure of his performance. Perhaps the best way to appreciate the drama of "Panther and Deer Woman" is to turn it into an oral text again by reading it aloud.

Features of Sociocultural Content and Style

Structurally this myth text is divided into two acts, which nicely mirror each other. In the first act, Panther loses, then regains his pancreas. In the second act, Wildcat captures the Deer's heart, then Coyote loses it. The first act of this drama begins with a stylized introductory phrase, "Panther was living with Deer Woman."[32] The information that "they were people at that time" was probably added for the sake of the visiting anthropologist; a culturally informed audience would know that myth-age characters with animal names combined both animal and human characteristics.

Right away we learn that all is not well in this household of Panther, Deer Woman, and Panther's younger, unmarried brother, Wildcat. Panther, the culture's finest hunter, is unable to get anything, so we know it is famine time. Deer Woman digs roots. So mundane a fact would ordinarily not receive comment but is stated in this instance because it will become an important item in plot development. "His brother Wildcat was always home, just laying around home." This provides the information that he is relatively worthless—or immature—as a hunter.

After returning home from an unsuccessful hunt, Panther observes his wife defecating in her root basket and piling the camas on top. Deer Woman cooks the contents of her basket in hot ashes. She serves the camas to Wildcat and the feces, which resemble camas, to Panther. Wildcat eats heartily, but Panther eats nothing. It is not apparent from the text why Deer Woman gives the real camas to her brother-in-law and the feces to her husband. Serving her husband such repulsive fare is clearly a hostile act. One wonders if the wife and her stay-at-home brother-in-law are having an affair. Notice how Panther indirectly confronts his wife by telling his brother that he has eaten someone's feces. Wildcat doesn't understand his brother's reference and goes outdoors. Although Panther displaces his hostility from his wife onto his brother, she follows its import.

Surprised and angered by her husband's comment, Deer Woman reaches inside Panther's anus and tears out his pancreas. Running away with the pancreas, she comes to the place where Deer are congregated so that people can't hunt them. Adding insult to injury, Deer Woman takes Panther's stolen vital pancreas and gives it to the Deer to play with. The Deer play with the pancreas daily, treating it like a ball, which they throw a long distance and then race to see who can reach it first and throw it back.

Barring the possibility of an affair, to a cultural outsider Deer Woman's hostility toward her husband does not seem well motivated. Coquelle explained that she was mad because Panther had "no business to tell her that way when she try to get food for them." But this doesn't explain why she serves her husband feces in the first place or why all the Deer are making themselves scarce. Comparative evidence may be of some help to us here. Fortunately, Edward Sapir recorded a Takelma version of this story at Siletz from Frances Johnson in 1906 (1909a:42–54). In the Takelma version, "Panther and His Deer-Wife," we learn that Panther has hunted so many Deer that they are in danger of disappearing. So the Deer sends a "deer-girl" to be his wife. "When he had married that deer-girl, then he found no more deer." Eventually, Panther finds out that his wife was a deer and tries to shoot her but misses. Then she steals his pancreas and takes it to "where the deer [are] assembled together." There everyday they play shinny-ball with it. The Takelma version indicates that Panther would have died if Wildcat had not restored Panther's pancreas. We can only speculate that perhaps at one time the Upper Coquille version contained such an explicit motivation for Deer Woman's aggressive behavior. It would certainly be consistent with one of the themes of the second act of Coquelle's story: the importance of a respectful attitude toward game animals.

The story now shifts focus from a marital to a sibling relationship, that of older brother to younger brother. After being ill at home about a month, Panther tells his "Sunday brother," Wildcat, to go and hunt. "Sunday man" was an epithet meaning ugly, lazy, or disliked person. Government agents were referred to as "Sunday men." This is the second suggestion that Panther entertains some hostile feelings toward his younger brother. The first is when he tells him, untruthfully, that he has eaten feces.

Wildcat goes to hunt at Panther's behest. He shoots a large buck on each of three successive hunting trips. But just as he has it butchered for packing home, two large men drive him away and take the meat. When he gets home and Panther asks if he has seen anything, he doesn't answer. He "hate[s] to say, 'No,'" that is, to lie, but he is ashamed to admit that he was frightened off. Wildcat digs and cooks roots for Panther as he has seen Deer Woman do. After the third loss of his kill, Wildcat goes home crying. Panther inquires why he is crying, and Wildcat tells his brother what has happened. Thompson laughed at this point in the story. The incongruity of Wildcat's successful hunting and his timidity with the two who rob him of his kill is a source of amusement. It also provides a striking contrast to Panther's courage and efficiency, even in his weakened condition.

Panther tells Wildcat to take him to the place where he was robbed. They go, Panther walking very slowly. They arrive at the house of Waterdog and Big Black Fly. Panther confronts these two and demands that they return the meat—and hides—to Panther's house.

In the first part of the act, Wildcat lays around the house, keeping up the fire. Then he hunts successfully for the first time, but his luck in hunting and his pride in his first kill is canceled out by his inability stand up to the two bullies. Panther's defeat of Waterdog and Black Fly marks a turning point in the maturing of Wildcat.

From this point in the story, Wildcat acts as a mature, responsible adult male. In the next scene Wildcat dreams of the whereabouts of Panther's pancreas. The importance of the dream as a source of prophecy and supernatural power in Upper Coquille culture now receives direct mention. Little Wildcat dreams about his brother's pancreas. Someone stands by him in the dream and tells him that Deer play with the pancreas on the other side of the mountain and advises him to go get it. Their manner of play and how he can retrieve that pancreas are detailed in his dream. When he awakens, Wildcat goes to look and sees that the Deer actually play at the place his dream has described. Then he tells Panther of the dream. Panther advises Wildcat to get the pancreas and run home with it.

Wildcat follows his brother's advice, and in a suspenseful episode he sneaks up on the Deer: "He's pretty close, he just 'long ground like cat." Note another—and more striking—simile: "Oh, Deer run there just like thunder." While such figures of speech are rare in Northwest states oral traditions, they are characteristic of Coquelle's performance style, as we have noted. Even though the Deer are on the lookout for Wildcat and Panther, Wildcat manages to grab the pancreas, run home with it, and restore it to Panther's body as his dream had instructed. The retrieval of Panther's pancreas by his now fully adult younger brother signals the end of the first act of this myth-age drama.

Although Panther is now well and able to hunt, he is unsuccessful. The Deer are still congregated in one place, and the animal people are beginning to starve. To compound the problem, a big snowstorm hits. At this point Coyote is introduced to produce a moment's laughter. "Coyote, he was there, he couldn't do nothing, he worse one to starve pretty quick." Coyote's appearance also provides the transition to the next major action.

Wildcat has another power dream, telling him where he can find the Deer congregated. His dream also instructs him to tell the people to tap all over his belly. Coyote, hearing Wildcat's request, proceeds to slug him with his fist! Coquelle laughed at Coyote's antics, explaining: "Coyote always done wrong, he tricky man." Wildcat's dream informs him of where the Deer play with their heart and how he can steal it from them. This appears to be a collective heart, perhaps a symbolic expression of the relationship of all Deer to humankind. If anyone can get that heart, he won't have to hunt anymore but can simply call to the Deer, "Come get your heart." It is an external heart that is thrown like a ball. Again, the Deer have prescience, warning one another, "Look out for Wildcat, he may take our heart." Being able to hunt Deer merely by calling to them is a nice example of wish fulfillment.

By following his dream's instructions, Wildcat returns home with the Deer heart and one small Deer with which to assuage the hunger of the household. He tells Panther how to call the Deer. They prepare a strong door to keep the Deer from trampling the place down, and Panther calls, "Deer, come get your heart." They kill ten or twelve and let the rest go. Note the explicit statement that they do not call the Deer again until all the meat is smoke dried and the hides put away. This is an ethical statement on the importance of not being wasteful and the need to maintain a proper attitude of respect toward food animals. Amusing moments occur in which Coyote from time to time wants to do the calling. This is fine comedy to the Coquille people, who laugh at the mere mention of Coyote.

Panther calls again, "Deer, come get your heart." Earlier when the Deer ran for Panther's pancreas, the sound of their hooves was described as "just like thunder." Now the recitalist says of the Deer responding to Panther's call, "Oh, they came, just like ocean coming." This change of simile is the subtle indicator that the denouement is beginning.

A small scene covers the period while Panther and other strong men are gone taking food to upriver villages. Coyote again becomes the focus of humor, but interestingly, he here performs as a plot expediter as well. Although Panther admonishes that no one is to call the Deer until his return, Coyote insists on calling the Deer, which come and take their heart from the inept Coyote. As the Deer leave with their heart, all the dried meat, hides, and even the bones disappear.

In anger and frustration Coyote impudently asks why his feces don't depart. The feces do so immediately, whereupon Coyote adds the insulting taunt, "Why don't you bust my belly?" His belly bursts, and its contents disappear.

Halfway home Panther and his men meet the Deer that are traveling toward the ocean. Panther realizes that Coyote has been meddling disastrously and suggests that they pursue the Deer. Panther is such a good runner that he catches the last Deer just as it leaps into the ocean. He butchers it and packs it home. More importantly he plants the hairs from that Deer hide—an arresting motif—so that Deer will grow in the land in the future.

The story reveals several cultural themes. Chief among them are anxiety in the culture regarding famine and rules for the proper attitude toward food animals, with Panther, a kind of culture hero, exhibiting the proper behavior expected of a headman and Coyote providing an example of how *not* to act. Minor themes concern the maturation of a lazy, immature younger brother into a respectable—even heroic—adult male and marital discord and its consequences.

Stylistically, the text contains a number of traditional elements and a few innovative ones. As a traditional Northwest states oral narrative, it is action oriented, moving rapidly from scene to scene; there are no flashbacks or flash-forwards. Although the story begins with a stylized opening phrase, it lacks a stylized ending word or phrase. It does contain what Melville Jacobs labeled a myth epilogue, that is, a statement that tells what became of myth actors (e.g., all but one Deer return to Deer country across the ocean) and how the country was to be in the modern era (e.g., the "planting" of one Deer's hair accounting for present-day deer in the land) (M. Jacobs 1959b:222).

References to nature for description's sake are absent, and references to movement and travel are minimal and succinct. Personality characteristics are more often deduced from an actor's behavior than stated explicitly. Humor, primarily generated by Coyote but also by Wildcat, punctuate the story in several places.

Other traditional stylistic features include repetition, syntactic parallelism, rhetorical lengthening ("Then he holler, ho⋯lle⋯r"), and extensive use of dialogue.

But Thompson's performance style went beyond the region's traditional elements to include several nontraditional features, no doubt arising from years of telling the stories in English. Although statements regarding characters' feelings are not as rare in Northwest states oral traditions as Melville Jacobs would lead us to believe, nevertheless they are usually implied by a character's actions (M. Jacobs in Seaburg and Amoss 2000:99). In Thompson's stories the feelings, thoughts, and motives of characters are prominently featured, for example, "He [Panther] lay down, he don't feel good about what his wife doing," and "Oh, last time it hurt him [Wildcat] awful when they drive him 'way."

Coquelle seems to have delighted in descriptive details with respect to indications of time ("I haven't eaten anything for about a month now" and "He sneak in there. It's 'bout one o'clock now") and distance ("he run to that tree about fifty steps" and "When it got dark, Deer lay for two hundred yards thick all around"). Such depictive detail would have been absent in more traditional recitals.

All these stylistic features—and others we haven't discussed—work together to realize a story that is fully *performed* by the storyteller.

Panther and Deer Woman

From Jacobs's Upper Coquille Athabaskan field notebook 5 (pp. 85–105). The title is Jacobs's. For a cognate text, see the Takelma story "Panther and His Deer-Wife" (E. Sapir 1909a:42-54). A close analogue to the episode in which Coyote disastrously calls the Deer appears in the Coeur d'Alene text "Calling the Deer" (Reichard 1947:135–38). See also Hymes's insightful discussion of myth-age Deer in his essay "Coyote, Polymorphous but Not Always Perverse" (2003:228–42).

Panther was living with Deer Woman;
  they were people at that time.

Panther hunt,
  he don't seem to get anything at all,
    kind of bad luck.
His wife go get ts'ənɛɬa [a root], x̣ásdjɛ [like camas],
  gʷusɬ'ɛ [sweet camas], everyday.
Panther hunt everyday,
  but get nothing.
His brother Wildcat was always home,
  just laying around home.

When Panther come home, two, three in the afternoon,
  he stood in brush watching his wife dig camas.
He saw her take that basket to the side hill and defecate on that basket,
  then get up,
    put roots dug on top;
      it made a full basket.
Everyday she was doing that way.

She go home,
  she cook that ts'ənɛ́ɬ'á [a root] in hot ashes.
That Wildcat kept the fire up.

Panther came home,
*   he got in house,*
*   don't say nothing.*
He lay down,
*   he don't feel good about what his wife doing.*

Wildcat sat on one side of fire
*   and Panther and his wife on other side.*
Wildcat was sitting there,
*   waiting for his sister-in-law to give him something to eat.*
Panther was lying down,
*   studying the matter.*

She cook that camas,
*   blow [on] it nice,*
*   give it to her brother-in-law.*
Then that feces from the bottom of the basket,
*   which seemed indeed to be camas,*
she put before Panther, her husband.

Wildcat ate, ate.
Panther don't touch anything,
*   just lie on back, legs crossed.*
His wife sat down there,
*   with grub right there.*

Panther watched his brother;
*   he eat, he eat.*
When he done, Panther say,
*   "You done eat now?"*

*   "Yes."*

*   "That's pretty good,*
*   you eat somebody's feces."*

Oh! That woman was nearly knocked down,
*   she so surprised.*

Oh, she's mad, of course.
He no business to tell her that way
*   when she try get food for them.*
Wildcat didn't know what his brother meant.
*   He went out,*
*   walked outdoors somewhere.*

She's mad,
*   she just sat there,*
*   right by his thigh.*
I guess he know what she going do.
*   She just reach right in his butt,*
*   tore out all his té lɛ [pancreas].*[33]

Then she went, ran away.
*   She took that with her.*
*   She became a Deer.*
*   She went to where Deer had come together everyday at*
*   one place.*
That's why that man had never got any Deer,
*   because they didn't go 'round,*
*   just stayed together in that one place.*

Now people were starving,
*   no one could find any Deer,*
*   they were all in one place.*
She ran there,
*   gave that télɛ [pancreas] to the Deer.*

Her man lay there paralyzed because it gone,
*   nobody know how she get it out.*
The Deer played with that every day.

That man sick 'bout a month.
Then Panther told that Sunday brother Wildcat,[34]
 he told him,
  "What you doin' layin' 'round house all day?
   You take my bow and arrow and go try get Deer or
    something, go and hunt!
   Can you hunt?"

 "Oh, yes."

Wildcat take bow and arrow and go hunt.
He have good luck,
 he find Deer, big buck,
  he went to head of creek come down slow,
   he sneak up, shoot it.
That Deer come down.

He go to work,
 cut it,
  cut it.
Oh, he glad!
He never killed Deer before in his life.

He cut,
 he got one side cut,
  he turn 'round, going to cut other side,
   he saw two men coming.

Right there they came.
One big black fellow said,
 "Here! What you doing?
  Don't touch my Deer!
  Get out of here."

One had big, long knife, arm length.

"Go home, that's my Deer!" he told him.

Wildcat had to do it,
*   he had to go home,*
*   he was scared to death [of] that little thing.*
*   They drove him away.*

He got home before dark.
His brother asked him,
*   "Anything you see?"*
He never answered.
*   He hate to say, "No."*

Two or three days later he hunt again.
His brother told him,
*   "You'll have to try hunt.*
*   I'm getting hungry.*
*   I haven't eaten anything for about a month now."*

Wildcat try hunt again.
Every time he go, he get one Deer,
*   but every time he had it half cut,*
*   come two men, same men!*
And he would have to go home crying,
*   big fat Deer he had lost.*

Well, black man just talk rough,
*   big heavyset man,*
*   he'd scare anybody.*

Wildcat studied, studied.
Wildcat went out and dug some x̣ásdjɛ [like camas] and
*   gʷusɫ'ɛ [sweet camas],*
*   cook for his brother like he had seen Deer Woman do.*
He go get water,
*   he eat something.*

He went nearly every day,
*   he had got three big buck.*
Oh, last time it hurt him awful when they drive him 'way.
Oh, he cry,
*   he think,*
*   "They ought to give me a little piece to take to my*
*   brother."*

He came back crying,
*   sat down,*
*   don't say nothing.*
He had killed three now!

Panther asked,
*   "What's the matter,*
*   you feel bad about something?*
*   You don't see any Deer?"*

Now *he* cry*!*
He say,
*   "Your brother killed three big Deer,*
*   but they took them away from me." [laughter]*

"What you cry about it for?"

"Well, I feel bad,
*   three good Deer they have taken away from me."*

"Well, who took it away from you,
*   man or something?"*

"Yes, two men.
*   One big black man, tall, heavyset man,*
*   had big, long knife that long [arm length].*
*   They want to cut my head,*
*   they scare me,*

they tell me to get out! Run home!
So I have to go home."

"Is that all they do to you,
    tell you to get out,
        go 'way?"

"Yes."

"Well, how far is that?"

"Oh, right down here."

Now Panther knew who it was.
He kind of get up,
    he can't do much 'cause that tέlɛ [pancreas] gone.
He walk slooooow.
He say,
    "Take me where you kill Deer.
        I want to know where it is."
All right, he took him.

"You pack that arrow and bow too," he told Wildcat.
They go slow.
Wildcat said,
    "Right here I kill Deer, this place."

"Which way they [the men] go?"

"This way." [pointing]

Panther went down a little ways,
    he saw the house.
Wildcat went too.
They saw a man come out of the house,
    then another came out.

Panther asked,
  "Are these the people who bothered you?"

  "Yes, yes."

They went to house.
Panther said,
  "You fellows steal meat from my brother.
    He kill Deer and you take it!"
They can't deny it.
They say,
  "We don't know he's your brother."

  "Well you know now*!*
    You take that good meat,
      pack it up good,
        pack it in my house!
          You know where I live!"

  "Yes."

They got to do it.
That was Waterdog, ts'áq'ə́l.
  He got big knife, big tail you know,
    bə́ntc'u, Big Black Fly, the other one.
They take all the grub back, except bə́ntc'u [Big Black Fly's]
  grub,
    it was full of maggots,
      bə́ntc'u [Big Black Fly] too lazy to take care of his food.

But ts'áq'əl [Waterdog] took care of his good,
  he take it back,
    and take three hides back.

Now Panther and his brother went home.
They got home,

ate meat, grease, nice Deer meat.
That sick man pretty tired,
*   can't hardly breathe,*
*   he's awful short of wind.*

Little Wildcat went again to hunt.
His brother tell him,
*   "You might see fresh Deer."*

He hunt all 'round,
*   he didn't see anything.*
*   He come home without.*

At nighttime he dream.
He dream of his brother's télɛ [pancreas].
Someone came and stood by him and tell him,
*   "Your brother's télɛ [pancreas]*
*   Deer play with it on other side of that mountain.*
*   A whole lot of Deer play with it.*
*   They sling it way up there,*
*   whoever gets there first picks it up.*
*   They sling [it] way back again.*
*   Oh, Deer run there just like thunder,*
*   all want to get there first to pick it up!"*

When he wake up, he went,
*   he watch them from top of mountain.*
He see the deer do that.
*   He watch.*

When he come back, he told his brother his dream,
*   because now he believed his dream.*
*   "Well, I dreamed that way last night."*
Panther said,
*   "It must be that way,*
*   they got my télɛ [pancreas].*

That's why I can't do no work,
   I can't breathe good.
You try to get in,
   just sneak in,
     take your time!
       Sneak in there.
You know where that thing drops when they throw it?"

"Yes."

"Well, you just sneak in there,
   when you got it, you run back here."

Wildcat said,
   "All right, I can get it."

Early next morning, he tell his brother,
   "I go now."
Panther warned,
   "When you got it, just run right here.
     Don't go anywhere!
       They won't follow you here."

He go,
   he get down there,
     he watch them,
       soon as daybreak they were already playing,
         Deer.

Oh! They sling back, way up that way.
Wildcat sneak in slow,
   take his time,
     he knows how far they throw,
       where it drops.
He sneak in there.
It's 'bout one o'clock now.

He's pretty close,
  he just go 'long ground like cat.

Now they sling it back this way.
He had to lie flat on ground.
Deer nearly jump on his head,
  they never notice.
They just after that télɛ [pancreas].

One said,
  "Pretty soon that Panther, dí·tc'u,
    goin' to come get his télɛ [pancreas],
    we have to watch, watch."

Oh, they come like thunder!
First man pick up [pancreas],
  he sling [it] back again.
Now Wildcat had chance to get on exact spot
  where that télɛ [pancreas] had dropped.
Deer were warning over at other side to watch out for Panther,
  too.

Wildcat was ready now!
They throw!
He hear them coming.
That télɛ [pancreas] drop right by him,
  right where he is!
He pick [it] up and run.
[Those Deer] holler,
  "Hey, he already got it! Catch him!"
No, they can't catch him.

One small Deer almost catch him
  just as Wildcat ran into open place by his house.
That Deer had to turn back from there,
  it daren't run on that open place.

He had dreamed last night how he would put it back.
When he got home, his brother asked,
  "Did they follow you?"

  "Oh yes, run halfway here,
    they have to turn back."

  "They better not follow you here," Panther said.

Wildcat put it back,
  just quick,
    however he dreamed.
Panther said,
  "Yes, indeed, I am all right now."

Now Panther hunted,
  he hunted over that way,
    but he never see no Deer.
He had got better.
That [is a] sign of no grub,
  when Deer stayed one place.

They starve,
  grub all gone,
    what he got from Waterdog.
All people starving now,
  couldn't hardly walk.
Come big snow, oh, *big snow!*

Coyote, he was there,
  he couldn't do nothing,
    he worse one to starve pretty quick. [laughter]
People all lay down one big house.

Even Panther can't get nothing,
  he couldn't even find tracks in that big snow.

He their best hunter,
  but never find Deer trail.
Wildcat went with his brother all [the] time.

One night everybody sleep,
Little Wildcat, he dream, dream.
His dream said,
  "Why are all you people starving here?
    They got lots of Deer here,
      can't you go find them?
  If you want to go there in the morning,
    I can show you where it is.
  When you wake up, tell people to tap [tasult'əm]
    all over your belly."

Now in the morning Coyote Jim said,
  "Say! You fellows hear what he say.
    He say tasult'əm [tap]."
Then Coyote Jim got up.
  Coyote Jim hit him hard, with his fist.
    He hit him!
  "Hey, what you doin'?" Wildcat protested,
    "I don't mean that,
      just take your finger and tap me."

Coyote always done wrong, he tricky man. [laughter]

He won't tell nobody what he dream.
That dream told him,
  "Whole lot of Deer there,
    they play with their own heart,
      they play with it.
  They sling over that way,
    they sling back.
      Now you can get it,
        sneak in there.

"But when you get his heart,
　　you don't want to run home here,
　　　but run to a little tree with that heart.
There's lots of little trees there where the Deer play,
　　get up in a little tree with it.

"If you ever get a Deer heart,
　　you don't have to hunt anymore,
　　　you just holler to Deer,
　　　　'Come get your heart,'
and that Deer has to come to your house.
That's a good way to hunt,
　　so I have helped you that much.
　　　You have to do what I tell you."

He went, morning,
　　where he was told to go,
　　　he had to go there.
Everybody weak, can hardly walk.
He could hardly run if he were to get that heart.
He watch,
　　he watched all day where those Deer played.

So Deer call his name,
　　they call,
　　　"Look out for Wildcat,
　　　　He might take our heart away."
They play,
　　they come,
　　　just like thunder.
First man to get heart,
　　he sling it back again.
They play all *day long that way, all day.*

About five o'clock,
　　it 'bout March, snow times,

two or three more times left for each side to sling.
He hear them talk,
  "Three times more this way,
  three times more that way we'll throw."
They call his name,
  "Look out for Wildcat,
    he may take our heart."

He sneak in there,
  he's right 'side of them now.
They come like thunder,
  oh, lots of Deer.
He thought,
  "This time I'll get it."

He got ready.
They sling one more time,
  it drop right by him,
    he pick it up,
      he run to that tree about fifty steps,
        climb up, limb, limb.

Deer came all around.
One Deer ran to get roots,
  dig up with hooves,
    he got hurt,
      he fell down dead right by tree.
Those other Deer never notice him,
  they push each other 'round,
    they go 'round,
      lay down by tree.

When it got dark,
  Deer lay for two hundred yards thick all around.
Wildcat don't know how he goin' to get out.
It got dark,

he never move,
just sat in that tree.

Come 'bout ten o'clock, he sitting there.
He move little,
oh, all Deer rared up, stand up,
pretty soon they all lay down again.

He did that again,
just before twelve,
they all jump up,
just that quick. [clap of hand]
Then all get quiet,
lay down again.
Well, he fix good,
he don't want to drop that heart.

'Bout two o'clock he move 'round,
Deer all snoring,
all sleep.
He moved more,
nobody stirred.
He think he can get out now all right.

He come down slow,
he come to that dead Deer.
He pick up Deer,
put on his shoulder,
he go 'long, stepping between Deer.
He get out.
That's way Wildcat can move without anybody know.

House only little ways,
he get home before daylight.

Coyote Jim have to wake, you know.

He got up,
   cut that Deer quick,
      cook, cook,
         everybody get up,
            get one chew anyway.
They cleaned up that little Deer,
   it don't go long ways.

Wildcat told his brother,
   "I dreamed that way,
      you have to fix it.
         Fix up good strong door for when Deer come [to the]
         house."
His brother fix it.

Coyote said,
   "Let me holler, call Deer!"

"Oh, you don't know nothing." [laughter]

"Why, I can holler, good as you can," Coyote said.
"Oh no, you wait," they told him.

So Panther, he hollered,
   He ready you know,
      "sɛ·ƚʸi nsɛ· xʷaɣi·yá·ƚ"
   "Deer, come get your heart."
Coyote Jim said,
   "I can holler that way."

Now they saw all kinds of Deer coming.
They kill ten or twelve right there,
   other Deer went back.
      That was all they wanted.

Lots work,

    cut Deer all day,
        all next day they cut Deer,
          they dry lots Deer.

Everybody eat,
    drink lots soup,
        get stout.
Work good.
When all finished,
    hide all put way,
        then they holler again.

Coyote want to holler,
    no, they won't let him,
        he in way! [laughter]

"sɛ·ƚɣi nsɛ· xʷaɣi·yá·ƚ"
    "Deer, come get your heart."
Oh, they came,
    just like ocean coming.
They open door,
    Deer come in home,
        Deer come in,
          heart hanging in back.
They kill twenty, rest go back.

Busy! Lots Deer meat to dry.
Have to build fire three, four places to dry quick lots meat.
Put big stick over top,
    get heat too,
        dry easy that way.[35]
They busy, busy, everybody put little meat away.

Panther kind of boss,
    he say,
        "Any people live that way?"

"Yes, lots. Maybe they starve now."

They had called Deer three times now,
*   so he sent men,*
*   three, four stout men,*
*   to pack meat to Indian village.*
Leader went, pack dry meat.

Panther left word,
*   "Don't bother Deer,*
*   don't try to get any more till we come back."*

Soon as gone, Coyote want to call Deer.
Some said,
*   "No, he told us not to bother."*
Wildcat say,
*   "Better not do that,*
*   boss say not do it.*
*   We might make mistake,*
*   do it wrong, can't tell."*

Those leaders one day gone.
Second day, Coyote said,
*   "I want fresh meat.*
*   I not goin' eat dry meat.*
*   Fresh meat for me!" [laughter]*

Well, nobody stop, they can't stop him.
About two o'clock he want holler.
They let him have it.
He kind of boss while leaders gone.
He take Deer heart down,
*   pack 'round outdoors,*
*   then he holler, ho⋯lle⋯r.*

Pretty soon Deer coming,

Deer coming,
just crowded on top each other.
Finally they reach that heart,
one Deer just grab that heart,
just run away.

Everything went,
bones *go,*
dry meat go,
everything go.

Coyote say,
"Well, why don't my shit go?"
His shit gone already.
"Why don't you bust my belly?"
Bust his belly,
everything go.

Now those leaders halfway back.
They met Deer going to ocean.
Panther said,
"Oh, already that Coyote has spoiled things.
Let's run after."

Panther started after the Deer,
he followed them,
he good runner.

The rest of the people go back in house,
no bones,
no hide,
no meat,
nothing,
everything cleaned up.

Those Deer go back home across ocean.

The last Deer that jumped in water,
    Panther caught.
He cut its throat,
    packed it back.

He brought it home,
    he planted that Deer hair all over mountain,
        plant hair all 'round, no more Deer.
So he plant, just like potatoes.

Even all people's sa [shit] had become Deer and gone back across ocean,
    because Coyote Jim had got mad and said,
        "Sa [shit], why don't you go too?"
Also his sa [shit] in his belly had become Deer because he say that.

Where he planted hair, Deer grow.
That's why deer this country now.
Otherwise,
    be no deer,
        because all had gone across ocean.

5. Oral Traditional Texts

This chapter presents forty-three myths and tales as told by Coquelle Thompson to Elizabeth Jacobs. Each text includes a headnote consisting of a brief abstract of the story followed by a list of citations of cognate texts, primarily from the Northwest states and the Yuroks and the Karoks of northwestern California. With the exception of John P. Harrington's unpublished versions of stories from Thompson, I have restricted bibliographic citations primarily to published cognate and analogue texts. The citations of cognate stories are as complete as time and patience have allowed, but they are an incomplete inventory none the less.

The texts are arranged in the order they were told by Coquelle Thompson and transcribed in Elizabeth Jacobs's field notebooks, perhaps the least arbitrary of a multitude of possible arrangements.

I have included in the endnotes section phonetic transcriptions of Native words and phrases recorded by Jacobs during her transcription of the stories. Since so little vocabulary from southwestern Oregon Athabaskan languages has been published, these items may be of interest to fellow Athabaskanists. A guide to interpreting Jacobs's 1935 transcription symbols is included in appendix 2.

The Flood

The story presented here is taken from Jacobs's Upper Coquille Athabaskan field notebook 1 (pp. 1–14). The title is Jacobs's. This is a tł'ənxácdən, "Myrtle Point," story, but Thompson noted that "all told it." The first section of this myth concerns the flooding of the world and its gradual repopulation when the floodwaters recede. For parallel versions of this portion of the text, see the Kathlamet story "Nikciamtcā'ac" (Boas 1901:20–25), the Hanis Coos "The Flood" (Frachtenberg 1913:45–49), the Miluk Coos "The water got high" (M. Jacobs 1939:58–59), the Galice "The ocean kept coming" (M. Jacobs 1935, 1938–39), the Chetco "The Ocean Rises" (E. Jacobs 1968:192–93), the Tolowa "Test-ch'as (The Tidal Wave)" (Bommelyn 2002:67–76), the Yurok "The Flood" (Kroeber 1976:430), the Karuk "The Flood" (Kroeber and Gifford 1980:55–56; Bright 1957:263), and the Shasta "The Flood" (Farrand and Frachtenberg 1915:210–11). For an international perspective, Dundes (1988) has assembled an excellent collection of articles regarding flood myths from around the world. The second part of Thompson's narrative involves Coyote as culture hero, traveling around and transforming features of myth-era conditions, inhabitants, and objects to be as they are in the present world. Parallel incidents involving people-eating Crawfish, homicidal Spears, castrating River Mussels, and other such myth-era abnormalities are widely distributed in Northwest Indian oral traditions.

"Noise-under-Ground, are you home?"[1]

"Yes, I'm home, Big-Fat-Person, I'm home."[2]

Big-Fat-Person [said], "The ocean is coming."

"Yes," Noise-under-Ground [replied]. When the flood came the people were all in their houses.

"Run outside!" they heard someone holler. "Get your boats ready. Hurry up." One boat was already in the water. They already got into their canoes. "Hurry!"

Some had already gone. They hurried toward the mountain. People were crying. Some tried to hang onto the canoes of others, but they let go and drowned.

The boats all turned into snakes. If they had rubbed their boats with shit, they would not have turned into snakes. That always happened in the flood. The paddles must be rubbed [with shit] too, or they became snakes.

That first young man had no wife. He ran up on that high mountain. While he was going along, the flood nighttime came. One naked young woman ran to that same place.

All came together on the top of that mountain. She [the young girl] heard noises [and] was afraid. But the animals were all gentle [there together on the mountain]. The woman was afraid.

[The young man said to her], "Let's go to there [to the peak]."

[She asked], "What's making that noise?" Everything had come together there. Birds were making noise. [They sat so thickly on the trees that] they almost bent the branches. "What can we do now? I am cold!" [she said].

"He's not mean.[3] He won't bite you. Let's get warm by him," [the young man said to her]. Right there they [the man and the woman] lay down. They slept there. She was not afraid.

Now it was getting daybreak. The birds were making noise. Everything, Panther, Elk, Bear, and Grizzly never got up. There was no room [on that hill-top]. They [the animals] were almost in the water. Everywhere it's wet. Maybe they [the animals] knew that the flood was coming.

Near sunup someone came paddling along. His wife, his daughter, and his son sat in the canoe. Right close they came. They pulled the boat ashore with the mother and his sister in it. That old man had everything [he needed], arrows, a knife—only no fire. The others lay down to sleep. The man walked about, smelling all around. [When it was] almost noon something was swimming this way. They watched it. Little wisps of smoke [arose above it]. It was a little ways, a little ways out. Now it swam out. [Red Squirrel] brought fire.[4] He is red on the back of his neck where he carried it [the fire].[5]

"Get grass, moss, hurry! Blow on it." They built a fire.

The old man said, "What can we do? Nothing to eat."

"Oh, [there are] lots of deer. Here we can get one," [the young man said].

"How [can we] get one?"

"Give me the knife. I'll get one." He picked up [the] smallest one, hamstrung him so the deer couldn't move or kick. They skinned it, cut and cooked the meat over the fire. Then they ate. That ocean stayed just the same.

Come five days, [the] ocean's stayed the same. Then, just at daylight water went in a flash. About a week later [the] ground [was] still soft—couldn't walk [on it]. [The] ocean went just like running downhill. No houses; nothing [was] left.

When the ground [was] getting dry, they had lots of meat dried. Then [the] animals went away [to] pick in [the] grass. People went down to build a house. Two men and two girls, they married. Nowhere—[there were] no more people anywhere. Everything [was] cleaned up.

They raised children who intermarried. That's how people came to be again. They raised the people. There came to be lots of people. [They] went back to the Rogue River. [They] populated the Coquille, Umpqua, Siuslaw [rivers]. When they got to a different place, they would have a different language: Coos, Umpqua, and so on. Siuslaw, Yaquina, Siletz [are] all different languages.

Coyote came to each of one [of these settlements] and named it: Tututni, this one Joshua, and you, mouth of the Coquille, mouth of the Coos.[6]

After that, Coyote came again to see how people [were] getting along. One place he came [to], one little town, everything [was] mean in that place. He came to see about it. He came to one old lady. Somebody caught all the water— no one could get [any]. In the house [were] one old lady [and] one little girl.

He asked [the] old lady, "Where [are] all [the] people?"

"Crawfish got all the people who went for water."[7]

He [Coyote] said, "Little girl, go get water. I'm dry. I'd like a little drink." The old lady cried. She didn't want that little girl to become dead, to go get water.

Coyote said, "Here's a bucket. You go get water. I send you. If anything catches you, cry loudly. I have sent you." So she went. She started to dip water, but something caught hold of her hand. She [started] crying, squealing.

Coyote ran down. "What is it?" She was already halfway in [the] water. Bones were piled up there. Coyote said, "Give me [the] bucket." He went to [the] water, picked up Crawfish, put it in the bucket. [He] put Crawfish in [the] fire, cooked, cooked, [and] cooked it all good. Then he said to the old lady, "Eat!" He said to Crawfish, "People have to eat you. You don't have to kill people." He made it be that way. Then [the] old lady ate, he ate, [and] the girl ate. That Crawfish was all fat and nice.

Now he sent the girl to get the water again. She [did] not want to go, but he said, "Yes, yes, you go now. Nothing will bother you." So she went—Crawfish were swimming around, but none bothered her then. That was settled.

Now Coyote went. He came to [where] he saw smoke. He came right there. He saw two women pounding acorns. He saw they did not look right. Both [were] blind. He sneaked into [the] house [and] got a handful of acorn meal.

Pretty soon they got [to] thinking, "What's the matter? Someone's getting our meal." They felt about with their sticks. They couldn't feel anything. "But there's someone here! Who are you?" Coyote felt sorry [for them]. Both [were] blind, trying to make a living.

"Well, I am here," he said.

"Oh, that's you, Coyote? All right. Will you help us?"

"I'll help you folks now," he said. He went out [and] got thin, sharp glass on [the] river's edge. He said, "Lean back, open your eyes. I'm going to cut [them] open," he said. He cut [them] open, both eyes. "Now you look!" he said. So they looked. Oh! They're glad! Those two old women were Grouse. He told them, "You don't have to pound acorns. You go to [the] top of a tree and croon everyday, 'hm, hmp, hmp.'"

"All right," they said.

"People will call you grouse." Now he had settled that.

He went along by the river. He had one town where someone had tried to get camas. He said, "What [are] you doing?"

"Oh, I just want to get camas; see if any [are] here. I'll come back tomorrow and dig them. Where are you going?"

"Oh, I'm going along the road to settle things."

The man said, "Oh, you cannot go past that little creek. Men never pass there. I never go by there."

"Well, all right," Coyote said. "I'll try to pass." He had a little stick. He asked the man, "What is it, Bear or something?"

"No, Salmon Pole. [There's a] spear on it. It shoots spears at men and kills them that way."

Coyote said, "Maybe he can kill me all right." Pretty close to [the] river, Coyote went slowly. He watched. Now he got there [and] something came, "Z-z-z-z-z." He hit it with a stick. [Here] came that spear, but he whipped it. "Now he won't do that anymore." He took that spear, put it back [on the pole], took [the] pole, and went and speared salmon. Lots of people came then. That man had told them. He speared six or seven salmon. Then Coyote said, "Now that is how people will use you, to spear salmon. You will not kill people." Salmon Pole was whipped right there. That was settled.

Coyote, he went on. Sometimes he camped right on [the] road. He saw nothing traveling for a long ways. Finally one morning about noon he heard someone hollering.

"Come here, I lay down here. Come here, I lay down here." He went in. He saw a woman flat on [her] back. "Come on," she said. [She was] River Mussel, who killed men [by] shutting [her] vagina on a man.

"What [are] you doing?" he said. "You can't kill anybody. You'll just be river mussels." He threw them in the river. Now he had settled that.

Some places he [Coyote] did nothing, just talked to things. Some Deer tried to hook him. He said, "Stop." They would not [stop].

Deer said, "I want to kill you."

"No," said Coyote, "I'll stop you now. You will have to be killed and eaten yourself. You cannot kill anybody. You will be deer." Now he had settled that.

Moon

In this myth text Coyote plays the role of a mature, responsible headman, who leads his people in a successful battle against the Moon people, shortening the number of months in a year and hence the number of winter months people will have to endure. At the end of the text he takes on an announcer role, transforming the animal people of the myth era into the animals of today.

The story presented here is taken from Jacobs's Upper Coquille Athabaskan field notebook 1 (pp. 15–19). The title of the text is tc'ǝɣálsi, "Moon." Harrington (JPH, reel 027, frames 0342–44) also recorded a version of this text from Coquelle Thompson in 1942. For a published version of Harrington's text, see Whereat (2002:33–34). For a partial cognate, see the second half of the Galice text "Coyote and his grandmother lived together" (M. Jacobs 1935, 1938–39). Cf. the Shasta text "Coyote Destroys the Moons Who Kept the Earth Frozen" (Curtis [1924] 1970:204).

That time,
*   that year was fifteen months,*
*   a long winter.[8]*
Coyote would not stand for it.
He said he would travel and see about that.
He held a council with all the people,

two or three thousand people.
He would pick up the mean, hard-to-get-along people—warriors.
Picked up one thousand and said,
"We'll go tomorrow morning.
Get ready.
We'll kill that Moon.
You people don't like a long winter.
Fifteen months is too long."

Very well.

In the morning they started traveling.
They travel night and day.
They went where Moon comes [from].
Finally they got to the ocean.
They camped there.

Next morning they got ready—
he told his people,
"Get ready!"
Some said, "How can we go on the water,
on that rough ocean,
how will we go?"
Others said, "He must have some way,
we don't know,
I guess Coyote knows."

They got bows and everything ready.
High tide came—ocean very rough.
Coyote walked around—
to teach his people what's right.
"Hold tight," he said.
"Everybody ready," he said.
"We go now."

Before he touched water,

he picked up a handful of sand [and]
   threw [it] in front.
Ground rose out of the ocean—
   a strip about forty feet wide.
"Come on," he said,
   "we'll cross on this."
Soon as they had passed,
   the water would be behind them again.
For two or three days
   they traveled in that manner
      on the ocean.

"We're nearly there now," Coyote said.
   "Don't make any noise.
      It can never get dark where Moon is.
         It's bright all the time."

Now they were all out on sand.
The men said, "Oh, how will we ever return?"
   They were scared.

Now Coyote held a council, very quietly.
He said, "Now you stay right there in the sweathouse—
   where the wind comes in
      that's where you'll be.
         You must eat!"
Big-Eater[9]
   That's what he went for.

Two Mice: "What you going to do?"[10] Coyote asked them.
   "I'll go and steal—
      I'll get in any little crack."

"That's what I hired you for," Coyote said.
   "All right, you go now.
      No one will notice little Mice.

You fellows cut every bowstring in every house
so Moon cannot kill us."

It was a big town there.
So those two went,
went to houses together,
they helped each other.
They got into big otter skin,
cut bowstring in two or three places,
then went to next [house].
They had to go to fifteen, twenty houses.
In very little time they told Coyote,
"We got it all done."

Now everybody went to line up to fight.
Coyote would hit one [Moon] on head
as he went to [the] sweathouse after eating,
and he would toss that dead one to Big-Eater.
He killed seven or eight,
and then one came
who seemed to know something was wrong.
They got him—
threw him to Big-Eater,
who chewed him just like candy.
They killed several.

Then one of them was smart.
He came to [the] sweathouse door and left—
came and went away ten times,
because he smelled blood or something.

Now they tried to fight outdoors,
but no bows—strings all gone.
That fellow come in last—
when he went out, he got hit in one hip
and cut a little off.

That's February—the shortest month.

After that there were shorter winters.
They had killed off several Moons.

Getting daylight now—all quiet.
Coyote called all his men.
    Now everybody come.
Coyote's people shot and killed several.

When they left, Moon's people were following,
    but Coyote threw sand again,
        and the water closing in behind
            kept Moons from following.

Big-Eater stayed behind
    to lay around in the ocean and eat.

He paid everyone when they got home.

Now he made a rule,
    "You people are animals, not people.
        I am people, I have mother and father,
            they die long time ago.
        I'm alone, I'm traveling.

Now Deer, I'll make you for people to eat.
    Go be deer.
Now you have to be bear,
    you will be wild,
        people will kill you and eat it."

Everything he changed then.

Pitch Woman (2)

A man in training to be lucky at gambling is captured by a Pitch
Woman, who wants him for her husband. He escapes from her pack

basket into a tree and offers to fulfill her desires in exchange for
quantities of Indian money. He tricks her out of her money and
then runs home with Pitch Woman in hot pursuit. Upon reaching
home, he jumps into a waiting boat. She wades out after the boat
and drowns in deep water.

This is the second in a series of four Pitch Woman stories Jacobs
recorded from Thompson. The story presented here is taken from
Jacobs's Upper Coquille Athabaskan field notebook 1 (pp. 27–33).
It is titled tł'ɛsétc'u, which Jacobs glosses as "Pitch Woman." Har-
rington recorded an untitled version from Thompson in 1942 (JPH,
reel 027, frames 0333–36).[11] *For partially cognate versions, see the*
Hanis Coos text "The Giant Woman (Second Version)" (Frachten-
berg 1913:77–83) and an unpublished Chetco text, "Wild Woman,"
recorded by E. Jacobs in 1935.[12]

[There were] all kinds of Pitch Women. [They lived in] wild country. [They were] eight or ten feet tall. Sometimes [there were Pitch] Men. [At] one Indian town one man was training for gambling. They were training [and] training. He was a good man, a good gambler, and a good man [for] running. Before daylight he went to get a buckskin a yard and a half wide. [He would] put it down to gamble on.

This fellow went to get wood for [the] sweathouse. He tied it up [in] two places, put it on [his] head to go. He didn't see Pitch Woman standing there. In the same way [as in the previous story] she threw that wood off his head, picked him up, and put him in her basket.

Then she went. She went downhill, not so far, two [or] three miles. Then [she came to a] kind of brush, maple limbs, [and] she went down in under [that]. This fellow caught on the limbs [and] pulled himself out of [the] basket. Pitch Woman went on. She never missed him. Then this Pitch Woman nears this open door [and] she's mad.[13]

She says, "Husband, my husband."[14] That man could see. Pitch Woman laid that basket to one side, picked up another basket. She ran back and passed him, ran way out [to the place] where she had caught him, and passed back under him. [It] only took her thirty steps [to cover the distance]. Once more she came back and forth under him. About a dozen times she ran back and forth before noon, hollering [and] hollering, "My man." At last she passed him again.[15]

Pitch Women were said to have lots of money. He thought he could beat [her] running, so [the next time she passed under him] he dropped a little stick. He was going to show himself. Pitch Woman went by, [and] the stick dropped on her head.

"Oh, my husband, right there you are! I've been looking for you [for a] long time. Come down, my husband, come down." She rolled around on [the] ground. "Oh, hurry! You've got to come down and sleep with me. Oh, hurry!"

The man said, "Oh, you want me so bad?"

"Yes," she said, "I'll give you all the money I've got."

"Well, here it is. Fill up that deerskin hide," he said. Pitch Woman looked around, studied, looked everywhere.

"All right." She picked it up, she ran, [and] she hid. Then she picked grass and held it before her so she could watch him so he couldn't run away. But he could see her doing it. She'd go a little ways, then do it again. Two or three times on the way to the house, Pitch Woman did that. The man heard the door open. Pretty soon she ran [back] with a string of dentalia.

"Here you are."

"Put it down there," he told her. "I said to fill it up." All right [she would] fill it up. Pitch Woman get [kept] running and watching.

The man said, "Hurry up now, go get money." She watched all the harder now because she had put Indian money there. He could always hear [the] door open. Now the skin was nearly half full.

He said, "You better hurry now. Then you can have me." Oh, Pitch Woman was glad. She jumped around. She was to marry this nice man. She went back again. She didn't watch anymore. She ran right back. The man could hear [the] door open, but it took Pitch Woman ten or fifteen minutes to dig up her money.

At last she said to him, "There—that's enough."

"No, you got to fill it up," he said.

"Well, I only got," she said, "big, long money left."[16]

"Well, go get it," he answered. She brought it. [She] walked slow, not fast like [the] first time. She put the long Indian money in there. She's gentle now, not looking back anymore. So he jumped down to see how many more he could carry.

"Well, two more, then I go," he thought. He climbed back up. He heard the door close, knew Pitch Woman was coming.

She said, "This is the last now."

"Oh, no, you got more," he said. He thought, "I'll go now." "Oh, you go get anything. I'll take anything you have."

Pitch Woman said, "Oh, I have lots of things. You have all my money now, but I have lots of things."

"Well, go get it," he told her. She had fine woodpecker headdresses.[17]

[As] soon as she had gone halfway, the man jumped down, tied up his hide, [and] ran [and] ran. [He] came up [to an] open place. He heard, "Husband, my man!" He heard her, "My husband, my money," he heard.[18] He ran, already half[way] on [across the] prairie. She came out [of the woods]. She could see him running.

That fellow thought, "I'm going to beat her, running all [that] I can." She knew what he thought.

"Yeah, you beat me all you can," she hollered at him. "Ill get you." Whatever the man thought, she would holler out at him.

He thought, "Ill beat her."

"Yeah, you're going [to] beat me," she'd holler. Now [he] came to [the] top [of a] little hill above [the] Indian town.

Then the man hollered, "Make ready a boat," he said, "I'm [being] followed."[19]

"I'm [being] followed," she yelled back.

He ran down fast. Two men [were] ready with a boat there. Some people were still sleeping in [the] sweathouse and didn't get up. She thought that fellow went [to the] sweathouse, but he had gone [in the] boat. He had fainted, out of wind when he reached the boat. She thought he had gone [to the] sweathouse. She picked it up, the sweathouse, [and] threw it in the water. Those people asleep in it were drowned. She waded in the deep water—it was only halfway up on her. She walked with [her] head out [of water]. She followed [and] followed. Finally, water came over her head, [and] she drowned. She just followed where the boat was instead of running along the bank.

They all divided the money. The chief got the most.[20]

Pitch Woman (3)

Pitch Women visit a pregnant woman, left alone with some children to keep her company. She invites the Pitch Women in to sing and dance and manages to set their pitch dresses afire, and they flee the house, pursued by her two dogs. The woman and children die.

This is the third of the four Pitch Woman stories Coquelle
Thompson told to Elizabeth Jacobs. The story presented here is
taken from Jacobs's Upper Coquille Athabaskan field notebook 1
(pp. 33–36). The title, tɬ'ɛsɛ́·tcʻu, "Pitch Woman," is Thompson's.
For a similar tale, see the Coos text "The Giant Woman (Third Ver-
sion)" (Frachtenberg 1913:83–85).

[It was a] big town, lots of people, along about July. One woman was pregnant;
she got sick; she got a baby. Everyone, in ten or twelve houses, [all the] people
were going to get camas. Some little boys and girls were left with her to keep her
company—about a dozen [of them]. She went to get wood, pitch, making ready
for [the] baby, keeping a fire at night. The children made lots of noise playing.

[It was] getting dark, getting night now. Two dogs watched on each side of
[the] door. They feed [the] dogs, then they [the dogs] go back and lay down
by [the] door. About ten o'clock the house seemed to be making a noise. The
woman listened.

She heard talking outside, heard "Pick 'em up."[21] "Oh," she thought, "Pitch
Woman has come to scare me." Now she knew Pitch Woman.

"Quick, quick," they'd say.

The other said, "Pretty soon, pretty soon." All the kids were scared. They
all got in between baskets—no more noise now. Only the woman [was] left
[visible].

[The] Pitch Woman was saying, "Hurry up, hurry up."

The [pregnant] woman called out, "My friends! What are you talking about
outdoors? Why don't you come in and give me a dance? Come in! Maybe
you'll get me after a while, not now."

"Let's go," one said.

"All right, let's go give a dance." So they decided.

[The] woman opened [the] door, slid it to one side. "My dog, don't get mad,"
she said. "Don't get mad, my dog." The dog kept still. She made a bigger fire,
planning to melt their pitch dresses.

Now they came in. "My friends, wake me up. I'm sleepy. I want you to
dance for me." They were ready. They backed away from the fire; their pitch
was dropping. She said, "Sing something." So they sang,

sɛ'nuɣəlɛ' danícyɛ
tɬ'ɛsɛtcʻu danícya[22]

They'd get together and whisper, "Ready now, we'll get two and go."

The other, "Later, later." They danced two hours or so—sweat!

She [the pregnant woman] told them, "That looks good when your backs come together. Come together good, dance right there." Then [she] put flares on them—pitch goes up [in flames] good. They ran outdoors. She sent her dogs, one after each of them, one up, one down. One dog never returned. The other came back with one eye out.

But those children all died, standing there, and that woman had to tell those people. She told what she had done; then she dropped dead. So, whatever happens, one mustn't tell or he'll drop dead. That's [the] Indian rule. Never tell about things until one year. After one year you can tell.[23]

Pitch Woman (4)

When Pitch Woman comes to get a man's children, he asks to be taken along too. So many people similarly attach themselves to Pitch Woman that they are able to hamstring her, and she falls dead under their weight. Her body transforms into a mountain where she falls.

The story presented here is taken from Jacobs's Upper Coquille Athabaskan field notebook 1 (pp. 46–47). tł'ɛsɛ·tc'u, "Pitch Woman," is Thompson's title. Thompson noted that Pitch Woman was never a man but always a woman, that there were always two of them, and that she gave no power to people.

No one knew where she took boys and girls. She had nearly cleaned out all the boy children. Beginning one day she came in the morning. They didn't know any way to fight her. She picked them up [and] put [them in her] basket.

She took one man's children, and he said, "You take me too. I'd like to go too." Then another one came and stuck onto her. Then lots of people [did the same]. Finally it was getting too heavy, she couldn't pack them. [She] can't hardly walk. Still more [were] coming, stuck on her arms, stuck anywhere [they could]. Maybe thirty [people] stuck on her basket, head, back, and front. She could hardly move. Well, she could hardly move her legs. [She] couldn't make it.

One old lady, blind, [and] one little girl [were] right under her legs. That's why she couldn't move her legs. She [the old lady] had a little flint knife.[24] Grandma put the little one's hand there [with the knife], and they hamstrung

[Pitch Woman].[25] Then they went back in [the] house. The little girl watched her.

"Oh, now they're falling down," she told her grandmother. Now [Pitch Woman] was dead, and the people all got off. There's a mountain there where she lay down.

Mean Warrior

Mean Warrior shoots an arrow into the air; it lands on his head, splitting him into two people, brothers. They constantly practice fighting. His brother tries to beat Warrior, is unable to, and Warrior leaves him. He encounters a woman looking for Warrior to protect her family from enemy warriors. Warrior marries the woman, kills a multitude of enemy fighters, and decides to settle in his wife's village. His Wolf powers clean up all the people he has killed there.

The story presented here is taken from Jacobs's Upper Coquille Athabaskan field notebook 1 (pp. 37–45). The title, q'i·tc'uɫdən tc'ətdú·nic, "[a placename] warrior (or mean person)," is Thompson's. For a partially parallel story, see the Miluk Coos story "A young man grew up alone, and then he split himself" (M. Jacobs 1939:53–54).

People couldn't hit him. He could shoot one arrow through ten men. He fought all the time, all around, they said.[26]

[Warrior] had a sweathouse [but] no wife. [He] lay down in the sweathouse alone all [the] time. He shot into the air [once], and [the] arrow hit him right in [the] head, split him in two. Then he turned around [and] saw a man standing there.

"You are my brother," he said. Now there were two. Now they practiced fighting every day. They practiced shooting arrows every day. When done, they went back to [the] sweathouse. He had a money purse, a little canoe five feet long, [full] of Indian money. Nobody dared touch it. He kept it in [the] sweathouse. His brother didn't touch it.

Come summer, his brother told him, "I think I'm going to whip you." He [Warrior] laughed at his brother.

He said, "No, you don't want to do that. I don't want to try [test] you that way."

"I think I'll beat you. I think I can run you down."

The brother wanted to so bad, he said, "All right. [If] you want to try, we'll go out. Get your arrows!" He [Warrior] got ready; he put on [elk-skin armor], a fighting coat of elk skin.[27] [It was] white. [An] arrow wouldn't penetrate it. [An] arrow would penetrate only tough spots. He put it on.

His brother had already walked away. Now they would come together. Now his brother was shooting at him. For a long time he dodged all his arrows. [This is] a Big Bend story, told at Rogue River get-togethers. His brother nearly whipped him. [Then] they got together to fight with knives. His brother had a war knife as long as [your] arm.[28] [His brother] hit [struck out] two or three times [but] missed.

Then he told his brother, "That's enough now. We'll stop."

Now he went and lay down [in the] sweathouse, all night; [he] never got up. His brother didn't come to [the] sweathouse. He felt bad because he couldn't whip his brother [Warrior].

About ten o'clock he [Warrior] got out, got ready, took [his] knife, arrows, war coat, [and] told his brother, "I'll go now. You'll stay here. You can have the Indian money. Take all I have—it's yours. I'll go." He put [his] war coat on [his] shoulder and started upriver. He felt bad.

About noon he lay down on the trail to rest. [There was] nice grass. [He put his] arm over [his] head, [and] he rested. He heard something make a noise. [It] sounded like someone crying. It came from the direction in which he was traveling. He heard a woman crying, approaching. Pretty soon she came close, about ten feet away. She stopped crying [and] sat down [with] her pack basket of Indian money. That fellow never moved, never looked.

She asked, "Where [do] you come from?"

"Oh, I come from home."

"Do you know where that fellow, War Man, lives?"

"Oh, I don't know, maybe he lives down below here. What do you want of him?"

She said, "I'll tell you. I've come to see him. They are going to kill my mother, brother, and sister. There is war all the time.[29] I've got money to pay him, my basketful of money. I'll pay for myself and my sister, [the] only ones left. Just last month they took my brother [and] my sister for slaves." He thought about it. She asked, "How far [does] that man live?"

"I don't know," he said, "maybe down below."

"Well," she said, "I have to go. I'll try to get back today." She packed up,

[and] she walked away. Then that fellow got up; he shook his war coat—it made a noise like thunder. She turned around and looked.

"That's my name," he said, "I am [the Warrior]."[30]

"Oh, it's you. You hid it from me. Why?" she asked.

"Well," he said, "we'll go now. You got me all right." He's hungry for a fight; he's mad. She packed the war coat, going in front. She's his wife now. He packed the money. They gooooooo, get on top of a mountain, [and] look down. Oh! People, people—[there were] a thousand people.

"Oh, they're abusing my father now," she said.

"That's all right. I'll fix it," he said. "Tomorrow morning I'll fight all right." Oh, that woman was glad.

Well, they sat down there and watched. He heard those people talking about him.

They said, "Maybe that woman went to get that [Warrior]."[31] He heard them hollering [and] hollering. They said they would kill the old man that night, after supper. They [the Warrior and his wife] went to the old man's house, right by [the] river. They went there fast, in [the] dark.

"Give me a little bit to eat," he told the old man. The old man told them to sit all around the war fighter. [The Warrior] ate a little, not too much. [The Warrior] wanted to sweat.

The old man said, "I'll go with you." He said, "Maybe they'll kill me right in front of you." They went in [the sweat]house. He took a big rock [and] put it in the sweathouse.

He said to the old man, "Sit down maybe here. When [the] men come in, roll this rock back and forth and say, 'Not too thick, one at a time come in and kill me.'"

Now those people were coming to the sweathouse. Now lots came. This war fellow [was] ready, sitting by [the] door. Arrows came shooting into [the] sweathouse. Arrows went over him [because] he was so low. One man came in, [and] the old man wiggled the rock and groaned, and the war fighter pulled him [the entering man] apart with one pull and threw him aside. Now that sweathouse was nearly full of dead people behind the old man.

He told the old man to holler, "Come one at a time."

The old man said, "I'm alive yet."

"Yes," said [the Warrior], "you'll be alive yet tomorrow morning. It's nearly daylight." They killed them as fast as they came in. Now there was no room left to move that stone. And it was getting daylight. All those people wanted to kill [the Warrior].

Now he put on his big war coat [and] something [a mask] in front of his face. He got ready. He studied. He decided, "I'll run to an open place, way down there. They'll think they have scared me, and they'll run after me all right." Then he raised up [out of the] sweathouse and ran. They started to run after him and shoot. It was like tch tch tch where the arrows hit his coat but didn't go through. Then when he got to [the] open place, he turned around; he took his knife, [and] cut a head off, cut the next one's head off, [and continued to] cut heads off. He used his knife all right. He fought there all morning, ever since daylight. His knife [was] just getting black from blood. His arm was bloody to [the] elbow. He fought there all day. Hardly any people came—hardly any were left.

Well, about two, three, four o'clock, there were four, five men coming right towards him. "Don't kill us," they said, "we want to talk to you." So he stood there.

"Well, I am your brother-in-law," one said. It was his wife's brother. "Now you have cleaned up everything, you've cleaned up all, all right." He had blood all over his war coat.

"If there are any more of these people, tell them to come kill me," he said. Now they went to the old man's house. They saw dead people lying around there just like cut brush.

So they came back to the house. Well, he looked around [and it] seemed like a prairie, [on the] other side, nice. He decided [to] stay there. [He] had a wife there now. "If anybody bothers [me], I'll kill them." That's how he thought.

That night he was getting tired. He had to sleep in the house—no sweathouse [was available]. Now he called Wolf—he had good powers—to eat the dead people, clean up the place. About ten o'clock he heard Wolves, wooooo, circling the town. They all came down, a thousand Wolves, Ocean Wolves, too. In no time they had cleaned it up. So they slept sound. Nothing bothered them.

Maybe [he] went around the world. I don't remember any further.

Star

Coyote and five companions spear a whale, which tows their boat
ten days before dying and beaching them on the shores of heaven
[the land of the dead]. They meet a man in charge of strangers

*there, and he introduces them to Spider, who agrees to return
Coyote to the earth below. Coyote transforms his five companions
into stars, is cautioned not to open his eyes while descending on
Spider's belt, but looks anyway. As a result, he drops to the ocean,
dies, is washed ashore, and is revived by the bite of a worm.*

*The story presented here is taken from Jacobs's Upper Coquille
Athabaskan field notebook 1 (pp. 49–52). The title, x̣átɬ'ətc'ɛ,
"Star," is Thompson's.*

Coyote, he went [to the] ocean, and he had five men. And they saw a big whale.
They speared it. [It was a] good-size boat they got. That spear pulled the boat.
That whale went night and day for ten days; [it] never stopped. Finally, [the]
whale kind of stopped. They felt low water, [and] they pulled [the] boat out on
land. [The] whale was dead [by] then.

There's no one around; all [is] quiet. They didn't know what place they got
ashore at. Now they slept. Then [at] daylight they saw a big mountain.

"Let's go that way." All right, they went—six of them. He's boss [Coyote].

Coyote saw a man, who asked, "Where [are] you fellows going?"

"Oh, we just came ashore here," Coyote said. "Yes, any more people there?"

"Oh, not much," he said. "Go that way. There's lots of people there. I'm
looking after this place. I take care of strangers," the man told him. "Aren't
you people dead?"

Coyote, "No, we're not dead."

"Do you know where you are?"

Coyote, "No!"

[The] man said, "You're in [heaven], here."[32] They hadn't died so they didn't
see much.[33]

"How many days have we been here? Oh, about three days," Coyote said.

The man told him, "You've been here three years already."

"Well," Coyote said, "I don't know."

"This is a different place, that's why," the man told him. "It's different from
the place you came from. This is [heaven]."

Coyote said, "We've got to go back."

"How are you going to go back?"

Coyote, "Boat, I guess."

"You can't get home—no way," the man told him.

Coyote, "Well, I don't know how we'll get back. I don't know."

"Wait a minute, I'll go see this fellow." [It was his] partner. "You are in a different world now; you have to do things differently. I'll go see this fellow." Then that fellow came out.

"Let's go a little ways on that bank," he said. They all went. "Now you look down. You see [the] ocean, *way* down [there]. Now you see [the] ocean where you came from. You can't go back. It might take you ten days to go back. Maybe you'd drown somewhere."

So then they asked the partner, "How [do] *you* think we [can] get home? How long [do] you think it [would] take us from here?"

"Oh, maybe ten days after you get [to the] ocean."

Coyote said, "Who'll take me down?"

That [partner] fellow [Spider] said, "I'll take you down."[34] Now he [Coyote] turned around to the five men.

He said, "Now you, my men. I'll leave you here. I won't take you back. Everyone here must see you. You will be Morning Star. You will be Evening Star."[35] [There were] three left. "You'll be traveling, the three of you. One [will be] dipper, one sənɣatdə́ł, [and one] sənx̣ástł'u.[36] [The] three [will] come up in [the] evening that way, traveling. That's all right. I'll go now," Coyote said.

Spider said, "Step on my belt. Don't open your eyes, or I'll drop you. I have no power to pack a man who looks around everywhere. I have no power for that."

Coyote, "All right. I'll shut my eyes." Coyote [was] no fool, you know. So he took him down on his string.

Coyote, "How long [will] it take us?"

"Oh, about ten days," Spider said. "It's a long ways." Oh, he was pretty tired, that Coyote. He'd like to look. About halfway [down] he looked. There! [He] dropped off [the] string, down head over heels, down, down. Oh, I laugh [about it]. He [had] no business to do that. [He] dropped down [to the] ocean, dead. [The] water took him ashore, dead [and] stinking. Worms bit him.

"Oh, who could wake me up?" he said. "I was sleeping so good." He arose up. That's the end of it.

Coyote and God

"Coyote and God" is divided into two major sections. In the first section the world is bereft of fire, fish, and berries. Coyote and fol-

*lowers travel across the ocean to the land of God, challenge him
to a game of staying awake, and succeed in securing fire, fish, and
berries for the world of the animal people and for future human
beings. In the second, larger section of the myth, Coyote impreg-
nates a girl, who gives birth to ten Coyote sons, then attempts to
drown them. Coyote rescues his sons but is unhappy with the last
and scrawniest one. As punishment for Coyote's dislike of their
youngest brother, the sons immolate themselves, but the youngest
son survives. Coyote finds his dead sons' bones, resuscitates them,
and then searches for the missing youngest one. Coyote finds him,
orchestrates his rescue from a snake's belly, and is finally recon-
ciled with all his progeny.*

*The story presented here is taken from Jacobs's Upper Coquille
Athabaskan field notebook 1 (pp. 53–69). The title is Jacobs's.[37]
Harrington recorded a version of the myth from Thompson in 1942
(JPH, reel 027, frames 0345–47). For parallel texts, see the Tututni
story "The Theft of Fire" (Farrand and Frachtenberg 1915:242),
the Hanis Coos "The Stealing of Fire and Water" (Frachtenberg
1913:39–43), and an episode in the Miluk Coos myth "The trickster person who made the country" (M. Jacobs 1940:210–13).*

God's home [is] where fish come from.[38]

Everywhere [there was] no fire in this world. Coyote Jim heard that [God]
had fire. [Coyote] got people, one hundred [of them] ready, [the] best men, to
go there. He went, took his people. He threw sand in [the] ocean, [which] made
land come up to walk on; water closed in behind them.[39] How many days they
traveled I don't know. They got there.

They went in a big house. It would hold any number of people.

Coyote Jim told [God], "I came to play a game with you."

God said, "All right." Coyote saw a fine fire there. It never went out. [It was]
just burning night and day [with] God sitting there.

Coyote Jim got ready. God got ready. They were going to sit on beds across
from each other.

Coyote Jim said, "I'll bet you money."

God said, "What do you want me to bet?"

Coyote, "I want fire, I want fish, I want berries—strawberries, huckleberries, blackberries. I want all kinds of berries." Oh, they saw in the house there all kinds of berries. Everybody looked around. Berries hung down. They wanted to eat them. Fish played right in [the] house [in] water there. This was where fish came from.

Now they fixed a bet. Coyote Jim sat down. He put a stick behind him to lean against. They had to play ten days, ten nights. Coyote Jim put in a star for [one] eye. He [was] smart. He slept. He did that for five, six, seven, eight days.

Then he told his people, "Watch it now. You grab that fire and run away with it when I catch him." [It became the] ninth night. All day they sat there. Coyote Jim [was] not sleepy. [It became the] tenth night. The fire [was] burning all [the] time; nobody fixed it—it just burned there.

"Soon as I jump him, you grab [the] fire." There's going to be a fight. Come daybreak and Coyote Jim jumped him. God had kind of shut his eyes.

"I win, I win," Coyote said. He tried to get in to where [the] fish played. He knew if he could get some of that water the fish would follow him. God tried to hold him back. Finally Coyote Jim got into that water, [and] then the fish followed him. Mud Turtle already had the fire outside.

Coyote Jim threw sand [and] made ground. They crossed. Then the ocean closed behind them. The fish followed them. They got ashore. They kept running back to that home river. Coyote Jim got there. All kinds of fish [were] coming in: steelhead, Chinook, silverside, trout—all kinds. [There were] millions of them. Now, no fire yet.

"Where's [the] fire?" Coyote said. People were hungry. They needed to cook fish.

"I gave it to that fellow." Coyote asked that fellow. Again [in the same manner], about a dozen [people] it had been passed on to. At [the] last [it was] Mud Turtle [who] would not give it up. Coyote [was] mad. [He threatened to] cut him [Mud Turtle] all to pieces.

Turtle squealed, "All right. I got it."

Coyote, "Where [did] you put it?"

"I put it in willow roots over there."

Coyote, "Go get it." They go get it, take moss, [and] build a fine fire. Everybody ate.

"Now," Coyote said, "nobody [is] to take fire till I say so. Pretty soon I'll issue that fire." Everybody was satisfied.

He [Coyote] told them, "Go get fish. Cut them. Cook them." They caught fish, cut them nice, put them on sticks. They cook.

"Every river fish must go into. [In the] wintertime [they will] all go in creeks, spawn there, lay eggs, in every creek. When fish get old, white backed [and] ready to die, they [will] go back to [the] ocean. They'll get fresh when they hit salt water. They'll get home. You must not abuse fish, just eat [them] right away. Every one of you gets a little fire. Go home [and] make your fire. Make your home. [You will] get fish, get deer, there will be lots of everything now." So everyone had to go home.

"You people do not have to plant. You do not have to work. Berries will just come for you every year. God will send them."

Coyote Jim went everywhere from there. He found [caught] a girl right by the river. He stole her, got her in [the] family way [pregnant]. She had a baby. But [the] girl had a family. Coyote Jim ran away.

"How can we sever the cord? We have no knife."

"Use sharp grass," Coyote called from outside.[40] Ten sons were born then. No girls, just boys.

The [girl's] father said, "Coyote's smart. We can't hurt him. You can't kill all those children."

Coyote scratched his head. "Give me a good house," he said. First thing, a big house [stood] right there, good fire [and] everything.

He scratched his head. "Next thing I want is a good sweathouse. Get me a good sweathouse." A fine sweathouse stood right there ready. Coyote didn't [have to] work [for these].

Coyote ran downriver, got a fine little fish basket, [and] made a little fence [weir] to watch there. Those people had thrown his sons in the water to try to kill them. He sat down there. He had made [the] sweathouse warm [and] nice. Soon one [son] came, like a fish, came into the trap.

He [Coyote] called [to] it. "My son," he said. There he stood, a young man beside him. Another came [about] ten-thirty. [He] called to him, "My son, get to one side." Another one came. The old lady had thrown them in. Every little while one came. He'd call him by name as soon as he got there. Now [it was] nearly daylight, [he] had nine. Then one came but turned [and] swam back again. Oh, it made Coyote mad.

He said, "What's the matter?" He saw water splashing around. The fish did that ten [or] twelve times. Now [it was] just daylight. At last he came in [into the basket trap]. [He was a] small fellow.

Coyote said, "I'll call you Spáyul," he said.[41]

Now he's done. Coyote tore down the salmon fence [and] took his sons [to the] sweathouse. He did not care much for Spáyul—too small. Pretty near noon they sweated; then [they were] ready for breakfast. They go back in [the] house—breakfast, acorns, everything [was] ready. Coyote [was] just like Jesus—whatever he thought, it came about like that. They eat. He tells his sons all about everything.

"I used to be a hunter [and] kill elk, deer, everything."

"Well," they said, "we can do that."

Coyote, "All right. You boys hunt, but don't go so far." Everybody had arrows [and an] arrow sack. All ten of them, Spáyul, too.

They hunt all day. They saw lots of deer, but they missed them. Spáyul, he came behind all the time. He'd shoot deer. He had [needed] only one arrow to [kill] each deer.

Spáyul thought, "I [will] kill nine anyhow." Spáyul [was] smarter than the rest, but Coyote Jim thought he [was] nothing because [he was] small. Well, he killed nine deer. Then he thought, "I'll go back." The nine brothers each packed a deer, and he carried their arrow sacks. They put [the] deer down by [the] door. The old man grabbed [the] deer [and] told all the boys to go [to the] sweathouse. They sweat before supper. [The] old man went up three, four hundred yards where his children [were] born [and] told [the] folks to come get meat.

"All right." [The] old man and woman came, but [the] girl didn't come. They packed lots of meat. He gave them hides, too, to make blankets. Now those people lived good. [The] boys hunted all summer. [There was] lots of meat getting dry. They had a good home. [They] killed [deer] every day, every day. One month they did not hunt. [They] hunted most of June, July, August—fat deer.

One day [still] Coyote didn't like that Spáyul—too small. The oldest son noticed that. [One day] the oldest son sent all [the] kids to eat supper. He remained in [the] sweathouse with Coyote.

He asked, "Why don't you like Spáyul, my brother? [Do] you think [that because] we pack so much deer, we killed them? *He's* the one [who] killed them all. We just pack [them]. Why don't you like him?" Coyote did not believe it. Though, he noticed that the boy [Spáyul] didn't eat much.

Coyote Jim said, "I've killed everything. But one thing I've never killed, that's a white deer." He's lying, ha! ha! He never killed anything. He never hunted. He just made [the] boys hunt. They all knew now that he didn't like Spáyul. That day they all went [to] hunt.

They said, "What [are] we going to do? We don't have to stay with him if he doesn't like our brother." That Spáyul just stood there, saying nothing. He never opened his mouth at all.

The oldest brother said, "Build a big fire, here. They got a whole lot of dry wood [and] made a big fire! They [were] ready to *do* something.

When [the] fire was half coals, the oldest son said, "I'll jump in there—you boys can follow me." All right, he jumped in there. He burned up there. Then the next one jumped [into the fire]. They kept on that way. At last only Spáyul [was] left standing there. He said nothing. He had a bow and arrow there. They punished the old man that way. At last Spáyul jumped. He had a power. He went down many feet under ground [instead of burning].

He thought, "I ought to die too." [He came to a] big lake, like the ocean—rough. [There were] lots of snakes there [in the water]. Soon as snakes smell you, [they] make [the] water rough [and make] lots of wind. Now Spáyul hung his blanket and arrows up on a tree, ready to jump in.

He thought, "Someone will find them." He knew he'd never get out [because] the snakes would swallow him. So he jumped in. [He] swam nearly to [the] middle of [the] lake when a snake swallowed him.

Now that evening the old man saw his ten sons all coming, packing deer. He ran back in [the] house to fix up [the] fire. He heard them put the deer down right by the door, nine of them. But nobody came in [the] house.

"What's [the] matter?" He ran out! No deer! Nobody! But he'd seen them, he'd heard the deer fall. Now that old man, it made him crazy. He knew his children [were] dead. He went down to [the] ocean. He thought they [had] drowned. Half [of the] ocean [was] dry, but no, they're not there. When he cried, it made [the] ocean half dry. He kept on that way, crying right where [there was] rough water. It would dry up—no, nothing. Just like wind he traveled, crying [and] crying [but] never [finding] anything.

He cried, "My sons, gone." Ten times [he cried like that].[42] Oh, he punished himself. [He would] eat nothing. [The] old lady, [his] mother-in-law, tried to feed him. He can't eat, just cry.

Now, [the] next morning he [was] going to track them. He found that fire. He found those bones. Well, he took those bones, put them all together in an elk skin. [He] put [them] in, put [them] in—every bone. He took them to [the] sweathouse [and] put them together [assembled the skeletons] where they slept. [There were] only nine. One was gone. Oh, he had to go back again. [But] no, [he] couldn't find it at all. Well, he [would] have to do something, [even if there were] only nine. They sweated, sweated. Five nights they sweated. Soon as daylight [came], he went out [and] sat on top [of the] sweathouse.

Then he heard them talking. "Open that door." Now his oldest son came up, then the next, the next. [They] kept on that way. Only nine came up, one's gone. Oh! He felt bad.

His oldest son said, "You don't like my brother. See what you get! Why [did] you do that?" Coyote [was] crying.

"I don't know," he said. "That's my mistake. I don't know why I did that. I just thought this way, 'He's too small. He can't do anything.'" That's what Coyote said. "I didn't say I don't like him. Now I'll get ready. I'll go hunt till I find him. Then I'll be satisfied. I'll hunt all over up to Coos," he said.

He went hunting [searching] where they [the brothers] had burned. Then [he] went to [the] water. He followed his trail [and] came upon his clothes, arrow, and bow hanging there.

"Let me try," Coyote said. He cried [and] cried, [but the] water didn't dry [up]. He did it five times, [but] no, [the] water didn't dry [up]. Now he called Fish Duck, [who was a] good traveler.

He said, "Go get your partner, Gray Eagle, and I want you too, Fish Duck.[43] Now we have to get a whole lot of food [because] about a thousand people [will be] coming together. They won't go near that water, but camp away from it."

He said, "Tomorrow at sunrise we [will] get there." All right, [when it became] daylight, people [were] running around. They [were] scared [when] getting near there [because the] water [was] getting rough. [The] snakes smelled them.

ts'ɛɣəltc'u [Gray Eagle] [has] a good eye. He said, "Well, your boy [is] right here, in that snake out in the middle."

Everybody said, "Well, what can you do? You can't catch that snake!" They held a council, talked, talked, [and] talked it over.

Then Gray Eagle said, "If I had good help, I could bring up that snake."

"Oh, that's what I want," Coyote said. "We'll get you help, whoever you want."

"I want that fellow," he said, pointing to Fish Duck.

"Oh, all right, everybody be ready." Now those two got ready. They had long talons, both of them. They went up [to the] top of a tree to look down. They saw by [the looks of] the snake's belly where [the] young man was. They talked.

One said, "You go first, I'll come behind. You take the tail, I'll take the head. We'll get him up." Now the people saw Gray Eagle diving down into [the] water just like a bullet. Behind him [came] Fish Duck. They hit [the] water together. Now [the] water [was] getting rougher and rougher. They saw Fish Duck's feathers coming up.

Then finally they brought that snake right ashore. Coyote Jim [was] talking so glad. He said he'd give those birds all kinds of money—anything they wanted. Now no one [would] touch [the] snake. All [the] people [were] standing around. Snake [was] dead, [but] no one would touch it. Coyote Jim took a big knife. He [was] going to cut that snake. Oh, it's just like stone. [The] knife didn't go in it at all. The knife [was] getting broken.

"If anyone can cut this, I'll give so much." No, nobody tried.

Well, one young fellow said, "Maybe I can do it."

Coyote laughed. "You can't do it," he said. [The] young fellow didn't say much. [The fellow was a] little lizard, poisonous.[44]

He [Lizard] said, "I've got a flint knife. I can do it."

Coyote said, "All right, boy, my mistake, you do it." Lizard cut it just like a fish. [He] opened that snake's belly [and] Spáyul dropped out.

"There you are," Lizard said, "[you who] make fun of me."

"Oh, I'll give you lots of money. I just said that," Coyote answered.

So they took that young Spáyul [to the] sweathouse. [He] sweated night and day for four or five days.

Coyote said, "Call me in [the] morning. I'll open [the] door for you."

Come morning, someone called him, "Open [the] door." Now his son came up, went down [to the] river to swim, [and] came back. Now Coyote Jim petted him. [He was a] big thing now. [Coyote would] never be mean [to him] anymore. He [Coyote] called everybody [to a] big place [and] paid out lots [of money]. Now he settled right there [with] his sons. He never lived [with] any wife. He just got a girl once in a while, got her knocked up. He just traveled around the world that way. Sometimes they kill him, but he [always] comes alive again.

Coyote

Coyote travels around, finds an old woman home alone, and rapes her. When her sons return home, they launch Coyote in a boat out on the ocean, where he becomes stranded. Seal and Whale approach him, and he alters their appearances. Whale swallows Coyote, and Coyote kills him. He cuts himself out of Whale when Whale drifts ashore in the land of the dead. Coyote reenters Whale and drifts ashore again. There he encounters a menstruating woman, skins her, and dons her skin. He sleeps with her sister, abuses her, then runs away and hides in a hollow tree, where he becomes trapped. Coyote escapes by dismembering himself and throwing the pieces out of a hole. He reassembles himself, but his guts are stolen so he closes his anus with pitch, which catches fire when he jumps over burning fields, and he burns up. Revived by a bug's bite, Coyote hunts deer for his grandmother. Transformed by his powers into a headman, Coyote joins the dead people's round dance, where he is trapped and killed. Panther joins the dance and escapes, the only man to do so.

The story presented here is taken from Jacobs's Upper Coquille Athabaskan field notebook 1 (pp. 70–100). The title is Jacobs's. Harrington (1942) recorded a partial version of this story from Thompson (JPH, reel 027, frames 0318–25). For cognate texts, see the Joshua story "Coyote and the Old Woman" (Farrand and Frachtenberg 1915:233–38) and an unpublished Chetco text, "Coyote," recorded by E. Jacobs in 1935. The episode of Coyote being trapped in a hollow tree, dismembering himself piece by piece, and reconstituting his body is widely told in the Northwest—as well as in California, the Great Basin, and the Plateau—either as a separate story or as one in a series of Coyote episodes (Thompson 1929:304 n. 109[m]).[45]

Coyote Jim was traveling. [He] finally came to the Coos River [but] found no one [there]. He [was] always traveling—never stayed in one place. Finally on top of a hill [he] saw smoke, close to [the] river.

"Oh," he said, "I'll find them." He came to [the] door. [He] looked in [the] door, saw one old woman there.

He asked, "Where are the people gone [to]?"

The old woman said, "My children have gone fishing down at the ocean."

"All right. You got any sweathouses here?"

"Yes," she said, "over that way."

"Well," said Coyote Jim, "I'll go lie down over there. When your children come back, tell them to wake me up. I'll go over there and sleep in that warm place." He said, "Don't holler. When I sleep, I can't hear anything. I sleep sound. You have to come in [the] sweathouse and punch me with a stick. Then I wake up."

About eleven o'clock the old woman saw a boat coming. Now she ran in [the] sweathouse, hollered, punched [him] with a stick. No, he didn't wake up.

"Oh," she thought, "what's the matter? [Is] he dead?" Coyote Jim was getting mischievous now. He wanted that old lady to come in [the] sweathouse. That's what he wanted. Now she was in the sweathouse. Then he woke [up].

"Now you go first," he said. "You go [in] front [of me]." He knew what he [was] doing. Two or three boys were watching. They saw what he's doing.

"Oh, that fellow—he's abusing our mother," they said. She didn't want to [do] it. He made her do it. He made her do it, that old lady, he got what he wanted. He went. He left the old lady there and went home.

Now already that boat had come pretty close. Those sons knew what he had done.

They said, "We'll fix it. We'll fix it." Now [that] Coyote had what he wanted, he ran down to [the] mouth of [the] river where [the] boat [would] come ashore, on [the] beach.

He hollered to the boys, "Come over here, come [to] this shore here. Now I [will] tell you boys. You fellows don't know. I'm [the] man to tell anything. Now I'm a stranger here. You boys take [the] fish out and fix [the] boat so I can lay down in it. That's the law. That's how you have to do it."

"All right," they said. They cleaned [the] boat out. He went to lay down there. They put a little wooden bailer there, some *old* baskets to sit on. That's all they left on [the] boat. They pinched each other. Now Coyote lay down, covered his face, [and] went to sleep. He had ordered them to pull [the] boat close to [the] house. Coyote heard the boat moving, making [a] noise. Those four boys were pulling it. He lay there a long time, maybe two or three hours. He felt [the] boat going way up and down. The boys had pushed the boat out, and the high tide had taken it out to the ocean, that boat. Now Coyote felt it going up and down.

"What's the matter?" he thought. He had told the boys when they got through to get out. Now he got up, about two o'clock. Oh, it pretty near made him crazy. He's out in the middle [of the] ocean. [There was] nothing but [the] bailer and old doubled[-up] baskets to sit on. That's all they left in [the] boat—no paddle, nothing. [The] boat [was] not going [moving] anymore. [It] just stayed in one place, way out in [the] ocean. All kinds of stuff [were] coming up to see him. A small Seal came right by [the] boat.

Seal said, "Hello, what's the matter?"

Coyote said, "Oh, your head's not so good-[looking]. The next time, you come by real close, and I'll fix you so you're all right." Seal went. Whale came. Oh, [it's] mouth [was] open that much [two arm's length]. [It had] no teeth at all.

Coyote called [to] Whale, "Come a little closer." Whale came [and] tried to swallow him.

Coyote said, "No, you can't swallow me now, not till after a while. Just now I want to see." Then Coyote got [the] basket ready. [The] Whale came back, opened [its] mouth, [and] water splashed way out. Coyote put [the] basket in his mouth, made teeth for Whale. Whale went around, [and] pretty soon he came back. "Now you got teeth," Coyote told him.

Now Seal came back. "Come close," Coyote said. All right. Seal came close. Coyote put [the] wooden bailer on his head, saying, "Now you go on. Come around after a while so I can see you." All kinds of fish came. Coyote no longer noticed. He had nothing to fix them with. He felt crazy. He sat down, began to sing. [He] sang,

> *"I got lots of friends where I came from,*
> *but I don't here now.*
> *I don't know what I'm going to do."*

Then he studied what to do. Now that seal came along.

"Come pretty close—I'd like to see you." Seal came close, raised up, oh, he [was] round-headed. Coyote said, "Oh, you [are] all right now. You look pretty good. You can go on now."

Now Whale came. Oh. [He] opened his great big mouth to swallow him.

"All right. I'm ready now," Coyote said. He had decided the best thing he could do was jump into Whale's mouth. He could not get out [of his predicament] any other way. Now Whale came. Now Coyote [was] ready.

"Come pretty close, come close to [the] boat. I'm ready now." Whale came, [and] Coyote jumped in. When he got in, it was just like a good tight house. Whale [was] going [and] going, no one knew where. Coyote did not know either. Coyote figured that since Whale always came ashore when [it] died, he wondered what to do. He scratched his head.

"I wish I had a knife." Right away he had a little flint knife.

Then he wondered, "Which way is his heart?" He had to decide which way to cut. Now he started right in [on the] heart. [He] cut down several inches. Oh, the Whale leapt. Coyote cut again [and] cut again. Now he had just like water, grease [flowing around him]. Now I don't know how long he was in the ocean, maybe two, three, four months or more. Then he felt [the] Whale roll.

"Oh, I'm on sand now," Coyote thought. He cut open the Whale [and] climbed out. [It was a] big open place. He could see a big beach. Now Coyote had to hide because people would come just as soon as they smelled that Whale. He didn't know what kind [of] people they may be. He hid in [the] sand [with] just [his] eyes and nose [sticking] out so he could see. Pretty soon he saw a man come running, a tall fellow. He looked around that Whale, walked around it. Then he *went* back, running back. Now Coyote looked [in the] opposite direction. Another man [was] coming [from] that way. He did [the] same thing, looked around [the] Whale [and] ran back. Coyote fixed himself better. The sand was warm.

Pretty soon people were coming from the first direction. Oh, just [about] one hundred, one hundred of them [were] coming. He heard them talking.

"Oh, what kind of Whale [is it]? Oh, alder or red Whale it is."[46] He saw knives as long as an arm. Everybody had a knife. Now [the] boss [was] coming.

He said, "Oh, something [is] wrong here." Now many people were coming from the second direction. People [were] thick around [the] Whale. [The] boss said, "Here, something's wrong. This Whale has a live person's smell.[47] It mustn't be touched."

Coyote wondered, "What kind of people can these be? They must be ghosts."

[The] ghost chief said, "Leave this Whale alone. It belongs to live people. All you [folks] go home." They all left. Now Coyote was there. They had not touched [the] Whale.

"Well, I must be in a different world," Coyote thought. "Those are not people; they are dead people." Well, he had to go back in that Whale's belly. It was [the] best he could do. He had some kind of stick, kelp. Now he had to sew up the hole on the Whale's belly.

He got in and said, "Now, my Whale, take me back where we came from." Now high tide came in, took [the] Whale away, [and] they went back across like fish. They went, maybe two, three months. Oh, just like water [the] grease [was] now. Coyote can't stand it now. He lay in it just like [it was] water. It melted his eyes. [His] hair [was] all gone.

Now it came ashore. He felt it. He can't see. He felt it roll.

"Must be on ground." Well, he had to get out. If he had to die, he [would at least] step on sand. He went up two hundred yards to the bank. He dug sand and got in it to stay. He can't see now if anyone comes. [It] must be nighttime [when] he got in there. Early in the morning, a moon-sick [menstruating] woman came around to swim.[48] She found a Whale there, saw tracks [leading] from [the] Whale. [She] saw a bald head. She wasn't scared.

She asked, "Who is it? Who are you?"

Coyote said, "It's me. I can't see anything. [I've] got no eyes. Lift me up." He caught hold of her hand. Of course, he wouldn't let go now.

"Who are you?" she said. "I've got people living a little ways from here. There are lots of people here." She said, "I'll go tell people the Whale is here."

"Oh," Coyote said, "it's too soon. You can go pretty soon. What [are] you doing? Are you a moon-sick girl?"

"Yes," she said.

"What do you do when you go back? How [do] you go back?"

She said, "Well, I cross a creek, and then I have to walk on a string [a strip of skin like a tightrope] and hold two trees in my hands and when I get there, I put one in one door, [the] other in [the] other door."[49] She's packing wood, bark on those trees. "That's what I do," she said.

Now he asked, "What's this—[the] top of your head?" He's feeling [around on her].

"Oh, that's [the] top [of] my head." He came down now. [Coquelle gestures with his hand.]

"What is this?"

"That's my ear."

Coyote, "Yes? Your ear? All right. What's this?"

She said, "My eye."

"What's this?"

"My nose."

"What's this?"

"My mouth."

"What's this?"

"My throat." [Coyote] kept on [asking].

"My shoulder." "My arm."

Coyote, "What do you call this?"

"Oh, my hand."

"What's this?"

"My breast."

Coyote squeezed [them]. "Oh, you got good ones," he told her. "Keep on that way. What's this?"

"My belly." "My thigh."[50] He's holding her hand all the time, using only one hand [to touch her].

"What's this?"

"My knee." "My leg." "My ankle." He's just fooling [with her]. "My foot." "My toes."

"How many?"

"Five."

"Five? All right." Now [he started in on the] other side, all over again—[the] same thing.

"Top of my head, my ear, my eye, my mouth, my chin, my throat, the hollow of my neck."[51] She [was] getting tired. "My breast, my arm, my stomach, my thigh, my knee, my shinbone, my ankle, my foot."[52]

"What's this?" [He was] touching her vagina.[53] That's what he [was] after. He held her all [the] time. [He] made her turn around [and] went down [her] back, all [the] same way [asking about everything]. Now he got ready. "Stand up straight," he said "[and] look over that way." She did. Now he caught her skin at the top of her head, tore it off her, [and] stepped into [it] himself. [As] soon as he put it on, he could see. That woman died there, naked.

Now Coyote went [and] got the two trees. "I think I can make it. If I don't make it, they'll kill me," Coyote said. Another moon-sick girl was laying in the bed.

The girl had told him, "My sister and I lay together." That's what Coyote

[was] after. Now Coyote got on that tightrope. The women were sitting outside.

That girl's mother said, "My girl is coming back. Now, we'll watch her." He lifted those two trees, climbed on that tendon, [and] he walked. Now [the] trees unbalanced him a bit, right in the middle. That old lady saw it.

"Oh, what's [the] matter?" she said. "My girl never did that way before. Something's wrong." Now Coyote straightened up, came right to the door, put one tree [at] one door, [the] other by [the] other house.

Now [that] girl had told him, "[As] soon as I do that, I go right to bed." He had to do that now. He went in [the] house to get in bed. Now the sister was supposed to get up [and] go swim. Now [it was] pretty near 10 a.m. Nearly all the people were gone to cut that Whale. Just one boy [was] left to feed his sisters. [The] old women always stood by [the] ladder in [the] house. [A] person had to go down backwards.

[The] boy noticed [and] said, "What's the matter [with] my sister? She's got something hanging down between her legs." [It was] Coyote's balls.

[The] old lady said, "Don't talk to your sister that way. What's [the] matter with you?" Coyote went and got in bed. [The] other sister got up and left for her swim. Now that old lady made breakfast, acorn soup and so on. Now when the sister came back, they ate together.

That girl [the other sister] went to bed before sundown because she was a moon-sick girl. Coyote Jim [was] already in bed. He's glad now, a young woman [was] coming to bed with him. He ought [to] be hanged.

Now half a mile away, where they were cutting [the] Whale, they hadn't found that girl's body yet. Now Coyote had bothered that lady all night. [The] next morning he [was] afraid. He ran. When they found that body, Coyote [was] already gone. He ran, looked back, and saw them chasing him.

He ran into a hollow tree [and] said, "Come together, my stick."[54] That stick came together. [They] didn't see him anywhere now. People got there looking for him.

He heard them say, "I saw him run right here but no tracks here, over there" and so on. Coyote listened.

He thought, "They can't get me." Then the people went back. They had followed him four or five miles.

Well, Coyote stayed there from October, when he went in, four or five months. He heard spring birds holler. He had stood there all that time.

He thought, "Oh, it's spring. I'll have to holler." He started [to] holler. He hollered two times for a bird.[55] [The] second time he hollered, a Rabbit came.

He said, "Who is it?"

"It's Rabbit."[56]

Coyote, "Go on now. I didn't holler to you." He hollered again. Each time he hollered, something came.

Pretty soon, "Who are you?"

"It's me."

"Who are you?"

"Deer."

"Oh, no, I don't want you, go on." He hollered again. Some bird came, a little bird.

"Chk, chk, chk."

"No, I didn't holler for you. You birds go on. You fellows [are] too small." [He] hollered again. Now something [came]. "Who are you?"

"I'm Owl."[57]

"No, I don't want you. You can't do anything; go on past. Go on now." [He] hollered again.

"D'it, di·t', d'it." [full of breath]

"Who are you?"

"I'm Fisher."[58]

"Go ahead, pass on. I don't want you. You can't do anything." He hollered again. Coon came.

"Who are you?"

"Coon."[59]

"Go on, I don't want you. You can't do anything." He hollered again. Somebody [was] coming.

"Di·t, dit, dit."

"Who are you?"

"Elk."

"I don't want you. Just go on. I didn't holler for you." He hollered again. Someone [was] coming. "Who are you?"

"Bear."

"I don't want you. You can't help me in any way." He hollered. [As] soon as he said, "I don't want you," that thing passed. He hollered again. Blue Jay made a noise.[60]

"Go on. I don't need you Jay bird." He hollered again. He heard [something] plain. "Who are you?"

"Beaver."[61]

"Go on. I don't want you." [He] kept on that way, hollering [and] hollering. All morning he hollered. Now he hollered three times, and nothing came. "Oh, what's the matter? What'll I do? I'll have to die here," he thought. [He] hollered again. Then he heard something, k'ə, k'ə, k'ə, way off. "Oh, I've [been] hollering for you. Come on here, this way." It was Woodpecker.[62] "I want you. Start in a little below and chop wide enough for me to get out."

Woodpecker said, "All right." He chopped [and] chopped. That stick [was] rotten. Woodpecker chopped just like a sharp ax.

Pretty soon Coyote could see out. He saw. "Oh, a nice place, just like a prairie. Oh, I wish I could get out." Now about head size [was the] hole. Pretty soon he could get his head through. Now he said, "You chop a little more." Now he noticed those pretty feathers. Now he's [the] devil. He thought, "Oh, I'll pick out at least half of those feathers. I'd like to wear those red feathers." He picked out half.

Oh, "kə́, kə́, kə́." Woodpecker flew away.

"Oh, come back. I [was] just teasing you."

No, "kə́, kə́." Woodpecker flew away. Now what was he to do with just that little hole?

Well, he talked to himself. "Oh dear, I ought not've done that." He talked to himself. "Well, anyway I'll save these feathers. If I see a girl somewhere, I'll give them to her." Oh, [he's] thinking about girls I guess. Well, he didn't know what to do. He just troubled himself now, punished himself. Finally, "I wish I had a little knife," he said, scratching his head. There he had a little knife in his hand. "Now I'll cut myself up and throw [the pieces] out." He cut himself [and] threw [the pieces] out. He cut his breast [and] threw it out. He cut his gut out, slung it out.

He heard some bird holler, "Kaw, kaw."

"Hey, don't come around this way. You might take my guts. Don't come around here," Coyote had to holler. That bird took it away anyhow, a big black bird—not a crow—a mountain black bird.[63] He took them.

At last, Coyote took his head off [and] threw it out. He rolled around there [and] rolled around there and became a man again. Only one thing [was] gone. He didn't know, or else he didn't care anyway. He can't help it. He went. [It was a] nice day, the sun shining fine. Oh, he saw lots of strawberries. He crawled around on his knees [and] ate [and] ate [and] ate. He's hungry. He went about thirty yards and ate all he can eat.

"Fine strawberries!" Now he got up, thinking he had [had] enough. Now he looked back. "Oh, strawberries." They were strewn all along behind him. Now he didn't know what to do.

He thought, "I'll go in [the] woods and look for pitch." He went. He found that [pitch and] put it in his anus and closed it. Now he went again [and] ate strawberries again. When he had enough, he looked back. This time [there were] no strawberries on the ground.

Now he went. He went around [the] field. He knew where to go, I guess. "I'll find a house somewhere," he thought. He found where someone was burning grass. Every year people kept the place clear by burning [it] over. All around the field were fires. Coyote had to jump over these fires. He jumped over. He made it all right. [The] pitch [from his anus] kind of melted on him, ha, ha. He didn't notice it. Finally he jumped over a big one, [and] that pitch caught on fire [and] set him on fire. Now he ran! He's running [and] burning [something] awful. He knew where deep water [was]. He had to run there and get in. He went and got in.

Now people from one direction had good strong powers, [and] they wanted to poison Coyote. Well, he got to the water. Now he jumped in [the] water— [the] river went dry.

He thought, "Ill have to go [to the] ocean. [The] ocean is never dry." He ran to [the] ocean [and] jumped in [the] ocean. "My stick stand up for me," he said. Now his thing [penis] stood up, and he balanced on it and burned up there. He punished himself that way. He [was] just crazy. He burned clear up. [His] bones fell in the water, drifted in on [the] sand [and] lay there for two or three months. [A] bug came [along and] bit him.

"Oh, who's bothering me when I'm having such a good sleep," he said. He's an old man now. One thing [about] Coyote—he never killed any men. He [was] always mischievous about women, that's all! Well, maybe he raised [created] more people that way.

Well, he got up. He went [and] took the trail, going on again. He was going back to his grandmother. He knew where she was. We don't know. Well, he found his grandmother.

The old lady said, "I have nothing to eat. You go hunt." She gave him what little she had. He ate.

"Grandma, I'll go hunt now." Well, he killed a deer [and] packed it in. Oh, [the] old lady grabbed him. Good times! He lay down [to] go [to] sleep. [The] old lady [was] working, cutting meat. [The] next morning he went again [to] hunt. [The] old lady got mashed acorns, made supper for [her] grandchild. He killed one deer [and] packed [the] meat in. Oh, the old lady [was] glad, happy. Well, he hunted two, three, four days. Now [the] old lady had just a full house [of] drying meat. "That's enough, grandma. That's enough," Coyote said.

Well, he lay down in the full moonlight. It was like daylight outdoors. He lay down [to] sleep. [The] old lady knew all about it. But he didn't know women were dancing away a little ways [from there]. Coyote heard [the] noise. Oh, it made him crazy. He got up [and] ran outdoors. A little ways away was a round dance [and] singing. He saw a girl singing. Oh, that was just what he wanted, a girl! He ran in [the] house.

"Well, grandma, I've got to go."

"Where [are] you going?"

"Oh, [the] round dance up here. I've got to go to it."

She told him, "You can't sleep tonight, tomorrow, [or] the day after. Those people never rest. You can't stand it. It will kill you. They go all night long, [and] they go fast." That old lady knew; she had heard about those people.

"Well, I think I can stand anything. I've got to go."

Grandma, "Oh, you don't want to go there. It's nothing, nothing! All they do is kill men! You'll never come back. But you can go if you want to."

"Oh, I've got to go." [As] soon as he heard [the] sound, you know, it made him crazy. He heard them plain. It's just [as if they were] a little ways [on the] other side [of the] mountain.

He went. He ran [and] went on top of that mountain. [He was] panting, a little tired. He didn't hear it anymore at all. Pretty soon he heard it, way [on the] other side [of] that next mountain. [The] same song they [were] singing. Go! He went, running, not walking, just running. He got [to the] top [of the] mountain. No song at all! He stood there maybe two, three minutes, getting a good wind [breath]. Now he heard the song, just a little ways [the] other side [of the] next mountain. He ran. [It was] getting daylight now. He heard birds making little noises. He ran [and] got on top of that mountain—nobody! Singing all gone now. Pretty soon he heard a little song, just a little ways [on the] other side [of the] next mountain. He ran again. In not a very long time he was on top of that next mountain. No song, nothing. Now it was daylight right there.

He had to rest a little while. He just thought [it was] only nighttime [that] they danced. He thought he'd have to wait there. But pretty soon he heard singing.

Now he thought, "I'll go now. I don't want to wait. I know where they are now. I've got to go." He ran *all* that day.

His grandma had told him, "You can't get there so quick." [The] next night he ran all night too. It always sounded just a little ways away. [He ran] the next night, all night, and then the next day all day again, just running towards that singing. [The] next day [when it was] getting daylight, they're still singing. He ran till ten, eleven o'clock [and] came out on top [of the] mountain. Oh! He saw people, people. A thousand people [were] standing around there.

He didn't know what to do. "Well, I don't know. I don't have any clothes. No chief's hat, no arrows, no bow, no elk skin. I can't get it anywhere. Well, I'll try." He sat down right there. He defecated. "Now, my feces, what [am] I going to do?" It didn't answer. "Say! What [am] I going to do? [There are] lots of people down here." No answer. Now he mashed it with his foot—[he was] mad. "I'll try another one." He sat a long time. [In] twenty minutes came a little [feces].[64] "What [am] I going [to] do?"

[His] feces said, "What [do] you want?"

"Oh, I want elk skin, a good feather hat, a good otter skin, [and] my bow and arrows."

"All right," [his feces] said, "there it is, right there."

"I want a big, long knife."

"All right, right there." He had a long knife.

"Now let me try," he said. He put [the] elk skin on [and] tied it up good. [He] put on a fine feather hat. "How do I look, [feces]?" he said.

"Oh, you look fine, you look good. They'll call you 'chief' as soon as they see you," his feces told him. He had a skin full of arrows, everything.

He said, "[Feces], I want one thing more. I want woodpecker heads on each shoulder."

"All right, they're there."

"Now, how [do] I look?"

"Oh, you look good. [As] soon as they see you, they'll call you 'chief.'"

"All right. Now I'll go. Good-bye. I'll go." He can't stand it. He saw them dance just a little ways away. He went, with his fine feather chief's hat.

When he got close, the people said, "Look! Someone's coming. It looks like a headman [is] coming."[65] He came among the people. People were all around, a thousand people [were] standing. He saw a moon-sick [girl's] dance. Just women [were] dancing. It made him crazy. These were ghosts' round dances. They never change their song! They sing a fine song [but] just that one song they sing.

> * əné si'wi·lɛ, si'wi·lɛ́'*
> *si'wi·lɛ əne··*
> *əné si'wi·lɛ, si'wi·lɛ́'*
> *si'wi·lɛ, si'wi·lɛ́' əné*[66]

Coyote Jim got excited. He wanted to dance.

He said to [the] men, "Why don't some of you fellows dance?"

They said, "Oh, we just look on. We don't dance with these people." Oh, he went around, he looked around, he saw lots of dead people's bones. As soon as they catch hold of you, you never get out. Coyote Jim stood there. That day he [had] got there at noon—he stood all that night till the next noon. Then he couldn't stand it anymore. He *had* to dance. He liked that moon-sick girl with the pretty big feathers. [The] people [who had been] all looking [had] gone away. Coyote decided he'd get into [the] circle right there where that moon-sick girl was.

"[The] next round I'll go there," he said. He [was] all ready. He put his knife in [the] arrow skin [quiver]. He was ready. When they got around again, he got in [the] circle right by [the] moon-sick girl. Good-bye now—he'll never get out alive. He [was] dancing [the] round dance, making good motions with his head. Everybody looked at him. Now he went two nights and one day dancing. [He] never rested, just circling around and around. About twelve o'clock they pulled [Coyote's] arm out, threw it away. [They] pulled [his] other arm out, threw it away. They never [even] looked at it. They just went [kept on dancing]. Now one man kind of got mad.

"Well, what kind of power have they got?" A whole lot of people [were] there still.

"I've [got a] notion to try," that man thought. "I think I could get away." That man [was] a big, rawboned, stout, slim fellow, Panther.[67] [He was] nothing but sinew, stout. He studied. He'd been there two, three, four days. He had seen men killed there, out of wind. Now they had killed [a] chief. Well, Panther got ready. He's mad that chief [was] killed for nothing and nobody looked when they threw them [the arms] away. Panther [was] mad.

He thought, "I'll get in where the moon-sick girl [is]." He got in, early in the morning. He danced two nights. Then [the] second night, twelve o'clock, he [was] out of wind. He tried to get out, but he can't [let] go, held like [he was] chained. Finally, he did get out, outside [the circle]. They didn't even look at him. He's out of wind now. He had gotten away all right. He was the only man to get away from that bunch. Any man [who] got in there, he's a dead man. He can't get away. Coyote had to stay dead till someone bit him, after he gets stinking. He probably [will] not try [that] anymore. Ghosts—that's what the women were.[68]

Wind Woman

While gathering bark from a tree, Wind Woman discovers a baby, whom she adopts and raises as her brother. The young man becomes a fine hunter. Rejecting all suitors, he leaves home to seek a wife, who happens to live across the river from the powerful and dangerous Thunder. Thunder insists the young man stay with him and his two daughters but attempts to kill him by means of eight son-in-law tests, the last of which the young man barely survives. Wind Woman comes to his rescue, destroys Thunder, and scatters his remains.

The story presented here is taken from Jacobs's Upper Coquille Athabaskan field notebook 1 (pp. 100–117).[69] The title is apparently Thompson's translation of the Upper Coquille word Its'i·. Harrington (JPH, reel 027, frames 0419–25) also recorded a version of this text from Coquelle Thompson in 1942. For a cognate text, see the Galice story "Wind Woman" (M. Jacobs 1935, 1938–39). The Shasta text "Thunder and His Son-in-Law" represents a partial cognate (Farrand and Frachtenberg 1915:211–12).

Wind Woman stayed alone. [She had] nobody, no folks at all, just she alone. Once in a while she got wood in a basket, got lots of wood, kept it on hand all the time. One morning she went [to get wood]. There was a big tree. She ran around it. It was hard to get that [tree] bark. She had a long pole. She sawed the bark open in that one place. She pulled there, then she twisted, then the whole bark came down, and one baby dropped out. She threw the pole away; she picked the baby up. That baby just cried, cried, and cried—never quit crying. She held that baby; she told it, "You are my baby." Everything [different kinship terms] she called it. At last she told it, "You're my brother." Then that baby quit crying.

She had all kinds of things in the house: beaver skin, coon, rabbit skins. All [were] nice, everything. She made them for [the baby].[70] Now the baby's all right. [She made a cradleboard] for packing the baby.[71] He slept there at night. Then [she] cleaned it, took it [the baby] out again. Finally that boy got to be two, three years old, can walk around, play. He was good company to her. She thought about a little bow for him. She made him a tiny bow and arrows. She had everything. She gave it to him, [and] that little boy would play [at] shooting, outdoors. Oh, that woman was glad.

Now when he was ten, twelve years old, she made a bigger bow, bigger arrows. She told him, "Now you go around over to that open place, you look around. [When] you see a rabbit sit up on his hind legs that way, you shoot him."

He went. He saw a rabbit, but he missed [and] he lost his arrow. He came back, "Sister, I lost my arrow. I want another arrow."

"Oh, all right, I'll make you another one." She made one, gave it to him.

He went around again, every day. Finally he killed one rabbit. Oh, it tickled him. He hollered. He put a string on it; he packed it on his back like deer are packed. He took it to his sister.

Oh, she hollered. She said, "All right, now, you're old enough now to kill deer. You have to hunt. You are old enough, now."

He went to hunt now. "Give me only one arrow, not two," [he said]. She dug up the best arrow she had. He never missed anything. [It was a] big bow he carried. He hunted. He fixed his own sweathouse. He slept there then.

That young man went [hunting]. About ten o'clock he [would] bring a big deer home. Oh, that young woman almost danced, she was so glad. I don't think she had ever been married.

She heard in the evening, someone coming. Her brother had already gone to the sweathouse. She thought, "I wonder what he wants? What's he coming back for?" Then she saw a woman standing outdoors.

The woman asked, "Does Wind's brother stay here?"

"Yes, I am Wind." Wind thought, "Well, she is a pretty woman." She said, "You can come in."

She took that good-looking woman in the house and fed her. It got late. They went to bed. In the morning they arose, cooked; that visiting woman was lively. She wanted to get that boy. She wanted to marry him.

That boy came back about ten o'clock. He saw a woman sitting there with his sister, but he never noticed her. He ate his breakfast, got his bow and arrow, and he went. He never noticed that woman.

His sister told him, "This young woman came to see you."

He never answered his sister. He went to hunt. About eleven o'clock he brought one deer. That Wind Woman was busy. She was a stout woman too.[72] He never noticed that [visiting] woman, just ate, went away again to hunt. [He] just kept on that way for three or four days.

Finally that pretty woman left. She told Wind Woman, "Good-bye. I guess your brother doesn't like me, so I don't have to stay here." She knew that boy didn't care for her.

About two, three, four o'clock two women came in. They had heard his name, [and that] Wind's brother was a good hunter, a good man. They came in the house. That young man didn't stay in the house. He stayed in the sweat-house, but he saw two women coming by. They were good-looking women.

They asked her, "Is this Wind Woman's house?"

"Yes."

"Well, we've come to see your brother."

Wind Woman said, "You folks come in, eat something. My brother never stays in the house; he stays in the sweathouse."

He came to supper, saw two women sitting there, eating. He said nothing, did not greet them or anything.

Well those two women talked to each other. Each said, "Well, I don't have to stay here and take care of him if he doesn't like me." Then, "Let's go," they said. Then they returned home.

He packed deer in all the time. Pretty soon there were lots of hides. Wind Woman worked on those hides. She's so stout, she made them soft, just like a blanket. She worked day and night.

As that young man hunted, he studied: "Well, I've got to go away now pretty soon. I have enough food for my sister, now." One day he sat down in the house [and] asked his sister, "Can I go away? Can I get a good woman somewhere?"

She laughed. She said, "Why, lots of good women came here to see you. You didn't sit down, talk to them, or anything. Why's that? What kind of woman do you want?"

He didn't answer. He just said, "Oh, I must go away, somewhere."

"Well, when are you thinking of going?"

"Oh, I might go in the morning," he said.

"All right. I've got everything ready for you to wear. You have to go like a man, not like a poor person. You take your arrow and bow."

He went in the morning, but she had told her brother, "Now you watch right across the river. Thunder lives right there. I know where you are going to see a girl. You better watch or he'll pick you up and kill you. Hammering-All-the-Time—he's a dangerous man."[73]

He answered his sister, "What do you think I am? I'm not a coward. I'm no coward." By that he meant he had his power. He's got a power to get away from any place. He went. He was traveling all day, all afternoon.

Now she had fixed a stone [pestle]. [She had] tied it up in otter-skin strings, and tied it to the front of the house, the line stretched across the house. She told that stone [pestle], "Now, if they abuse my brother over there, or he gets into trouble, you have to fall down, break that string."[74] That fellow was gone, that Wind Woman sat night and day, working.

Finally he arrived. Now he heard *dul*, *dul*, that hammering. Now he got to that house [in the] late evening. No one was around outdoors. He thought, "That [Thunder] fellow hasn't seen me."

But [Thunder] had seen him and said, "I'll fix him all right."[75] So the next morning, not early, around breakfast [time], Thunder opened the door where he [the young man] stayed. "Who is it here?" Thunder [in a harsh voice] said, "I've come to get my son-in-law. You people are no good!" The boy had stopped at the next house [across the river from Thunder]. "I have two *good* daughters. Come on, son-in-law." Then that boy had to go. That old couple was afraid to answer a word to Thunder.

That boy went with him. Now they went, crossed in a canoe. Thunder took him in the house, where pretty women were. One woman had fingernails *that* long [seven inches]. She was the one who killed people. This young man thought, "I'll have to be ready for her and for old man Thunder." He [the boy] had his power in his hand all the time, but no one could see it.

Now Thunder told the young man, "You go over there a little ways. I've got a [fish] trap over there. You'll get all kinds of eels there and bring them here."

"All right."

He got there. Oh, all kinds of rattlesnakes [were] there. He took his power, he took a stick and strung those snakes on the stick and took them [back].

Old Thunder was sitting by the fire. The young man opened the door and threw them [the snakes] right in the door, said, "Here's your fish." That old man got scared, jumped up. He had expected those rattlesnakes to kill that young man. Now the young man came back in the house. The old man took those snakes and threw them back down to the river. Those two women sat, one on each side of the fire. The one was ugly, but the other one looked pretty good.

Now the young man knew they would try a different way. The old man said, "Let's sweat."

"All right," the young man answered.

So they went to the sweathouse. That sweathouse was awfully hot. Old Thunder kept moving around. He was getting ready to do something. Well, the old man got out, so the young man got out too. Then they went to the river to swim.

"Dive!" the old man said.

Now the young man knew what he [Thunder] was going to do. The young man dived. Thunder caused thick ice to cover the water. The young man tried to come up, but his head hit the ice. He swam up[stream] about fifty yards, put his power up through that ice—he had it in his hand all the time—and got out and sat down.

Down a little ways stood Thunder, laughing. "Ha! ha! You were going to beat me, eh? Now you can't get out."

Back home that [pestle] began to move. Wind Woman thought, "Oh, my poor brother. He's having a hard time, now."

The young man went back to that first house where he had been staying across the river. Now those two daughters [in this household] were his wives. They treated him good, fixed him food.

Near sundown Thunder made the ice go. He saw no one dead in the water at all. Now he thought, "Oh, that young man beat me, after all."

The next morning about ten o'clock Thunder came after the young man. He growled at those poor old people and scared them. "You have no business to keep my son-in-law here," he said, "You folks [are] no good, [you] got nothing."

The old man never answered. [He was] afraid. He had no boys, just two daughters.

Thunder said, "Come on, son-in-law, let's go back. You need not stay with these dirty people." He took him back across the river.

Thunder studied what to do. But that young man knew what he thought. Thunder said, "We'll have to wrestle, now." Thunder wanted to mash his [the boy's] ribs. He was stout.

The boy said, "All right."

Then they stood together, all ready. He [the boy] told his power, "I want big chest muscles, big back, a strong body like a log."

Thunder grabbed him, tried to mash [crush] him, couldn't do it. He tried to throw him down; couldn't throw him down. They wrestled for half an hour. The young man had beat him. He couldn't throw him.

"All right, son-in-law, let's go back in the house."

The young man had to do that. He went back in the house with him. They sat down.

That ugly looking girl said, "Let me look for lice in your head. Put your head right here in my lap."

He said, "All right."

He already talked to his power, had his head fixed for her. She looked for lice. She was [really] looking for a place to tear his head off. She tried it once.

He said, "What's the matter?" Her fingernails were all broken. She fell over dead. She [would] pull people apart and sling them down the hill. It was her own fault.

Now they were going to sweat again. They went in the sweathouse. Oh, [it was] hot! Just red, all those stones! Now Thunder jumped out quick. He closed the sweathouse door. It was burning up in there. He thought, "Now that young man will burn up."

Now that young man just took his power, made a passageway under the ground to the river, swam across.

Old Thunder stood in front of the burning sweathouse, laughing. "Oh! Ho! You thought you'd beat me, eh? Now you're burning now," he said.

The fellow [was] already back in the house across the river.

Back home that [pestle] moved. [His] sister thought, "My poor brother, he is having a hard time, now."

Now the next morning Thunder came again to abuse those old folks. He found no bones where the sweathouse had burned. He took the boy back across the river again. He took him back in the house and studied what to do. "All right, son-in-law, come on."

The boy acted like he didn't know what was going on. He just did whatever he was told. They went outdoors. Thunder caught hold of a good-sized tree, caught the top, and pulled it down slow. He sat on the top; he told the young man to sit near the base. "You sit here," he said. Now that young man knew Thunder would jump off. Thunder said, "All right, you set on good?"

"Yes."

Thunder jumped. The tree snapped up. That young man had jumped too, but Thunder didn't know it. The young man went back across the river while Thunder stood there laughing. "You thought you were going to beat me, but where are you now?" He thought that young man had gone way off somewhere like an arrow. He went back in the house.

In the morning Thunder came again [to the house where the young man was staying]. "Well, you'll have to come back with me, son-in-law."

"All right."

They went back again. Thunder told him, "I have a little bird's nest up in that tree. I want you to get it." That bird was making a noise to fool him.

Now he had to go. He pulled himself up that pole [tree trunk]. He never looked back. Finally he looked down. He was way up to the sky. He could hardly see the ground. "All right. I'll get out [of this situation] some way." He studied. He got a little moss, rubbed himself all over [with it]. He said, "I'll just be that moss, weigh nothing, wind will carry me down."

That devil Thunder was laughing, dancing around at his house.

Now that piece of moss rolled off. He came down, down, [for a] long time. "What's the matter? I haven't hit the ground yet!" He waited a long time. He opened that moss so he could look out. There he was, hanging on a maple tree. He removed that moss and jumped to the ground. It wasn't high. He went home across the river.

His sister watched that thing [pestle] moving. She thought, "Oh, he's having a hard time. He suffers now."

The next morning Thunder came for him again, saying, "Oh, I just came to get you. Let's go across. We'll have to hunt. I'd like [some] meat."

The young man thought, "I know what he'll do now," but he said, "All right."

They went. They went a little ways on the mountain, somewhere. It got cloudy, dark. Snow came down. That devil Thunder ran home. The young man came back slow. He couldn't tell where to go. He had to use his power to guide him. Now he came, came, [in the] cold. He got home, half dead. He scratched on the house by his wife [where she slept]. She opened the grass [and] saw his hand. They dragged him in. They built a big fire.

Back where his sister was, that string [holding the pestle] broke. Wind Woman cried. "I'll fix you!" she thought.

Towards daylight he was getting better. They gave him some hot soup.

He told his wife, "My sister will come here, pretty soon."

About ten o'clock they heard something, a big storm coming. It was coming now. Trees [were] just like straws [in that] big wind. The top of the house went [blew] off.

"That's my sister," he said.

Wind Woman took Thunder's house, mashed it. He [Thunder] broke in pieces. Wind Woman threw one part one way, another part, another [way]. She had killed him now. She had let her hair loose on just one side.[76]

Her brother told her, "These old folks don't have any wood."

"I'll go get some," she said. She went, didn't take long. She made lots of noise, brought two sticks, trees, right under her arm. She put them right by the door, took her pole, [and] chopped them right up, bark and all. "Now, I'm done," she said. She told her brother, "Now there'll be no more trouble. You need not travel anymore. You have two women now. You stay here, come home whenever you're ready."

They gave Wind Woman all kinds of food: Indian oats, dried berries, clams, [and] camas.[77] "I'll have to go back. I have lots of things at home," she said. Now she went back. She was all done there. She got home; everything was all right.

Rabbit's Son and the Grizzly Bears

Rabbit steals a baby from a berry patch and raises him to man-hood as his son. When out hunting one day, the young man's errant arrow lodges in Grizzly Woman's pack basket. She takes him home as her husband, where he is in constant danger from her man-eating brothers and sister. When Grizzly Woman's sister tries to kill the man, an infuriated Grizzly Woman decapitates her whole family. Later, remorseful for what she has done, Grizzly Woman tries to kill her husband but is herself killed by Snake Woman, who has befriended the man. Snake Woman becomes the man's wife, and they share quantities of dried food with both the man's natural parents and with Rabbit.

The story presented here is taken from Jacobs's Upper Coquille
Athabaskan field notebook 1 (pp. 117–30). The title is mine.[78] *Har-*
rington recorded a version of the story from Thompson in 1942
(JPH, reel 027, frames 0428–39). Unlike most of Harrington's texts
from Thompson, this one has a title: "Story of Rabbit's Son." For a
cognate text, see the Takelma story "Eagle and the Grizzly Bears"
(E. Sapir 1909a:123–43).

Once a woman was picking berries. She put her baby down and went around
[the berry patch], picked a basketful. She came back, and her baby was gone.
She cried around, ran home, everyone hunted, tried to find who got the baby
or if some animal got it. They never found out where that baby had gone. No
one knew.

Rabbit had a home right there in the berry patch. [He] took the baby. That
baby grew. He could walk around, [was] growing good. Now he had [an] arrow—he's about ten, twelve years old. Rabbit made [an] arrow for his boy.
Now he shot everything, brought deer home. He's a man now, seventeen, eigh-
teen years old. [He] packed deer in [the] house. Old Rabbit got busy, made
good soup for his boy.

The boy had only one arrow, not two. If he'd lose that arrow, that would be
his last. He couldn't get any more at all. One morning he went. He went in [the]
brush. He saw [a] grouse drumming [hooting] there. He watched that grouse
sitting there. He shot! Gosh! He missed that grouse. He had never missed anything before. [There were] no more arrows now [as] he had only one. [This was
the] first time he ever missed. Now he had to follow in the direction he had shot,
to hunt [for] his arrow.

He went. He came to [an] open place. He saw one woman digging camas.
His arrow was stuck right in the edge of that woman's basket. He hated to go
there, but he had to go there.

She pretended not to notice him coming, but all the time she was thinking,
"He's bound to come." He got there. She said, "Say, were you trying to kill me,
to shoot me?"

[The] young man said, "No! I was shooting a grouse."

"You'll have to come to the house with me," she told him.

The young man said, "All right." She pulled the arrow out from her basket
and handed it to him.

"Here's your arrow." They went back to the house.

There were two houses there in [an] open place; no brush at all. They went [in the] house. She cooked dinner, all kinds [of] food, acorns, Indian oats, berries, everything she had dried.[79] She cooked then, gave him a good dinner. He ate.

"I'll tell you," she said. "You listen! I'm Grizzly Bear Woman. I don't eat people. I eat food like this, like people eat. Now my brothers, four, five, ten of them—they don't eat food. They eat people. Two or three times I've had men come in, and they've killed my men right before me. I'm sorry, but I never got mad at them. But this time, if they try to harm you, I'm going to kill every one of them—even my father and my mother. Now they're out hunting people. Whether or not they'll bring some live people, I don't know. They eat here. They'll be here soon. It's nearly time," she said. Then she told him, "You lie down here, and I'll take care of you. They'll dare not touch you." She said, "My sister, my smallest one, she's a good hand to tattle. She watches me to see if I keep [a] man. I just want to let you know, so you could be careful if you hunt tomorrow." Then she explained, "They never go south; they always go east where there are lots of people."

He told her, "People watch pretty careful. They can hardly kill people."

Now they hollered. They were returning.

"They're coming back now," she said to him. They came to that house. They put people down, eating guts and all—dirty. That little girl about seventeen, she's worst of all. She loved to eat Indians. She'd even cheat her own sister. At nighttime she'd come to her sister. She wanted to find out if her sister had [a] man.[80]

"I want to sleep with you, my sister," she'd say. She'd do that. Her sister sent her away, but she'd come back again; she smelled people. She'd come back, "I want to lie down sister."

"All right, you lie down by me." She'd lay down, turn around, and hug her sister. She wanted to feel behind her! Ha ha, [she's a] smart devil, you know. She felt the man lying there.

The next morning that man went before daylight to hunt. Now her sister got after səlnə́lgi and told her, "Now I've given you one more chance. Don't you tell your brothers I have a man here." She knew that little girl always told. "Don't you like to eat good meat, nice meat, elk meat, deer meat? Don't you like that? Now you eat people's guts—no good. No good!" she told her.

The man went hunting different ways. One deer [he] hunted one way, one deer he hunted another way. Now that səłnə́lgi, she had already told her brothers. She went with them because she liked to get the guts.[81] She [was] hungry. Oh, her brothers got crazy [to] hear their sister had a man. Those brothers never came to see their sister. Just only səłnə́lgi came. Now that man had hunted different ways. Some of those brothers tracked him one way; some of them went the other way to look for him. But they missed him. He got back, packing a deer.

Grizzly Woman was making baskets all the time. She put her basket away, went [and] got that meat, cooked, got everything ready. She asked him, "Which way did you go? Those folks were looking for you."

He told her, "I went south."

She advised him, "If they ever catch you, don't run elsewhere, run right here. Come right in the door here. I'll fix them." Her man lay down to sleep. He had hunted all morning. Now that səłnə́lgi had been watching to see which way he had come back so she could report. She came to the door.

"Got [any] meat, sister?"

"Oh, you go on, eat guts, go on and hunt." But səłnə́lgi had to come in anyhow, there was meat there, she had to come in, she didn't care. She took that cooked meat; she ate, just swallowed it right down. She saw that man lying there, her sister's man. Her sister pretended not to notice, but she was really watching səłnə́lgi very closely. Maybe [she] fed [her] mother, pa, I don't know—it doesn't say—but she had lots of meat.

Well, he [the man] had to go tomorrow morning, before daylight early in [the] morning on [the] mountain. He had only one arrow to use; he never missed any deer. He killed a deer, he got ready to pack it, then he heard the brush crackling. He looked. He saw two men coming; they had tracked him. He ran; he [was] already in [a] field. Now that səłnə́lgi, she was close behind him, that she-devil. Now Grizzly Bear Woman heard him coming. She put her basket away and got ready. She went out. There was little səłnə́lgi getting awfully close, running behind the man. səłnə́lgi had almost caught him. About two feet behind, the man [ran] out [of] wind. Just like a little cat, she [Grizzly Bear Woman] grabbed them and cut their necks off, each one as they came, first səłnə́lgi, then the others. Then she's mad. She went [to] kill [her] father and mother that way too.

Grizzly Bear Woman had something [a power]. She was a doctor. Well, she got them all cleaned up. They came back in [the] house. Her man sat there, head down.

"My man, do not feel badly about it. I promised that—it's their own fault. Now you are free to go hunt. You can go get plenty of meat for winter."

"All right," he said. He arose, ate his meal. She had everything ready, acorns, berries, everything she had dried. They lived good. He hunted every day.

About six months later, one day he hunted. He brought [a] deer, put it down by the door. When he was coming, he seemed to hear someone crying. It was Grizzly Bear Woman. He put the deer down, opened the door to get in [the] house. She can't look up at him. She held her head down, can't look in his eyes.

He thought, "She's going to kill me now. She feels badly about her brothers, sister, and parents." About noon he ate. She's different now, not like she used to be. She fed him, but did not eat with him like always, but sat to one side making her basket. Now he walked outdoors, walked around. He told his wife, "I'll leave my bow and arrow here and take a little walk." He went barehanded.

A little ways to the river, he went there. There was one good road, trail; he came back. He looked behind him, saw a nice woman.

She told him, "Stop awhile, I want to talk to you. Well, you have a wife; your wife killed all her people—sister, brothers, and her father and mother. Now she has turned around on [against] you, and she's going to kill you now."

"Yes?" said the man.

The woman told him, "You be ready tomorrow. You watch her. Beware [be ready] tomorrow."

"What can I do?" he said. "I can't help it if she's going to kill me. I can't do anything about it."

Then the woman told him, "If you can manage to beat her [running] to this road, you run right here. I'll be here, and I'll kill her for you."

"All right," he said. He wondered, "How can she kill Grizzly Woman? Has she an arrow or something?"

"Oh, you think I can't do much?" said the woman. "Watch me practice." There came [she turned into] a little rattlesnake about three feet long. It stood straight up, coiled itself, then shot out straight like a spear. "That's how I'll kill her," she told him.

"All right."

Now he studied how he could get away from the house. The woman had said, "Watch out for her tomorrow. It's the last day you have to pack for her. When you put down [the] deer, you go watch carefully. She'll be crying." [The] next day he hunted all morning. About one, two o'clock he came back packing a deer. He heard her. She was crying, just like that woman had told him. He put the deer down, opened the door; he was watching her. The roof was open at the smoke hole. There was a stick across the door that one always caught hold of in entering the house. But that man did not take hold of it. Grizzly Woman charged it.

"What's the matter?" That man was out the smoke hole and jumped twenty feet away. Growling like thunder, that Grizzly [would] make anyone so scared they'd fall down. But not him—he *ran*.

Grizzly thought, "He can't get away from me. I'll get him." She just trotted leisurely behind. That fellow ran past where the Snake Woman was. Then when Grizzly Woman went by, it snapped out noiselessly, and she fell down just like she'd been shot with a gun. Now the snake was a beautiful woman again. He was frightened of her too. He knew what she could do. Now they went back to Grizzly's house, where there was all that food. Grizzly was a good hand to dry meat.

Now that Snake Woman was pretty. Now they took over that house. Snake Woman worked just as good as Grizzly Woman, drying meat and all. She was his wife now.

She told him, "You have a father and mother just a little ways from here. Rabbit stole you when you were just a little baby. If you want to see them, I'll take you over there. It won't take long."

"Sure," the man said, "if my father is living I'd like to see him." She took him there.

He came in [the] door. The old man and old lady looked. A stranger had come. Then the woman asked them, "Did you lose a baby a long time ago?"

"Yes."

"Well, that's him, that's him. You see, your neighbor is Rabbit. He raised that boy. Don't you ever have hard feelings against Rabbit. He raised your boy fine. See how smart he is? He's a smart man now. Don't ever talk evil of Rabbit. Rabbit did a lot of hard work to raise him."

The man asked his father, "Would you like to come home with me? It's just a little ways. You need not stay there if you don't want to, but come get food."

"All right." Both of them came. They got in the house; they loaded them up good. Snake Woman packed dry meat, he packed that fresh deer, the old lady packed the dry hides. [The] old man carried dried meat too. They went that little ways; it wasn't far, maybe half a mile. They got down [to the] parents' home, put away the meat and skins and so on.

"Where do you have to be, my son?" the old man asked.

"Oh, don't worry about me; I'm here all the time. I don't go away. If you want meat or anything, you [just] come."

Snake Woman said, "Let's go see Rabbit now. He lives just a little way [from] here." They went there. Rabbit was eating grass. He looked. He knew he had raised that boy.

"Oh, have you come back now?"

"No," the man told him, "I've come to get you. You come get your meat." They wanted to get rid of some of that meat. They had more than they could use. They took Rabbit, who was a good-looking young man, except for his big head. He was big-headed, big-eyed too. They got there, gave him dried meat and food, all that he could pack.

He stayed [in] that house, his Snake wife with him. He had no more trouble. That's all.

The Woman Who Married the Sea Wolf

Shag abducts a young woman and takes her to the Sea Wolves' home out in the ocean, where she successfully passes several daughter-in-law tests with Shag's help before marrying a Sea Wolf. After her two boys are born, she and her family pay a visit to her natal family, bringing gifts of Indian money and whales. Her husband returns to his ocean home. After an extended visit she and her children also return to their ocean home with gifts for her in-laws.

The story presented here is taken from Jacobs's Upper Coquille Athabaskan field notebook I (pp. 131–39).[82] Harrington recorded a similar version from Thompson in 1942 (JPH, reel 027, frames 0410–16). For a cognate version, see the Chetco story "Si·čálni" (E. Jacobs 1977:269–73). Cf. the Tolowa notion of ocean cougars and mountain cougars in "The Man Who Caught the Ocean Cougars" (Curtis [1924] 1970:199). The theme of both women and men marrying nonhuman people is found throughout Northwest Indian oral traditions.

She was a moon-sick woman.[83] They, the Wolves [Sea Wolves], sent [Shag] boy to watch her and steal her and bring her to their house.[84] Everyday he watched her. But she'd come there, swim quick, get out, and run home. She had no time to talk, [she] told Shag. She didn't care for him. He'd think, "Next day, I'll get you." He'd walk around on [the] sand and [when] she was coming.

Finally, he told her, "I have to take you. You have to come with me. There's a man over there [who] wants you for his wife."

"All right," she said.

"Follow me." Shag told her he [was] going along to [the] ocean. She didn't see any boat, but pretty soon Shag said, "Come here, get in here." Oh, Shag had a nice boat, a fine boat. She got in. She had come down [because] Crow took her dress, took it to Shag, and that's why she had to follow Shag. So when she got in the boat, he gave back her dress.

Now there were fine elk[-skin] blankets there in that boat. Shag told her, "They sent these for you to use." Shag told that Crow good-bye, and he went. It didn't take long [for the boat] to get to shore. Oh, they saw on [the] sand lots of houses. It was [Sea Wolves'] place.

Now Shag told her, "Lots of girls I bring here don't know where to get water. But when they get inside, their mother-in-law hands them a bucket and says, 'Go get water. I want a drink.' Then they go outside. Can't find water at all. But you're my people; I want to tell you how to do [things]. When you get [the] bucket, I'll be lying down, wiggling my foot. You come along, push my foot aside, and there will be a spring there. You dip up water, give it to your mother-in-law, and oh! it will tickle her. Then they'll cheer you. They'll say, 'Smart woman!' If they give you a basket for wood, I'll be lying there. You push my head away—there's the wood right there. You put it in [the] basket and take it to your mother-in-law." He taught her that.

In the meantime her husband was staying in [the] sweathouse before being married. She got there and thought, "Which one is my man?" They were all coming back for supper. But now they were making supper. She was his wife now that she had got wood and water.

Now that handsome man came and sat by her. "Oh, that's my man, this good-looking man." She's ashamed then, hung her head. Now all the people ate. The old man talked; they ate together there. She was his wife now. Back home the old folks were crying. They [the Sea Wolf and his wife] didn't sleep together; he just went back [to the] sweathouse with [the] other men.

One day she walked on the beach. She saw a fresh Chinook salmon. She picked it up and put it in [her] basket. How those people hollered, "Oh, oh, don't you pack that whale. Stout woman you are, you pack that whale." She threw it down on the beach. Now everybody got a knife, cut that whale. She watched. She [was] half [Sea Wolf] now.

Now Shag told her, "They call that fish salmon in your country, but these people here call it whale. Here they call whale fish. That fish you had yesterday, well that was whale.[85] They are all surprised [by] what a stout woman you are." She stayed a year there.

One day she said, "Well, my man, come on, get [put a] blanket on [the] ground, lay down; I want to hunt for lice." All right, she sat down. He put his head in her lap; she looked, couldn't find any, at last she found one.

He said, "You find one?"

She told him, "Yes, I have one here."

"Well," he said, "you put him in your mouth, don't chew it at all, just swallow it down."

She did that; she swallowed it down. Then she got [in the] family way. She got a baby boy, nice-looking baby. She had to nurse it. They wouldn't let her pack water and wood anymore. She had to stay in [the] house and care for [the] baby.

When her baby could sit alone and play, her husband called her again, said, "Let's get my blanket and go outdoors. You look for my lice again." They went; she looked, after a *long* time she found one.

"I got one," she said.

"All right, you swallow it right down, don't chew it." She did.

"Now," he told her, "you'll have two boys, and you have to go back home." He had been around, Shag, and told her [that] her mother [was] all right. "That's all the babies you'll get." Shag told her, "They have to send you home. They're going to dance in your father's house because you [have] been gone one year."

So she got one more baby. [The] baby began to walk. They grew like grass— already they were big boys.

One day the old man said, "My daughter-in-law, you must go home and take your children with you." Now they got ready.

Her man said, "I'll come later. I'll be there in a couple days. I want to see their dances. Now what do you think your people want over there?"

"Take whatever you wish," she answered.

"But I must buy you. I'll have to take lots of Indian money and maybe I'll take two whales."[86]

"All right."

"You tell your father to go day after tomorrow, early in the morning to the beach, and he'll find those two whales there. He must go early in the morning." That's all he said to his wife. He told [them], "You folks can go now."

It took her only [a] couple hours to get home. When they got there, it was dark already. She went in; they asked her what she wanted. She didn't want anyone to see her good [clearly], there at the dance. She went in; it was before dance time. People in other houses were getting ready. The old people were wondering who had come in so early. They noticed two boys come in also.

Presently she grabbed her mother and said, "It's me, it's your daughter." That old man was glad.

He said, "I have to fix it where she can sit down. There will be a large crowd tonight. We have three nights more to dance." So they fixed [a place] for her to sit down, with her children by her. About ten o'clock those dance people were ready. They had already danced six or seven nights and were slow about getting ready. Now they started to dance. Oh, big time—big crowd! Now they had a good time, big time for her; they had thought she was dead.

Next day they gave a big dinner for her, had lots of people there.

She told her father that night, "Go first thing, early in the morning, to the beach. This is the last night of the dance, and my man is going to come." Before [the] dance, then, she went out towards [the] river. Her man already stood there, so she brought him home. He was a good-looking man, everybody watched that good-looking man. They stayed and danced all night. Nobody slept. They also began early, as they didn't want a new man to come in and think there was no one to dance. They sat up all night and looked on. Just at daylight they stopped. Now the dance was over; they'd had a good time.

Her father came back from [the] beach. He told his boss [chief] there were two whales on the beach. All the men went down to cut it. About a hundred people cut all day. They make a hole, tie a rope on it [the blubber] and cut huge slabs, pulling on [the] rope [as they cut]. They pack, pack, pack, pack whale, pack whale. They pile it up like bacon. Then [the] chief issues [distributes] it—everybody got two slabs. Then they cut meat.

[The] next day everybody made a big dinner. They made that man and his wife and children sit in [the] center, and they piled the food around them. Fine camas, acorns, all kinds of food—good time.

When he had just finished eating and everyone else was still eating, he told his wife, "Go get me a pan." She went and got a large dish, and he filled it with [the] largest money [beads] from inside his clothing, then put it before his father-in-law. Everyone clapped for him. They [were] glad!

He said good-bye, left in the evening. He told his wife, "Whenever you're ready, you come home."

Next day, they were busy. They were busy [with] maybe a whale a week. So much meat, so much whale grease. [Sea Wolf] let [the] remainder of his whale float ashore for [the] people.

The woman stayed home one month, and then the boys wanted to go home. "All right, we'll go home now."

[Her father asked his grandson,] "What do they want over there?"

He said, "You know, what I'm wearing, elk skin. They want that kind. But the kind they want most of all"—I don't know what they use it for—"is otter skins."[87] He got half a dozen otter skins. [The] chief gave him one; everyone gave him one. They rubbed them up good and tied them up.

At last they [Sea Wolf's wife and her children] were ready. They went down, right down in [the] ocean, right into [the] water, and presently could be seen swimming away as [Sea Wolves]. They got home, maybe [in a] half hour they got home. You see, everybody thought [there was] no land in [the] ocean, but those people had a home there, had land—different world it was then.

That's as far as we can go now.

Raccoon and His Grandmother

Raccoon steals food from his grandmother, lies about it, and is whipped as punishment. He runs away crying about being whipped, his tears creating dark circles around his eyes. He follows a trail to the Grizzly Bears' house, where he encounters a succession of five Grizzlies, the first four of whom he kills while pretending to paint their eyes. The fifth Grizzly, a shaman, dodges Coon's blow and chases him up a tree. As Grizzly uproots the tree, Coon jumps to another one and eventually escapes with the help of a man who carries him some distance away by traveling underground.

The story presented here is taken from Jacobs's Upper Coquille

*Athabaskan field notebook 1 (pp. 140–47). Thompson called this
story q̓á·ləc, "Coon." The title here is mine. Harrington's version
from Thompson was recorded in 1942 (JPH, reel 027, frames 0405–
8). The following partially cognate texts all share these same plot
features: Coon lives with his grandmother, steals her food (or fails
to share food with her), and is punished by her; this punishment
alters his appearance in some way. The remainder of the story
can differ markedly from text to text. See the Santiam Kalapuya
story "Pheasant whips her grandson coon" (M. Jacobs 1945:130–
32), the Clackamas "Coon and his father's mother" (M. Jacobs
1959a:423–30; 1960:318–21), the Wishram "Raccoon and His
Grandmother" (E. Sapir 1909b:153), the Kathlamet "The Raccoon" (Boas 1901:142–54), the Cowlitz "Coon and His Grandmother" (Adamson 1934:220–21), the Upper Cowlitz "Coon kills
Grizzly swallower, whips his lewd grandmother, the Ducks scold
her" (M. Jacobs 1934:179-83), the Kittitas Sahaptin "Coon boy
kills Grizzly swallower, he and his grandmother kill food swallower" (M. Jacobs 1934:217–19).*

Coon was a young man; he lived with his grandmother. One morning he did
something wrong. [He] stole food when he shouldn't [have]. His grandmother
came back from packing wood. She wanted to cook, [but] she missed the
food.

She asked him, "Did anybody come here?"

"No."

"Well, what did you do with the fish? Did you get that?"

"No, I never took it."

"Yes, you did get that. Now you tell me!" [In] those days children couldn't
lie; they had to tell.

So he said, "Well, yes, I did get it." The old lady whipped him for his mis-
chief. Oh, he *cried*! She kept on whipping, slap, slap. He ran out, ran down to
the river, crying:

> "She whipped me,
> She whipped me,
> She whipped me,
> My grandma."[88]

Now he went along crying. He wouldn't go back to his grandma anymore. One place where a log had slid down he picked up a sharp stone like [an] ax. He went along, crying again. He went, maybe two, three hours. He saw a trail leading down into the water. He [thought], "I'll go follow that road." He went up the road, came to an open place, [and] saw a house with smoke coming out.

He went to the door—nobody! "Oh, I think I'll have to get in anyhow." [A] fire was burning. He got in and sat down. Pretty soon he heard someone coming, dút, dút, dút, and [heard him] drop one big piece of [his] firewood load.

Then that person packing wood patted his stomach looking at Coon boy, and said, "That would be a pretty good breakfast for me." It was Grizzly. "Where have you been, boy?"

"Oh, I've been down to the river."

Then Grizzly looked at the black streaks on Coon's eyes, from his weeping, and said, "Oh, where did you get that black paint to fix your eyes up like that? Have you got any?"

"Yes, I got some."

"Will you paint me like you are painted?"

"Yes, but you'll have to shut your eyes and lay down here."

"All right." Maybe that Bear wanted to hurry lest another Bear come back too soon. He wanted to eat Coon himself.

"Shut your eyes good. Don't try to look. If tears get on it, it will make it no good."

"All right." Grizzly Bear lay down, shutting his eyes. Now Coon took out his sharp rock.

"You ready?" he called. He didn't want to miss.

"Yes, all ready." Coon cut right through his eyes. Grizzly Bear never moved, never squealed at all. He [Coon] pulled him outside and threw him down the hill. Coon was stout. Maybe something helped him, you can't tell.[89] Now he washed up the blood, cleaned the place good, [and] sat down.

Almost as soon as he had sat down, he heard another one come. This one threw down wood too. Tum! He came in, looked at Coon boy. "Where [have] you been, boy?"

"Right by [the] river I came down."

"How long [have] you been here?"

"I just got in here," Coon said. Bear knew there had been one ahead of him and couldn't understand why he hadn't eaten Coon boy. Now Bear was watching the paint. The boy looked good—oh, Bear liked that.

"You got any more of that paint?" he asked.

"Yes," Coon boy told him, "I have a little—enough to do you."

"You paint me. Hurry, they'll come back pretty soon." Both wanted to hurry but for different reasons. That boy was scared. He had to do something. He knew he couldn't get away from there; they'd chew him pretty quick.

"All right, lay down, shut your eyes good. You ready?"

"All right." He hit him, just like [you'd] chop [with an] ax. He [Grizzly Bear] never moved; he never said a word, just dead right there. Coon got busy, pulled him out, threw that fellow right down [the] hill, took that wood [and] slung it [the] same place, washed up that blood, [and] just sat down there when he heard someone coming. Goodness! [He] got scared now! He [Grizzly] came in.

"Where did they go, those people who came back? I thought they'd come back already." He was kind of mad. Maybe he smelled blood or something.

That boy answered, "I just came in. I don't know. There was no one here when I came."

"Where did you get that paint you painted your eyes with?"

"Oh, I got some here."

"Well, I want you to paint my eyes that way."

"All right, lay down." Coon was in a hurry. They were getting back quick. "Shut your eyes good." He took his stone, [and with] just one lick he killed him. Quickly he threw the body away and the wood after it. He hurried to clean the place. He was afraid someone would get there.

Sure enough, one came just as he sat down. A big man walked, dút dút dút dút. [He] threw [his] wood down. Oh, he [was] mad! "When [did] you come here?"

"Oh, I just came here; no one [was] here when I got in," [Coon said with a] tiny voice.

"No one here when you got here, eh?" He looked all around, suspiciously. He saw Coon's eyes. "That paint looks good on you. You got any more?"

"Yes, I got some."

"I want you [to] paint me that way. Hurry up, they'll be coming back. If both of us sit here with our faces painted that way, they'll like that. Maybe they'll laugh."

"Shut your eyes good." [As] soon as he said it, Coon hit him. He never missed. He got ready, put him away. He had killed four now. Their sister was a doctor, a Grizzly Bear doctor. She's a woman.

Now she came in. Oh, she could smell blood. She looked around, looked around. "Where did they go? Three or four men came back. I always come last; now there's no one here. What's the matter?"

"I just came in," he told her. He wanted to finish now; he wanted to hurry.

"How [did] you get that paint? Who painted you?"

"Oh, I painted myself."

"Have you got any more paint?"

"Yes, I got some more."

"Well, you can paint me right away." She wanted to eat that boy—she was hungry. "Hurry up, paint me before they come back."

"All right, lay down." Well, Coon knew that she was kind of watching him. That doctor kind of shook her eyes [her lids fluttered]. Then just as he got ready she shook her eyes more. "Shut your eyes *good!*" Then he hit! Goodness, if that rock didn't miss! She had dodged it quick. He just missed.

Now she jumped up, lunged at him. Then he got away, ran to the river.

"You can't get away from me. I'll catch you." He ran. Now he saw her coming. He was getting tired running—they had gone a long ways—so he climbed a tree. She came there. She knew he was there. "It's a good thing you have waited for me here," she said. She dug the tree up by the roots. It fell, but Coon was over safe in another tree.

Coon kept going that way; he went from one tree to another. Grizzly did not know how to climb. Grizzly saw Coon running over the hill. She saw a man standing with him, putting fire around. Coon got to that man. "Grizzly is going to kill me," he said.

"All right, jump on my belt." Then the man took him down underground. They came up way off somewhere else. They could see Grizzly's butt sticking up in the air where she was digging, trying to go underground.[90] Coon was going to travel.[91]

Panther and the Grizzly Bears

Panther and Grizzly Bear are mortal enemies, always fighting. After Grizzly Bear kills the last male Panther, Panther returns to life from a drop of his blood saved by his grandmother. Four successive Grizzly Bears attempt to fight the restored Panther, who

tricks each of them into swallowing a bag full of flint splinters from
which they die. The fifth Grizzly, a shaman, sees through Panther's
trick, and they fight, all the way to the top of a mountain. They end
up fighting on the moon, where they can be seen today.

The story presented here is taken from Jacobs's Upper Coquille
Athabaskan field notebook 1 (pp. 148–61). The title, dí·tc'u, "Pan-
ther," was given by Thompson. I have changed it to "Panther and
the Grizzly Bears." Thompson told a version of this story to Har-
rington in 1942 (JPH, reel 027, frames 0416–18).

Panther and Grizzly Bear can never be friends. They always hate each other.
[When] they see each other, [they] always fight and kill one another.

This last Panther, they killed him. Grizzly Bear killed him. But he missed
one drop of blood. They always had to clean up blood to prevent persons from
coming alive again. Panther had told his grandma to always look if he had
been killed—maybe she could find some blood. So his grandmother picked up
that blood, took it in the house, put it upstairs.[92] Then that Panther came alive
again.

Grizzly Bear came every morning. Now Panther hollered every morning.

Grizzly Bear asked other Grizzly Bears, "Do you hear that?"

"Yes, I heard that."

"Did *you* hear?" [he asked a second Grizzly Bear].

"Yes, I [was] just sleeping with my wife on my arm when I heard that."

"Did you hear?"

"Yes, I was just on top of my wife when I heard it."

"I was just through [copulating with] my wife when I heard it," [the third
Grizzly Bear answered].

The fourth [Grizzly Bear replied], "I was just going to start in when I heard
it." They sent a man over there. Old ladies were there. They didn't kill Panther
women.

The man came and asked the old women, "Did you holler this morning?"

One old lady said, "I hollered bɛ· bɛ· bɛ· bɛ·."

"Oh," said the Grizzly Bear, "it didn't sound like that.

Then the other one hollered, "What did you do to make me come alive
again? On the ground I got better. You made me come alive again."[93]

"Oh, it pretty near sounded like that." Then he [Grizzly Bear was] afraid.

Now, ever since he came alive, Panther had been grinding fine, fine flint arrows, [like] filings, to kill Grizzly. He wanted to make five of them. He knew what he was making it for. Panther would swim, come back, eat his breakfast. [He would] go back again upstairs, sleep, get up, work, work, making five little sacks of flint grindings.

Now tomorrow he would be ready. So early in the morning he hollered *plain*! [The] Grizzlies heard. "Oh, we'll get him now." The Grizzlies sent the man again. "We'd better go one at a time," they said. He came in Panther's house: "Did you holler this morning?"

One old woman said, "Well, I always holler in the morning, bε⁻ bε⁻ bε⁻ bε⁻."

"What did you do?" he said to the other. "Did you holler?" Then she showed him. "Oh, it sounds very much like the way it was hollered this morning." Now Grizzly sat down. He asked questions. "Anyone else around the house here?"

"Who has to be around?" Panther's grandmother answered. "There's nobody."

Now Panther moved upstairs, made a little noise. Grizzly jumped up. He saw Panther standing there. Panther was ready now.

"Well," Grizzly said, "you are there, son. Come on down. We'll go for a little walk."

Panther, "No, I don't want to walk. I can't get down there where you are. There's no way to get down." [He was] just teasing, I guess. "No way to get down," he said.

"Hold on now," Grizzly said. "I can tell you how. You can step on my head, right here." He stood right under Panther.

Panther, "I might break your neck. I can't step on your head."

"Well, how [about] this?" Grizzly holds out his hands. "In my hands—you can step in my hands."

Panther, "No, I might break your hands. I don't want to."

"Yes, yeeeeeees." Grizzly didn't know what to say. "Well, I'll tell you what you [can] do. I'll stand there. You step on my mouth. I'll open my mouth." He opened his mouth and stood there.

"No," Panther told him, "my foot is too dirty. I can't step in your mouth."

"Well," Grizzly said, "that doesn't hurt it, a dirty foot. That's the best place. You step on my mouth."

Panther said, "All right, I can step on your mouth all right, but I'm getting *ready* to do it." Grizzly Bear [was] glad, oh, he's glad. He knew what he was doing. Panther said, "Well, you ready?"

"Oh, yes, I'm ready. I'm right here."

"Well, open your mouth good now. I'm about to step now. Shut your eyes good. You don't want to look. Something might fall in your eyes."

"All right. Whatever you say goes," Grizzly answered. Oh, he was glad. He knew he'd get him.

"Ready now?"

"Yeeees." [Grizzly had his] hands out, [he] shut his eyes, [and he] opened his mouth. Panther held his bag ready.

"Now watch, don't look." Then Panther let all those filings pour in his [Grizzly's] mouth, [Grizzly] choking on them.

Grizzly said, "I knew you were going to do that, but I trusted you." He died then. Panther came down, pulled Grizzly Bear outdoors, [and] threw him down the riverbank. He came back, fixed everything good. No blood! You see. He went back upstairs again.

The old lady said, "Another one is coming now. You watch him!"

Panther said, "You keep still!" She doesn't have to scare him. He, Grizzly, came right in the door.

"Heiiiiiii yɛɛɛ, what [are] you, old woman, doing here? One fellow came this way this morning. Did you see him? Which way did he go?"

"Oh, he went down that way," they told him. "You can track him that way." Now Grizzly wanted to hurry. Panther moved upstairs. Grizzly saw him. He stood up, [his] hands extended in pleasure.

"Oh, that's good, I'm glad to see you. You come down, come down on my hands."

Panther, "Oh I don't want to step on your hands."

"Step on my head then." Grizzly stood up, his head nearly touching [the] upstairs.

Panther, "No, I can't step on your head—might break your neck."

"Well, how about my mouth?"

"That's a little better," that Panther said. He would beat him that way.

"That's the best way," Grizzly said. He stood up close, opened his mouth wide. Panther moved about a bit.

"Shut your eyes good," he told Grizzly. "I'm ready and something might drop in your eyes." Grizzly didn't answer. He had already opened his mouth. He wouldn't talk.

"You ready? Ready now!" Panther moved his feet around. "Now shut your eyes good, I'm *coming!*" [He] untied his bag [and] poured right down Grizzly's mouth.

"Eeeeeeeeeeeehhh." Grizzly fell over. "I knew you were going to do me that way." That's the last words he said. Panther came down, pulled him outdoors [with] no help; he's alone. [He] came back [and] cleaned up good where Grizzly scratched when dying. He knew someone would be there soon so he hurried.

Another was coming. The old lady whispered, "Another one's coming, here's another coming now."

"All right," Panther told her. "Sit down and keep still, be natural so you don't scare him." Grizzly came in [the] door, looked all around; he looked around pretty sharp.

He asked [the] old lady, "Anybody come here?"

"No."

"Well, it's funny. Two men were coming here; it's funny."

"Well, they went by, they went down that way." Grizzly stood around, he didn't sit down, he kind of noticed something I guess. That fellow Panther, upstairs, he moved. Grizzly saw that fellow. *Oh!* He nearly went crazy.

"Come down, come down, I was just wishing to see you. Come stand on my head, it's easy."

"Oh, no, [I'd] break [your] neck—can't step on [your] head—[I'd] break [your] neck."

"How about my hands? I [will] do this way to strengthen my shoulder."

"Oh no, I might hurt [your] hands, not your hands." Grizzly stood [with his] hands up, thinking about what he [would] say next.

"Well, you can step on my mouth."

Panther, "All right. I'll be ready in a little while. All right, now I'm ready." Grizzly wouldn't talk anymore now—he had opened his mouth. He wouldn't talk anymore.

"All right, I'm coming now. Shut your eyes good, something might fall in them." Grizzly stood up more [taller]; opened his mouth wider. Panther moved around a little more, just making noise with his feet while he untied his little bag. "All right now, shut your eyes good." He poured them in, he never missed, it just went down like water. Grizzly just fell down.

"I knew what you [were] going [to] do to me, but it's my own fault," he said. He died. Panther came down, threw him down the riverbank, [and] came back. The old lady helped him sweep up where Grizzly scratched. He went upstairs again. Now he's killed three. He had one more to kill. [Of] course, that doctor he can't kill—she's bound to catch him.

The old lady said, "He's coming now. He's walking awful fast." Grizzly came right in [the] door, got in [the] house.

"What [are] you folks doing now?"

"Doing nothing."

"Those people who came by this morning, did they come in here?"

"Yes, they came in for a little while, then they left. They went that way." This Bear was sharp.

He said, "Show me which way they went."

The old lady said, "They went out the door there, turned around that side of the house, [and] went down that way." He looked outside. He didn't believe them. He came back in [the] house again. Now Panther moved, and Grizzly looked up and saw him.

"*Oh*, I thought I heard you holler this morning. I was pretty sure it was you. You going [to] come down?"

Panther said, "Yes, if I knew where to come down I would."

"Well, I'll help you to get down," Grizzly offered.

"All right, how [are] you going [to] help?"

"Well, you step on my head. It's only a little way to step."

"Oh no."

"Well, in my hands."

"Oh no. [I could] never do that."

"Well, you can step on my mouth."

"Oh, all right, that would be the best thing for me to do."

Grizzly thought, "[As] soon as he steps on my mouth, I'll have good food right then." That's what Grizzly wanted.

But [what] Panther wanted: "That fellow [will] open his mouth wide and I'll fix him." "Ready now?" Panther said. He scuffed around, opening his bag. "All right, I'm ready. Open your mouth wide and shut your eyes *good* too, lest something go in your eyes. Now, when I step in your mouth, suppose your jaw broke. Then what?"

"Oh no," Grizzly said, "you can't break my jaw."

"All right, you ready?"

"Yeah, I'm ready, *any* time."

Panther, "All right, I'm ready now. Don't move. Open your mouth and shut your eyes good." He touched Grizzly's nose a little. "Watch out now. Shut your eyes good." He just poured it right down, never missed a piece.

"Grrrrrrrr. I knew what you [were] going [to] do, but it's my own fault." That's the last words Grizzly said. Panther came down, pulled that dead Grizzly Bear off, slung him down [the] hill. He cut the legs off—each one—as he threw him down in order to make tracks because that Grizzly Bear doctor man was pretty sharp.

He sent the two old ladies. "Get out right away; go along the soft dirt in the road making tracks." Oh, those old women couldn't go very far. They threw [the] legs down the hill and just got in [the] house when that Grizzly doctor came. He came in slow, looked around.

"Where [have] those people gone, anyhow?" he asked.

"Well, they came here a little while," the old lady said. "They stood around a little while, then they went out. They went in that direction. You can go track them that way." All right, he went [out for] a little while then, maybe two, three minutes. All those tracks were going that way, so he believed it. He turned around, came back.

"All right," he said, "you folks were telling the truth. Say, who hollered this morning?" Panther moved around.

He said, "I'm the one [who] hollered this morning. What are you going to do about it?"

"Well," Grizzly said, "I know you've been born again. Well, you better come down. Here, you can step on my head."

"No, no, I don't want to do that. I wouldn't step on anybody's head."

"Well, my *hands*, step on my hands."

"No, [I] might break your hands."

"Step on my mouth then!"

"Oh, I don't know. I have to get ready a little first." He had to fix himself now, his last chance. He had to take his arrow and put on what he needed to wear. He knew this doctor would get away from him—he just *knew*. He got ready, his last chance.

"Well, I can step on your mouth."

"All right." He opened his arms, opened his mouth. "As soon as he steps in my mouth I'll grab him," Grizzly thought. Panther got all ready.

"All right, I'm ready to step on your mouth now. Open it wide; shut your eyes good." But when that doctor shut his eyes good, he could see plainly what was going on. So he saw that Panther had that little sack. "Ready now!" He poured [but] that doctor dodged. Just like thunder he growled. They fought a little while in the house. Then they went out, around an open field three, four, five times. Hanging on to each other, letting go. Hanging on to each other, letting go. Just a big fight. [They] never quit fighting. They were going up a mountain now, fighting right up the mountain. They got to the top of [the] mountain. Both stood [there], gave up, talked.

They said, "We'll never quit fighting, we never will, we'll be fighting in the moon, and people will see us." When you see something in the moon, that's them. They're fighting.

Coyote Jim

Coyote, living with his grandmother, prematurely announces the beginning of springtime and throws away the remainder of their winter food supply. His grandmother, having secretly retrieved and cached the discarded food, eats in secret while her grandson starves as winter weather returns. Coyote hollers for help, and Spider Woman from the Sky Country provides them with a self-replenishing supply of fish.

The story presented here is taken from Jacobs's Upper Coquille Athabaskan field notebook 1 (pp. 162–66). The title is Jacobs's. For partial cognates, see the first half of the Galice text "Coyote and his grandmother lived together" (M. Jacobs 1935, 1938–39), the Joshua "Coyote Arranges the Seasons of the Year" (Farrand and Frachtenberg 1915:228–33), and the Shasta "Coyote and His Grandmother" (Farrand and Frachtenberg 1915:218–19).

He [Coyote] lived with his grandma. They had lots of grub [such as] dried fish, dried [salmon] eggs. One day he went out on [the] prairie, an open place. Oh, he saw flowers, flowers—fine flowers. Everything [was] nice and pretty.

"Well, it must be springtime," he thought. "Strawberries [are] nearly ripe, flowers." He ran back to the house.

"Grandma, [it's] already spring. Don't keep the food in [the] house anymore. It's getting old. Throw it in [the] water."

"Why, what's the matter with you now?" The old lady answered.

"You ask what's the matter! Why there's strawberries over there, flowers, everything is growing. It's spring now. You have to do that now, grandma. Sling that grub out in the water." [The] old lady never answered. She was mad. She knew Coyote was getting crazy in the head now.

"All right. You do as you please—whatever you say goes." Then she went down to the river with a long pole with a hook on it. Now Coyote Jim threw a bunch of fish in the water. [He] went back for more to throw in—he kept on [doing that]. Pretty soon, as the fish floated down, that old lady hooked them [and] put them aside. Coyote cleaned up in the house. She saved nearly all [the discarded food].

[The] next day she went out looking for a big tree with a hollow in it. She put that dry fish in there. She could get along now. Now, she took a little dried eggs and dried salmon, hid it in her basket [by] putting her cap over it. A big snow came the next day. She lay down. Snow [was] coming down [and] coming down now. [It was] two, three feet high [in the] morning. She lay down. He kept up [the] fire. He went to get wood. He fixed up [the] fire. [The] old lady lay with [her] back to [the] fire. He saw this thing, [her] chewing muscles, move. The old lady was chewing salmon eggs. Coyote watched that.

Finally, "What are you eating grandma?"

"Nothing! I'm not eating. I caught a louse. I'm chewing that."

"Give me a little, grandma. [Did] you chew it good?"

"No, I haven't got any. I swallowed already. Now you threw away all [the] grub, threw it in the water! What can I do? We [will] have to starve to death. You were going to get spring strawberries—go on! Get strawberries!" Oh, that hurt him. He went to get wood, packed wood in. She would eat good while he was gone.

"I won't give him a bite," she'd think.

Coyote went downriver to get water. He saw salmon jump, a big salmon. He ran over there, got water where [that] salmon jumped. [He] took it home and boiled that water, thinking it would have salmon grease in it. He boiled it. He wanted to give grandma some.

"You want to drink this, grandma?"

"What is it?"

"Oh, where fish jump, you know, I got that water and boiled that."

"No, I don't want a drink," that old lady answered. "I drank already." It snowed outdoors [and] snowed outdoors. Coyote got well punished.

He got up one morning. [The] sun [was] shining good. Oh fine! Well, he studied. He thought something.

He hollered, "Oh, they told me my grandma was in heaven. I want to get something to eat." He hollered three, four, five times. [There was] no answer, nothing at all. Pretty soon, [it got] kind of cloudy. He thought it [was] going [to] snow. He went in the house. Pretty soon a woman came to the door—one he had never seen before. She came in [and] sat down. Coyote sat with his head in his arms, starving.

The young woman said, "What was it you wanted? Give me a pan." Coyote got up, found the biggest pan he could get, and brought it. The woman reached in her pocket [and] brought out a little dried fish [the size of] a forefinger's two joints. She put it in that big pan. Coyote [was] kind of mad. He kicked that pan. The pan tipped over, [and] a whole lot of fish spilled out, just a panful spilled out. They gave the old lady one too.

Now he put them all in the pan. He ate. As he took one out, more came in, one panful after another. That young woman sat there saying nothing. She stayed overnight.

Then she said [the] next day, "I'm going home now. You'll get along with that fish now." She pulled herself right out of [that] house. She was Spider Woman.[94]

That's as far as I go.

The Wolf Person

A Wolf woman overpowers a Coquille man, who was out hunting one day, and takes him to her mountain home to become her husband. They have two children, and after a year she allows her husband to visit his human wife, children, and aged parents, with the proviso that he not touch his human wife. After a year's visit, his Wolf wife sends many deer to his village before taking him back. Although he never returns to visit his people, he promises to continue to supply them with meat.

The story presented here is taken from Jacobs's notes written on both sides of three loose-leaf sheets of paper, in my possession.[95] Harrington also recorded a version of this story from Thompson in 1942 (JPH, reel 027, frames 0391–93). Compare the Hanis Coos story "The Woman Who Married the Wolf" (Frachtenberg 1913:163–67).

When summertime comes, Wolves [come out of the ocean] onto land, where they go to the mountains to hunt for two or three months. In the autumn they return to the ocean, where they eat all kinds of fish and whales.

One time a Coquille man [was] married [and had] two children. This man hunted every day, packed deer meat [home]. One day he did not come back. He sat on a log. Elk [had] passed by already. He just rested there. Then he saw a woman coming by.

She said, "I caused you to sit this way. Don't think you just sat this way. I caused you to sit this way because I wanted to get you [for a husband]. Come with me." The man had to go. [She] opened the door, [they] came in, [she] shut that door in the [side of the] mountain. [It was a] nice house, elks came [nearby]; [there were] blankets, fire, skins hanging [about]. The fellow thought that the old man [there], the old father of his Wolf wife, must be alone.

"I'm not alone. My brothers will come," [the old fellow said]. He had to live with that woman till her brothers came. Two old ladies sat down; one old man sat there. The [Coquille] man didn't say a word. He didn't think [know] these people [were] Wolves. Necklaces of dentalia, maybe twenty strings, these people had on. He sat down. [The] woman talked to him.

"You're going to marry me," [the old lady said]. She started to cook dry meat in elk grease, acorns, camas, all kinds of stuff. They made him eat. The old lady ate with him; he's her man now.

In maybe one month, maybe two months, he doesn't go anywhere. Only a little ways [away is] his home. He could see it on an open place [on a] side hill. He had a different power [and] didn't think of anything.[96] [The] Wolf brothers came in packing seven or eight of them [elk].[97] [They were] not wolves [but] people.[98] They ate little elk bones just as if [they were] muscle. [They] threw no bones out.

[The] old man, [the Coquille] man's father, wept on the mountain, assuming the man [was dead]. People hunted all over for him. [The] man stayed about one year. [He] had two little boys. [He] never came back.

One day his Wolf wife [and] their boys hunted. They said, "Papa, I see people down there. One old man cries, one old lady cries too." He felt bad.

He said, "It's my mamma [and] my papa. They think about me; that's why they cry. They think I'm dead; that's why they cry."

[The] woman [his wife] said, "Let him go home for one year."

They told him, "You stay home one year but do not touch your wife. If you do, you'll die, [just] like that, right away. You can pet your children all right, but do not touch the woman." Every day those Wolf people hunted. The man got ready to leave. Every so often he'd find a deer. Those old Wolf women would pick up sticks on the trail, and then a deer would come, z-z-z. They'd choke him right there by themselves. His little [Wolf] children saw the man [preparing to leave and] jumped on his leg and squealed and squealed.

"Let me go. I'll stay with you." The old woman hung on to the man. He didn't take them; they had four legs.

[After he got home] he held his mother and father's hands. He saw his wife, his children. He petted his children. He wife got a big deer hide for a chair. He sat down. Every day his Wolf children gave deer for the old people [his parents] when they went to gather sticks. [There were] lots of people down below in Coquille City. They all came to see the returned man. Maybe one hundred people [came]. They wanted to see what he looked like now. Three or four houses cooked. Lots of people ate. Everybody ate.

The returned man did not eat; wouldn't talk to anyone. He sweated every morning before breakfast. [He] sweated before supper. [They] sweat, too, early before daybreak. Every man took his boy to the sweathouse because they slept warm.

He stayed one year at home. Then, [when it was] almost spring, all those different people visiting every two or three weeks—some from Coos Bay— caught fish, steelhead, everything. [There was] high water, rain. [There was] only dry meat, no fresh meat. [The] men in the sweathouse talked about him, thinking he's not there.

They said, "Why [is there] no fresh meat? The Indian Wolf is home. Only steelhead and so on [are available]." He heard them. [When] everybody [was] sleeping, before daylight, he left, went to the mountain for elk. [He] drove it down [and] killed it right in the doorway of the sweathouse. They heard the elk cry right in the doorway. He came up. He'd been swimming [and] was drying his hair. He didn't mention [brag] about his elk. The people fixed it, cooked lots, ate elk grease, soup.[99] Then everybody helped pack elk meat [and] fat home.

When [it was] springtime, about May or June, they went and camped on a big two- or three-acre gravel bed in a summer camp for eels and fish. They had to take [his] bed for him. He laid down on his belly and face. They fixed camp all the next day. About eleven o'clock they heard Wolves hollering all around.

"Something! Something!" the people said. The fellow just lay there on his face. They saw elk coming down the river. The people shot them and big deer, pulled them out on the shore. Afterwards, one more again [was] coming in the river. [When] Wolves holler all over the mountain, deer have to take to water.

[The] old people said, "Something's wrong." About two o'clock they killed ten deer, big bucks. Then just like thunder Wolves growled all over. That fellow just disappeared. The Wolf woman had sent that much meat to his people before taking him back.

He never returned to his people again. But at camas digging time, September, they went there for meat. They knew he didn't die.

The sons told them, "Go slow; we'll go ahead." But the fellow already saw his father and mother going. They heard Wolf, and pretty soon a deer would come by where they were sitting. Then they saw their son.

He said, "Don't touch me. I'm not dead. Don't cry. As long as you live, I'll give you meat." They saw his Wolf hair on his shoulders. He promised people to give [them] meat there [at that place].

Coyote and Wolf

Coyote's ten sons and Wolf's ten sons compete in a shooting contest for a bag of medicine that can resuscitate the dead. Coyote's youngest son wins the contest, but the medicine is stolen from the Coyote boys, all of whom are killed by Wolf's sons. Wolf and his sons abandon their home and head to Klamath River country with the medicine. Coyote follows them, finally catches up to their camp, and transforms himself into a high-class Klamath River headman. His disguise fools the Wolves. He steals the medicine from them, successfully eludes their pursuit, returns home with the medicine, and resuscitates his sons.

The story presented here is taken from Jacobs's Upper Coquille Athabaskan field notebook 2 (pp. 1–30). Thompson noted that "Coyote Jim [was] a regular traveler." The title is Jacobs's. Harrington recorded a version of this myth from Thompson in 1942 (JPH, reel 027, frames 0364–82). For a partially parallel text, see the Miluk Coos story "There were many people at that place" (M. Jacobs 1940:222–23).

Coyote had ten sons. Wolf had ten sons. Wolf lived straight across [the] river from Coyote. They faced each other. They heard so much [in Coyote's house] that they [people were] shooting [for] medicine in the East somewhere. Also, Wolf heard about that too. They both heard about it all the time. Of course, nobody can [had been able to] shoot that foot-long string. A bag of medicine— about the size of two fists—hung down from a precipitous rock over water by that string. That was how they heard about it, that no one was able to shoot that string and get the medicine. They heard that someone in the East had said that one drop of that medicine would bring one back to life when dead. That's why everyone tried to get that medicine, but they couldn't get it.

Well, one evening they came together. Wolf's sons and Coyote's sons on each side were talking. Coyote listened to his sons talking about that medicine. He listened.

Then he told them, "You fellows can never get that. You never *will* get it." Once in a while he would say that to his boys.

His youngest son, Spa·yúl, said, "Papa, you don't know. I'm going to shoot that string off. I'll do it too." Then the old man Coyote never answered anymore.

Over there, [to the] East, they worked [in the] daytime. [They, the competitors] stood around [in] different places. Then they stood them in a row to shoot. Each person was allowed just one shot [in] one day.

"Well, [in the] morning we'll have to go." Everyone [got] ready. Wolf's sons got ready. Wolf's youngest son was good too. Now Wolf's youngest and Spa·yúl [got] way behind because they were small.

Spa·yúl had told his brothers, "Let Wolf's sons shoot first, all ten of them."

Those brothers said, "All right." They got there. They traveled all one day. [The] next day they got there about noon. *Oh!* They saw people, lots of people. Now they got there where [the] boss was.

"How many of you Wolf boys?"

"There's ten of us."

"All right, you stand over here." Then they asked Coyote's sons, "How many are there of you?"

"Ten of us."

"All right, you stand over there, a little ways to one side." The people shooting stood on [the] left side in a bunch.

Now they could see that thing hanging over across [the] river. But they could scarcely see the string. It hung about two feet down from that rock, so people could see it good.

Now the boss told them, "You fellows want to shoot now? You just came. Do you want to rest until evening and shoot then?"

"Oh," the Wolf boy said, "we can shoot now, just the same."

"All right. Well, who's to shoot first? Who's oldest? He's got to stand here to shoot." All right, Wolf's eldest son went and stood there. He had a fine arrow. He's ready to take [an] arrow out. He had a good bow. Sooo [many] people were watching. Everybody watched. All those best shots were watching. Now he shot. He hit that rock. His arrow broke and fell. He had missed.

"All right, now Coyote's oldest son!" Well, he got ready. He's ready to shoot—oh, he missed about two feet. His arrow dropped down. People were down below picking up arrows that dropped. Those young boys got lots of fine arrowheads. Whatever they picked up was theirs.

Now [the] second Wolf boy had to shoot. Spa·yúl and his brothers stood together. Spa·yúl said, "I'll get it. When it comes time for me to shoot, you boys all go over near where that medicine is, and as soon as I get it and it drops, you pick it up and run as hard as you can." There'd be a big fight, you know, *bound* to be a big fight. [The] smallest Wolf boy said the same thing to his brothers. Those two youngest were to be last. Well, that day five Wolf boys and five Coyote boys shot. Then it was getting dark. I don't know where they ate or slept—nothing [was] said about that.

[The] next morning [at] nine o'clock everyone [was] out in the field again. Now the boss told them, "Strange boys [the strangers] will shoot today. There's ten of them. Yesterday they shot, five boys each. Today they have to shoot another five, that will be ten." That's what he announced to the people. Now everybody knew.

Always the Wolf boys got first shot. They were all too far off [target]. [They] didn't get near it. Coyote Jim's boys shot too. They shot pretty good but never touched that string. They'd keep [coming] up [to shoot]. Another one [was] coming up. Wolf boy came [up] front. He'd shoot—nothing doing! Two Wolf boys [had] shot already, only three [were] left. Now [the] second Coyote boy shot. He shot pretty good but didn't get very near it. Now Wolf boy again. Ready! He shot—didn't touch it. People [were] just *quiet*, just looking, all those people standing all had knives, arrows, everything. There's going to be a big war. Now Coyote boy stood in the shooting place. [He] shot right and straight, hit near the medicine, but didn't touch [the] medicine at all.

Only two [were] left now. Spa·yúl talked to his brother. He said, "Tell my brothers we'll talk [things] over." They came. He said, "Now we didn't come here for nothing. It will soon be my turn to shoot. Now don't wait for anybody. You see how they all stand and watch us. You be ready to run and get it." Spa·yúl knew that there would be a big war. Wolf boy had said the same thing to his brothers.

"Now [it's] your turn," [he said] to the fourth Wolf. He shot. Nothing doing. Now only [the] smallest Wolf [was] left.

"Now Coyote boy, come on, [it's] your turn now." Coyote shot. He shot pretty close. That boss, he kept watching. He said to [the] Coyotes, "You boys get pretty close all [the] time. These boys [Wolves] over here don't get nearly as close as you boys do."

Now the last Wolf boy, the smallest one, he told his brothers, "Now watch. I might cut that string off, you can't tell." He stood up good, fixed his arrow fine, ready to shoot, pulled back [his] arrow slow, [and shot]. That medicine moved. Oh, those people [were] excited. They thought sure that medicine would fall. Wolf boy almost cut it. It was pretty close.

Back home, Wolf had come to old Coyote. They talked, talked, [and] talked. They heard that no one had cut that medicine now [in the] East.

Spa·yúl came. He was a small man but a good shot. He told his brothers, "You go now. Act like you're looking for something. Just get over there without being noticed. You have to get ready to run. Don't wait for me. I'll run too." His brothers slid down below, pretending to pick up arrows and so on. Now Spa·yúl was ready. He put [an] arrow in his bow, pulled slooooow. Plop, [it was] just like somebody [had] cut [the] string. That crowd sounded like thunder. That Coyote boy got that medicine, [and] he *ran*. [When] he got where he had to give up, he gave it to his brother. They kept on that way.

Now all the people were fighting. They killed one Coyote boy. Those Wolf boys had turned against [the] Coyote boys in spite of [the] fact they were supposed to help each other. The people [the crowd] had turned back. They couldn't follow. At last Spa·yúl took the medicine. Those Wolves had killed all nine Coyote brothers. He jumped on a tree and climbed *way* up. He was almost back to the house. He was all alone up there—no help.

Down below those two old men talked. Wolf said, "I heard somebody holler, 'Coyote boys all got killed.'"

"No," Coyote said, "I heard it a different way. I heard *Wolf* boys all got killed." They argued back and forth.

"Well, we'll have to do something to settle the belief [what to believe]," Wolf said.

Coyote said, "All right, what shall we do?" They were standing outside the house.

"I'll have to [piss] over the house," Wolf said, "just like [a] rope.[100] Now if my boy got killed, it won't go over the house." Wolf did that, he pissed over [the house], just like string it went over. "Now you see, *your* boys got killed. Now you'll have to do that the way I did."

Coyote, "All right. I don't believe my boys got killed, but I'll do it."

"All right, you do it." Now Coyote urinated. He looked up to see [if] it went over [the house], and it just ran right in his own mouth. Coyote had to give up now.

Not very far off, at the top of the hill, was Spa·yúl, in the top of the tree. All the Wolf boys got together. "We'll have to kill him. We want that medicine. There's no help for it; we'll have to kill him."

"Well, we can't stand around here," the oldest Wolf said. "How [are] you going [to] do it?" As they spoke, the door opened behind them, and a big, tall fellow came in.

"What's the matter, boys?" he asked.

So they told him, "You see that fellow over there in the tree. We're trying to shoot him."

The tall man, "Well, give me an arrow. I'll shoot him." Measuring Worm was the tall fellow.[101] They gave him an arrow. "Oh, that's no good, that little bow. [It] can't shoot anything. Go get my bow and arrow."

They looked [and] said, "Oh, nothing here."

"Oh, it's standing right by [the] door," he said. Then they found it. Oh, [it was a] big arrow, big bow about six feet tall. They gave it to him. He stood straight, [and] he shot, hitting Spa·yúl right in [the] side. He rolled over and fell down.

The oldest Wolf boy warned, "Now don't run in there, don't go there, wait." They waited until Spa·yúl let go of [the] medicine, dead. He held it a long while. Those Wolf boys didn't want that tall man to know he had something so precious. They had to hide it. Then they went there and got that medicine.

Now they swam up, across, and took it over the river. They all went home. They hung it up in the house. Oh, a big thing they had done!

Their sister, an old lady, told them, "They'll fix you fellows for this. You never will beat him, Coyote Jim."

They said, "We'll have to go [to the] Klamath River, run to tatc'ɛ·. He can't go there. He can't go that far."

"All right," she said, "I won't say anymore." She kind of held for [sympathized with] Coyote. They had no business to kill those innocent people. Now they were four or five days getting ready. Old Wolf visited Coyote.

Coyote said, "How does it happen that they killed only my boys? They didn't kill a one of your boys?"

Old Wolf says, "I don't know."

Coyote, "That's all right. They killed my boys, that's all right."

For about four, five days, Coyote heard big noise across the river. Wolf boys make lots of noise when they're home. Then he didn't hear anything. Coyote went outdoors—no smoke over there. He went back in [the] house, lay down, [and] he studied. He studied pretty good [about] what he'd do. No one knew what he was going to do. He rose early in the morning, went outdoors. "If there's smoke there, they'll be home," [he thought]. But no smoke was there. It was *quiiiiiet*. Now he knew. "Now I've found out. You folks killed my boys." So he went back in [the] house, got ready. [He] got [his] arrow sack, bow, matches—everything he needed he put in the arrow sack, [with a] knife. [As] he got ready, he cried [and] cried. He knew now. He cried [and] cried. He got everything ready.

He crossed [the] river, went to Wolf's house, made a big fire. [He] saw an acorn paddle there, all kinds of grub, [but] he didn't touch it. He didn't want to eat. [The] fire got hot. He noticed that paddle [again]. He picked it up.

He said to it, the paddle, "Now you always know everything.[102] Which way did they go with it? Tell me, hurry up! I have to go." It never answered. "Hurry up, hurry up; I'll put you in the fire if you don't talk!" It never talked. "You don't want to tell me, eh? All right!" He put it right in the ashes [coals] of the fire. It was beginning to burn.

It said, "Oh, take me out! I can tell you which way they went." He took it out [and] held it smoking before him.

"Now, which way did they go?" It never answered. "You better tell me now! I'm in a hurry. I want to go. I don't want to wait on you. I'll just burn you up completely if you don't tell me." He put it in [the] fire. "You don't have to talk," he said. "You'll just stay there and burn. I won't take you out." Those Wolf boys had told that paddle never to tell if questioned by Coyote.

That stick hollered, "[If] you take me out, I'll tell you [for] *sure* this time." Coyote just walked around. "Hurry up, take me out!"

It was half-burned, and Coyote thought, "Maybe that's enough punishment now." So he took it out. [After] putting it down to let it cool, he picked it up. "Now you tell me." It never answered. Now three times it hadn't answered. "Hurry up now, tell me. I don't want to wait on you." [It] never answered. He thought, "It's just been fooling me. I'll make him tell this time." He put him in [the] fire. "All right, you *stay* there this time. You can hide it all you want to."

[The] stick hollered, "Take me out. I'll tell you now. I give up."

"No, you stay there. You've fooled me enough."

"Oh quick, take me out, I'll tell."

"All right." He held him right in front of him. "If you don't talk, I'll put you back. Now you tell me."

"All right, you want to know which way they went?"

"Yes, that's what I want to know."

"They talked about going to [the Klamath River].[103] That's how they talked. They said, 'Coyote can't go that far.' The old lady said, 'All right, you think [the] way you want [to].' So they went. Your youngest boy, Spa·yúl, they killed him just a little ways over here. They took that medicine. All your boys got killed on [the] way home. I just told you what they said. That's all I know."

"Now, which way did they go?"

"Pick up that rock [mortar]. Right there's how they went." Coyote picked up that rock. Right there was a big trail. Two, three o'clock [in the] summertime it was. He didn't talk to [the] paddle anymore. [The] next morning he got ready. He got on that trail; he went, tracking them. He came up about eight or ten miles from there on a mountain where they had gone up. He went right up. He sat down to rest. He cried [and] cried. There was a bird up there, hollering.

Coyote, "Oh what is it? Is it my boys?" He cried half an hour. [Then] he started on crying, "My sons, my sons."[104] He cried all day long. He came to where they [the Wolves had] camped. [Oh], lots of meat [was left there]. He cooked one leg, took [the] marrow out, [and] filled a little gut sack with the marrow. He put that away in his arrow sack.[105] He lay down. He ate nothing.

[The] next morning he started off without eating. He just thought, "I'll fix you fellows." That's what he thought. He traveled all day till evening. Again he found where they had camped. He sat down, built a fire. All kinds of meat was there. He cooked one leg again. When done he filled another little gut sack of marrow and put it in his [quiver]. He lay down, slept. [The] next morning, early [in the] morning, he started off, crying, cryiiiiiiiing. He went all day. In [the] evening he came to where they had camped. He had to cook one leg and fix a gut sack of marrow, fine elk marrow, [and] put [it] in his [quiver]. He lay down, slept.

He kept on traveling that way. [The] next day he traveled all day, then [in the] evening got to where they had camped. [He] cooked one leg, fixed a gut sack of marrow. [As] soon as he got there, he always did that right away. He put it in his [quiver]. He knew what he was making it for. [The] next day he traveled all day, not fast, just [fast enough] to get [arrive] by evening to where they had camped. Again he cooked one leg, filled a sack of marrow, put it away, [and] lay down. Always he cried all day, never missed a day, just cried [and] cried.

He kept on that way, traveling. [The] next morning [he'd] get out and go, travel all day, get there where they camped in [the] evening. [He'd] fix his sack of marrow, then he'd lay down. [The] next morning [he'd] start out again. [When he] got there [in the] evening, [the] first thing on his mind always was to fix that sack of marrow. After that he'd lay down and sleep. [He] slept harder because he had cried all day. [The] next morning he'd go again, [and] go again. He'd get there late in the evening, always fix what he had in mind, put it away, go to sleep. [The] next morning birds hollered around. He got up and went. [He] kept on slowly, traveling all day, get to where they camped, fix what he had in mind, break that bone, put [the] marrow in a sack just as it was getting dark, put it away, and lay down.

[The] next day he got up, went again. He just came right in there, maybe before five, he got there where they had camped. Oh, he saw the smoke a ways away down by the river. "Oh! Now I'll get 'em!" He was glad. He was more lively now; he hurriedly fixed one more sack of marrow—that made *ten*. He thought, "That's the last now. No more." He lay down. "I'll get ready tomorrow morning." The next morning he got up. [The] sun's way up now. "Oh, I forgot something. It's about my boys. I'll have to ask what I'm going to do." He sat down [squatted] a little ways away [off the trail] and defecated a little.[106] He stood up. "Now my [shit], you must tell me what to do, what's the best way I can do?"[107] It didn't answer. "You going to answer?" It didn't answer at all. "Now you tell me quick. I'll mash you if you don't tell me." It never answered. Now he cussed it, jumped on it, and mashed it. "All right, I'll kill you if you can't talk." He sat down again. A long time he pulled [strained]. Finally there came a little tiny bit. Now he got up. "Well, [are] you going to tell me what I'm going to do? What's the best way for me to do it? That's what I want to know."

Well, that feces answered. She said, "All right, I'll tell you. You can be chief. Those folks are bound to call you chief. Don't go straight down here but go around and come up to them from tatc'ɛ́tdən way. You come up from there, then they're bound to call you tatc'ɛ́tdən chief." Then she told him, "You must keep still. They'll take you in [the] house. They won't allow you [to] go [to the] sweathouse. They'll put you in [the] house with their sister. That medicine will be hanging right over your head. But don't look up because if you look at it, they might catch on to you. Now, another thing: You're not to cry. You mustn't cry. They'll have to tell you how they killed your boys because, of course, they don't know it's you, but they think you're tatc'ɛ́tdən."

"That's all I want to know," said Coyote

"What do you want now?" his feces asked.

"Well, I want a good elk skin, a chief's elk skin, a good one. I want an arrow, a full otter sack of arrows, and a bow fixed nice. I want Indian money to put over my neck. Lots of them, good ones. I want a hat, a feathered, Indian money–decorated hat, a nice one."

"All right." Everything was ready right there.

"I want a good pipe, a good long sack, a chief's sack, packed like a camera."

"All right." It was ready right there.[108]

"I want a fine knife, a chief's knife."[109] You have to pack [it] in your hand.

[His] shit [said], "Now they're going to [take] you [to] that woman. Now you'll have to talk tatc'ɛ́tdən talk. Let's hear you talk tatc'ɛ́tdən language."

Coyote, "Oh, I can't do that."

[His] feces, "Now you talk. I'll make you talk it right." Then he could speak the tatc'ɛ́tdən language plain. Because that Wolf's sister understands [the] tatc'ɛ́tdən language. Now everything was done, right there. It was just before noon. He was ready to go now.

He put that suit on. "How [do] I look now, my feces?"

"Oh, you look like a tatc'ɛ́tdən now. You look good. Good luck! They can't catch on to you."

Now Coyote went. He went a different way—he ran like [the] dickens to get around from below. Late [in the] afternoon he was coming there, 3:30 or 4 p.m. Those Wolf boys had been hunting. They had returned about 11 [or] 12 in the morning, all packing elk and so on. That woman was drying meat. Coyote hid his ten sacks of marrow where he would pass it again. Now they looked out from the house into [an] open space where they could see someone coming.

"Oh, someone's coming. He looks like a big [important] man." They were all ready to sweat.

The woman who was cooking said, "Now you fellows watch. It might be him [Coyote]. You can't beat him. It may be him, or it may not be him; you can't tell."

They laughed. "Oh, what [are] you talking about? He won't come around here."

"All right," she said, "all right."

Well, he came; he was close now, that man. A young man met him, made him sit on top of [the] sweathouse. [The] sun [was] way up now. Strangers always sat on top of the sweathouse, right by [the] hole to enter.

Now, Coyote took his pipe out. Oh, it looked fine. It was a chief's pipe. He smoked, then he put his pipe in his sack. Now he talked. He talked tatc'étdən. They were all listening. They were watching him close. But they couldn't understand him. Now they all believed he was genuine because he spoke tatc'étdən. They went and got that woman because she could understand tatc'étdən. Coyote talked. She talked to him.

He said, "I come from tatc'étdən. We don't know you people here. You have settled here all right."

She answered in tatc'étdən, "We have just come," she said. One brother told her to say, "We'll tell him how we came here at suppertime." She told Coyote that.

Now they told him, "You go back with that woman in the house. We'll come in pretty soon. We are all ready to sweat." So the woman took him in the house. Chief! Ha, ha, ha! Maybe he'll marry her. She cooked. He sat there. They spoke occasionally.

This fellow [Coyote] asked, "Do you catch any fish here in this river?"

She answered, "We just came here a little while ago. We don't know where to catch fish."

"Oh," the chief said.

Now [that] they were done sweating, they all came in [the] house, ten, eleven of them—the old man made eleven. They all came back in [the] house. They started in eating.

When nearly done eating, the oldest son began telling: "We kind of got away. We had trouble over there, so we came to a different place. I can tell you why. We had trouble from Coyote. My brothers killed Coyote's boys, all ten of them. They went way over there. They got medicine. Coyote's boy, the youngest one, shot that medicine string, [and] the medicine came down. One of his brothers got that medicine and ran off towards home with it. We fought all the way. We took it away from the Coyote boys; we killed them all." People bragged of exploits in this manner.

Oh, he was surprised, that chief. He never looked up till they showed him hanging over there that medicine. He didn't notice it much; he just kept on eating. Just like his feces told him, he had to do it just exactly as he had been told.

Well, those boys got ready to [go to the] sweathouse. They all went [to the] sweathouse, leaving only two [Coyote and the woman] there. She fixed a bed, made him lay down there, the chief. She got to work making a basket. She sat there making a basket pretty near all night. She was all the time that way. She was a mean one to watch him. She sat up all night to take care of that medicine. She didn't trust but what he might take it away.

He stayed there about a week. He never tried to do anything. She got used to him. Then the boys wanted him to go hunting.

"You come with us where we shoot elk. Don't take your hat, just your arrows and what you need to wear." She didn't want him to go.

She told her brothers, "Why are you taking him out? You might have trouble. Trouble is coming from somewhere. You folks don't know."

"Oh, don't talk about trouble," the boys said. "It's no trouble to hunt." They showed him where to sit down on a log and they would chase the elk down. All right, they went as Wolves do, always traveling. He heard them hollering here and there, "Wooooooo, wuuuuu." [On the] other side [of the] mountain, all over they hunted.

Now he hurriedly defecated. [He] got only a little. "Now what am I going to do, my [shit]?[110] It's nearly time for me to get away now. Now you tell me what to do!"

"Yes," she says. "The best thing you [can] do is kill yourself. You've got a knife. Chop yourself up and lay the pieces all around here." That's what he did. Guts lay here, arm over there, leg down that way, parts everywhere.

Now the elk [were] coming! Elk came past where [the] dead person was.

They pass—what [do] they care. One Wolf came, tracking elk. He saw elk dodging at that place.

"Oh, what's the matter? [Why does] he dodge?" He went there. He saw [the] chief's arms, guts, legs, head, laying around. Oh! He got scared!

His [Coyote's] [shit] had told him, "If you do that way, that medicine [will] be yours. One drop on you, it will be yours. You'll be a man again."

Now the others came. "Where's the chief?"

"Oh, come here! That chief got killed." They saw those arms, head, guts all laying there. Now they *all* got scared. They had to pack everything home, somehow.

When they got home, oh, goodness! She's mad. "I told you not to take that fellow. You can't mind; you're wild people."

"Oh, don't be scolding [us] about it. He'll be all right pretty soon. That's what we got [the] medicine for," they said. Then they put [a mat] down, put his head, shoulders, stomach, put [it] all together—[it] takes a long time—put him like a man lying there.[111]

Now they got that medicine. They held it straight over him. They dropped *one* drop, shut up the medicine, hung it up again. [As] soon as they dropped [it], that fellow stood up, no scars or anything.

Now they told her, "You believe now? You were mad a little while ago because we killed your husband. Now you keep [the] fire good, take care of him."

"All right," she said. They went [to] sweat, came back [at] supper time. He lay down; she interpreted for them. He wanted to know all what they did.

"Oh, that's fine," he said. "I became a man again—that's good. I don't know how I got killed." They came again [the] next day, ate, didn't talk much, didn't watch anymore. Coyote got up in [the] night, went around, went outdoors, walked all around. He went back in; the woman was still asleep. He figured he could get ready tomorrow night. He [would] claim he's sick. She [was a] pretty good watchman.

[The] next night, as soon as they went to the sweathouse, she was making a basket. Coyote blew a little, "P——f, p——f, I wish she'd go to sleep." She put her basket away, lay down, and went sound to sleep. Now he got ready, taking his time. He didn't want that hat anymore. He just threw it away. He didn't want his knife—he didn't want anything. He just left everything there. He took that medicine, put it on his back, [and] he went. He didn't run, just walked, taking his time. He went tatc'ɛ́tdən way.

The woman woke up near daylight. The man [was] gone. The medicine [was] gone. "Oh, I knew, I just knew it was him all right." She ran [to the] sweathouse. Her brothers all got ready. They went how Wolves run, just like [the] *wind*, they went after him.

Coyote, he walked kind of sloooow when he nearly got to tatc'étdən town. Those Wolves saw him. Coyote just ran in a house. He [had] already given the people one [bag of] deer grease. "Fight for me. Try to stop them."

"All right." They all fought for him. He walked on, got to another Indian town, gave people grease, [and] they fought for him. He kept going. [He'd] go in one door, out the back, and they would fight, thinking he was inside. They [the Wolves] kept on following him. They'd see him go in [a] house, then he'd go on, *walk*, not run. That was good pay to those people. They never tasted that kind [before]. [He] kept on that way to the tenth town. He gave his last grease.

"Fight for me; this is the last I have." Now he went on slower. "I don't care, they'll have to give up now." Those Wolves were getting weak, fighting with nothing to eat. He rested at the top of the hill now. Nobody came. It was all right. Those Wolves turned back from that last town.

Now he just took his time. He knew which way he [would] go. He knew which way [to] his home too. He walked along, camped some place alone. [He went on] steady [for] two, three, four days, steady. Finally he's home now.

Now he got busy. He hung that medicine up above. No one knew anything about it. Now he was going to look for his children. He packed bones in [the] sweathouse, put them all together good. He's *busy*, more busy. He put them all together. It made nine—one was gone. He went back and looked. He couldn't find him. That paddle had told him, but he forgot it. He looked all around. At last he remembered what the paddle had told him. He looked [and] sure enough, that fellow's bones lay right there. Now he picked them up [and] fetched them in [the] sweathouse, put [them] together, [and] put them together. Now it was all right. [There were] ten of them. Oh, he was glad. Now he put a drop on each one of them—ten drops.

Then he said to them, "You fellows call me tomorrow morning. I'll open the sweathouse door. You fellows sweat." Then he took the medicine back in [the] house, put it away.

Sure enough, [the] next morning he heard someone hammer [on the] sweathouse door. He got up, ran down, and opened [the] door. He sat down on top [of the sweathouse]. [The] oldest son came up, went down to [the] river to swim. Pretty soon another one came up, went down to the river to swim. Nine came up [like that]. Then at last he came up, Spayúl. Ten of them! He cooked all kinds [of food]. [When] supper [was] ready, they came in [the] house, ate— [they had] a good time! Oh, Coyote Jim [was] glad; oh, he felt happy.

How Land Came into Being

The world begins with no land, only water. From within a house descending from the sky, two men deposit in the water five flat plates, one landing on top of the other until, with the fifth plate, land, trees, sand, and so on appear. The leader of the two men makes a wife for his companion and builds them a house. The husband sleeps with her at night but is invisible. She has a baby and, thinking her husband has abandoned her, goes out looking for him, completely neglecting the baby's needs until her husband reveals himself and reprimands her. They raise a big family from which the earth is populated.

The story presented here is taken from Jacobs's Upper Coquille Athabaskan field notebook 2 (pp. 36–42). The title is Thompson's, from nən'ɛ nut'át hasɬsi·la, "no land, it came that way," that is, this is how it (land) came about. Anna Birgitta Rooth ([1957] 1984, reprinted in Dundes 1984:166–81) provides a concise overview of North American Indian creation myth types. For a cognate of Thompson's narrative, see the Joshua text "Creation Myth" (Farrand and Frachtenberg 1915:224–28, reprinted in Ramsey 1977:217–22). See also Ramsey's discussion of this text (1999:3–24). The Hanis Coos story "Arrow Young Men (The Creation of the World)" is a partial cognate text (Frachtenberg 1913:5–14).

[There was] no land, only water. Something came down from [the] sky [and] floated two feet above [the] water. They brought down a house from heaven. Two men were in that house. No one knows [their] names at that time. They took out one plate of land. They put it down on the water. That plate went down in the ocean. [There was] no sound at all—it just went down. They waited a long time—no sound at all.

Then one said, "Get another plate." He put down another plate flat on [the] ocean. [In the] same way he put it down. [In] the same way it went down—no sound at all in that deep water. They waited a little while, talked [it] over. There was *nothing*, only water.

One man said, "Well, try another one, another plate." They tried another, in exactly the same spot. It went just like the others; no sound came back.

"Well, how many plates before we see land?"

"Well, there will be five. Down where we put that first plate, land came into being. The second plate made more land come. The third plate brought another [layer of] land into being. There has to be five. Get another one," he said, "[and] hurry about it." The same way they put another [one down]. This time they could see the water splashing and stirring.

"Oh, now we're all right. We'll get land pretty quick now. Take out the last one, quickly!" Whatever the boss man told him, he—the other [man]—had to do it. "Now you put it down the same way. There's only one way to put it in." He put it down. Now, as far as they could see was land, trees, grass, creeks, everything. "Now [that] we've got land, we'll go on shore now and see what we can see." They got out on nice sand. There was good, fine sand.

Now they saw a track, [but] not a dog track. "Oh, we don't want that fellow. He means lots of sickness." They had seen a wildcat track. They went a little ways, [and] they saw another track.

"What kind of track is that? Same track?"

"No, that's a dog track. Well, let's go back. That's enough. There's no one around here, no people. We'll go back where our house is now." They came back in the house, [and] they talked.

The fellow said, "Boss, what shall we do now?"

"Well, I don't know. [There's] no people." [The] boss turned around. He made a woman. A woman stood there, a good-looking woman, fine. The boss said, "That's your wife." They [the couple] walked a little ways away to live by a fine creek. [The] boss said, "Right here is your house." They turned around and looked—there was a fine house standing right there. Everything was ready there when he took the woman into the house. The boss told her, "That's your home."

Everywhere they walked they could see that wildcat track and the dog track. They tried every way to kill that wildcat, but they never caught him. Now it was getting dark. She made supper ready, thinking her husband and his boss would be back, and [but] they never came back. Finally she sat down and ate. She got tired of waiting. She went to bed. She woke up. She felt someone sleeping beside her. She felt there, she felt a man sleeping there. [As it was] getting daylight, she slept again, and he got up and left. She cooked a little but saw no more of him. She didn't like it, but she couldn't help it, to have a man sleep with her at night and then see no more of him. She looked, [but] that other house—the heaven house—was gone.

Sometimes she'd go out, walk around on [the] beach. It was a nice place, but she was lonesome. Every night she would feel a man sleeping by her, but she never saw him. Now she was pregnant. [The] baby was born. No one ever said who took care of her—some unseen helper. She had to put [the] baby away; she had to get up.

She thought, "All right." She's not sick. She took care of [her] baby nice. When [the] baby was five days old, she made a baby basket. She put that baby in [the] basket. She was getting [ready] to go. She was terribly troubled, jealous. She thought, "That man must have another woman somewhere." She had never seen her man yet. [The] next day she went, carrying her baby in [the] basket. She just went. She said nothing. She felt jealous. "He must have another woman somewhere." She traveled, found no one, nothing, just a fine open place near the ocean. She [could] hear [her] baby crying. She'd shake herself [and the basket cradle on her back], "Shut up! I don't want any baby crying." That's all she could think about, her jealousy. "If [the] baby dies, I don't care." She never nursed the baby, never rested, just went on, just traveling night and day. Finally, she turned around, came right straight back. Still she had seen no one.

The baby cried; [it was] about dying. But that man was with them all the time. He was with his wife all the time. He wouldn't let her see him. He's just like [the] wind. He came behind. She never felt him. That little baby was hardly anything left, just [a] head. It would cry. She'd just shake it. "Keep still!"

She came to a pretty place where a fine little creek came down. "Oh, I'll take a rest here," she thought. Her man was behind her. She looked around [to see] where she could sit down. Someone from behind took the baby.

"You see this baby?" She saw the baby, [but it seemed to be] only [a] head, crying [and] crying. "What do you treat a baby like that for? You know, that's *my* baby." She sat down. "You untie this baby, you bathe him and nurse him." She saw the man now. She did that, she bathed the baby, nursed it. The baby became all right, healthy and nice.

He asked her, "Are you hungry?"

"Yes, I didn't eat anything in a long time," she said.

"All right, we'll eat now." He turned. There in front of them was all sorts of food. "Go ahead, eat!" he told her. They ate lunch there. They were going on now. The man packed the baby; she followed behind. It didn't take long to get home. They got home. He stayed with her now.

They had a big family after that. Every year they had one baby. The children married each other. They kept on that way. Now there were lots of people. They couldn't get along. They fought. They had to move away and raise [their] children elsewhere. People got on earth that way.

Now they got a dog. They raised dogs, and that man said, "You see the dog, see that dog's eyes?"

"Yes."

"You have to have a dog's eye, a black eye." Indians have black eyes. "But when white people come, the white people will have wildcat eyes."

[The boss man was] not sx̣áiyɛɬ'a.[112] [We] just called them the people who made the world. [It's] not Coyote. [The] boss man never came again. The Indians claim five earths [these five plates] made. Indians were all on the last plate.

A Man Followed His Wife to the Land of the Dead (Orpheus)

The story presented here is taken from Jacobs's Upper Coquille Athabaskan field notebook 2 (pp. 61–73). Jacobs's title from the notebook is "Man who followed his wife," perhaps from Thompson. Later she changed it to its present form. I have added (Orpheus) to her title. For an early comparative study of the Orpheus myth among North American Indians, see Gayton (1935a). A later, more comprehensive study is Hultkrantz (1957).[113] See also Ramsey for an analysis of the Nez Perce Orpheus story (1999:69–80). Coquelle Thompson's variant of the Orpheus plot is relatively unusual: the husband manages to successfully retrieve his dead wife and bring her back alive to the land of the living. This narrative is told, then, as if it were a historical account rather than a folktale or myth text.

A man was going to buy a woman from another country, a different Indian town. They [her people] brought [the] woman to his house, [had] a big dinner [and] a good time. His father paid money [to her family, and] those people of hers went back. They went around together, he and his new wife. They just hugged each other.

One day he said, "I'll go over that way and hunt."

"All right." He went. He went, taking arrows and everything. This woman stood outdoors watching in the direction her man had left. While she stood there, she died. No one knew what killed her. They put her in [the] house [to] see if she [would] come alive again. No. Her man came back. Oh! It hurt him. He didn't know what to do. He cried. They went to work and buried that woman. They had to hold that young man, talk to him [and] talk to him. He cried all [the] time—just couldn't keep still.

Finally, [in the] evening he studied and studied. He had heard in ghost stories that the ghost left the graveyard five days after it was buried. Now he studied. Late that evening, ten o'clock, he went to [his] wife's grave, sat there all night. He thought, "I can go where *you* go." [As] soon as [it was] daylight, he came back to the sweathouse, lay down, [and] slept. [He] never came back in [the] house. People came in the sweathouse, but he [did] not talk. People didn't know where he went after dark, but [as] soon as it got dark he went to the graveyard. He sat down, right on top by her grave there. [There was] no sound at all, nothing, just quiet. Come daylight, he came away. [It was] two nights now. He went [to the] sweathouse [and] lay down. That's all he studied. "Now I have to go with her; I have to catch her." [The] next night again, [as] soon as [it was] getting dark, he went there, sat there till morning. [There was] no sound—he heard nothing. [At] daylight he came back to the sweathouse. [The] next evening he had to go there again. That makes four. [He] sat there all night, never a sound, no noise at all. [At] daylight again he came back to the sweathouse. He didn't eat anything. He [was] not hungry, just studying that one thing. He wanted to get his wife—that's all.

It's the fifth night now. Now he thought, "This is the night," because he had heard it that way. He sat there. It came midnight. Near one o'clock he heard [the] movement of beads under him. "Now, now I'll get her." He got ready. About three o'clock [the beads] made more noise, stronger. He [was] ready right there now. Just at daybreak he heard her come up, his wife, [her] dress rattling.[114] She went. He tried to clasp her, but [he felt] just wind; he couldn't get her.

Now she went. He couldn't see [her], but he could hear those beads making noise [with her] running. Oh, he had to follow that. He ran after the noise of those beads. He heard her dress making noise. When they came to a mountain, that dead person went right through, but he had to go around or over [the] top because he's a live person. He went till [it was] getting dark. He had to stop wherever he was. He sat down and slept. [There was] no more noise of the beads.

[The] next morning she got up, right from his feet, [and] she ran. He went after her. He couldn't get near. [He] ran after, ran after, [and] ran after [her, but he] couldn't get near. It [was] getting dark now. He had to lay down. He knew she wouldn't go anymore at nighttime. He knew that. He went to sleep [as] soon as he lay down—[he was] tired. [As it] got [to be] morning, just a little ways off she got up, started off.

He just thought, "I'll go where you go. I don't care where you go, I have to go." Pretty close [to] noon, he could see her take [her] dress off, throw it to one side, and try to jump in black water. He had heard that dead people jumped in there, went to a house, and were given a panful of some kind of salmon eggs to eat. That's what he learned from his study. He grabbed her, said, "Don't jump in there."

She said, "You better go back now. I'm not your wife now. I'm dead. I'm dead. You are alive yet."

He told her, "Put your dress on again."

She did. "Oh, I'm dead now."

He answered, "Whatever you say, I'm going to go where you go. I like you; you're my wife! I have to go."

"Well, I don't know what will happen," she said. Finally, she kind of walked, trotted. He kept right on her heels, watching pretty close. He could see her now, as she ran. Now she got to a house. Right in [the] house an old man [was] waiting around. [He] got [had a] panful of something, some kind of louse.[115] They claim he's [the] man to holler across when dead people come, holler for a canoe.[116] That's his business. [The] government pays him I guess.

The boy kicked that pan, spilled out those lice, told her not to eat it. The old man saw him, looked at him, [and] noticed the man was a live Indian, but the woman was dead. The old man said, "You will have to go back. I can't put you on [the] boat."

But he hung on to his wife and said, "No, this is my wife. I have to go with her where[ever] she goes." [The] old man said no more. He couldn't say he could go. Live people were not allowed to enter the dead people's land.[117]

Now the boat was coming; the old man had hollered, "Boat, come, [there's a] woman here to go."

Across came the answer, "All right."

He hung on, hung on [to her]. At last he told her, "Put your arms around my neck this way so I can jump in the boat with you." So he did, he jumped into that boat.

The ferryman turned around and said, "Something smells on you."[118]

"Oh, shut up and go on!" He told the ferryman, "I'm not a live man." The ferryman had smelled him.

They got across, got out, [and] already [there were] people there ready to take her to [the] dance place. She had to go there. [As] soon as she danced, [he had to go]. [There was the] same kind of old man as the one who had the pan [of lice]. Because [the] husband [was] alive, he had to go to that old fellow. He went to see him.

[The] old man said, "I don't know, but I'll do the best I can. When I make your wife alive, I still don't know how you can go back."

"I want my wife," he told him. "I don't care if I stay here, but I want my wife to be alive, like a person." They had to hurry.

She was over playing a game, but the old man told him, "She'll come with that crowd in the evening to dance here. That's my business, to have the dance here. Now, your wife died over there, [is] that it?"

"Yes."

"And you could hear her in the daytime, but you couldn't see her?"

"Yes, I heard a noise."

"And as long as you could hear her, you wouldn't give up?"

"No, I wouldn't give up. Just as long as I heard the noise, I could follow that."

"All right, I'll do the best I can. You stay with me too; don't go anywhere. Don't go anywhere because people won't like you because they'll smell [that] you're a live person, and they don't like that." Then that old man told him, "I myself am a live man. I'm not dead. I'm a live man; that's why I'll try to help you."

It got dark. Now they were coming, making a big noise. "Now they're coming," the old man said. "You stand right by me, don't look around, just look [in] one place. Can you tell [recognize] your wife now?"

"Yes, yes, I think I can."

"Well, you just watch her, watch your wife. Now when they get done dancing, they make a little noise, and then those dance people all have to run out quick. Now you stand right here by the door, and when your wife runs by, just catch her in your arms and hold her. She won't squeal or anything. You just hold her, and they'll all [just] run past her."

[As] soon as the people went out, then the old man put some kind of strong medicine on [the] firewood, making thick smoke all around the place. Then for two, three hours the old man blew that smoke on the girl, all over her legs, everywhere. Then he took some kind of strong medicine, rubbed all over her. That young man [was] sitting down. He took some kind of water [and] sprinkled her face, rubbed all over her head. Pretty soon she sat up.

"Well, how do you feel now?"

"Oh, I feel all right."

"Well, where's your man?"

"He's sitting over there."

"Do you like your man?"

"Yes."

"Do you feel like you [would] like to go back home now?"

"Yes."

That old man said, "Well, you're not all right yet, but I'll work on you yet." Now it [was] two, three o'clock in the morning. He worked on her again. He made more of that kind of fire. Smoke again, he worked on her again, pulled on her arms, made [her] stand up, he rubbed her legs, even on the bottom of her feet he rubbed some kind of medicine. Then he brought something like a big bucket, [and] he made her stand in that. Thick steam came up all over her. She sweated and sweated. He rubbed on her in that steam, worked on her for half [an] hour.

Now he made her step out, then he slung it away. [It was] just like nothing, but before it had been steam. Now he opened something right there beside him. There was a spring right there. "Now you go swim," he told her. She went to swim. [She] swam quite a long while till she got cold. It was daylight by then. Now he made her stand by [the] fire again, worked at her again, dried her hair, dried her all over with some kind of buckskin.

Now he took her burial dress, he shook it in hot steam, shook it, brushed it good; everything she was wearing was cleaned. "All right, you put these on now, they're all clean, they're all right." She put them on. "Now you folks sit down." They sat down. He told her, "You are just like people now. You are a person just like your man. Your man was a person before but you were not; you were dead. Now you have come back, you're a person again; your body is all right. But you must eat." So he went and got all kinds of food, dried elk meat, dried fish, and acorn soup. "You folks eat now." He had everything. Maybe he [was] working for God—or something—must be.

They had to hurry. Before they ate, he told them, "You people must hurry and eat now. You won't have a chance to eat later [when] you have to go. I am going to see some people who go every other day to [the live] people's world and get camas. They told me on that hill, in an open place where they dig camas, they saw old people crying—an old man and woman they saw crying. I'll go see those people now." He went.

Now that man and his wife began to talk. They didn't know how to go back. They had water [and] everything, [just] like people. She was a person now. Presently that old man came back. He said, "I have men now, I have two men." Presently two men came in. The old man said to them, "Now these two people here want to go back. I won't tell you everything, but you know how it is. His wife died over there, and he followed her here. So I'm helping them. Now I'm trying to send them back. Will you take them back?"

"I'll try," one of the men said. He had great big wings. They nearly touched the ground. [He was] a great big bird said to have come from way across the ocean.[119] A kind of black bird—tame. Now they got ready. [The bird] said, "Now I'll tie my belt up tight. Put your feet in here." The other man took one of them. Now they rose up and went. They cautioned them, "You must never open your eyes, or I'll drop you right in the ocean." So they shut their eyes, kind of slept.

It took them only three or four hours. They went to where the old folks dug camas. "Now open your eyes." They opened their eyes. "Now you pile up lots of camas, old-fashioned food, [and] put [them] in the basket here. That's all the kind of pay I want." Now the birds left.

It was about two, three in the afternoon. They felt ashamed [embarrassed] to go back in the house. "Well," he said, "we've got to go back in." [There were] maybe ten, twelve houses there, all issuing smoke, lots of people. When they got near the house, some boys saw them [and] ran in the house.

"Somebody's coming." So a man ran out.

"Oh, my! That man is coming back with his wife that died last week." Now they went inside.

He told the old people, "Don't cry, don't squeal. It's me. I'm all right. My wife is getting better." They wouldn't let anyone cry. People kept coming from one house after another to feel of her. They could hardly believe it was her. Then they sent a messenger to run for her mother. They, her people, came and had a big feast and good time. They notified every Indian town. Everyone came; they had never heard of such a thing before, never seen that kind.[120]

Mountain People

Diminutive Mountain People play in creeks and dwell in a mountain home, living just like people. The Mountain People once took in fifteen to twenty Euchre Creek children. Two years later the lost children appear before a fisherman, explain their comfortable living conditions, and teach him a song and dance for the people to use. They are never seen again.

The story presented here is taken from Jacobs's Upper Coquille Athabaskan field notebook 3 (pp. 50–52). The title is Thompson's: náts'ən mɛ·dəné, "Mountain People."

They played in a little creek. When boys played around [that] creek, they saw little baby foot[prints] in the sand. Well, some little person must live up the creek. [The] next day again they [the boys] saw lots of baby footprints [and the] next day, [even] more. So they followed those little tracks in [the] sand. Now they saw those little spears coming down. They kept [on] going. At last they got to a little house [at the] foot of a mountain.

One little tiny man about a foot high spoke to the boys: "We made you come this way. You see lots of brush tied up? We did that, clear around here all the time. Come in [the] house." He took them right in a door in [the] mountain.

Oh, [there were] lots of two-foot [tall] people, little women [and] little men. [The] little people thought maybe they'd be carried home [to the boys' home] because [they were] small. They hunted like men, those little men. [They did] no harm. [They] fed people. [The] next time the boys came around there, no tracks [were seen] at all. [They] couldn't find them again. [They] lived just like people. [They had] all kinds of bear and elk blankets, just like people. They couldn't give any power.

At [Euchre] Creek, fifteen or twenty boys and girls played at the mouth of the creek every day.[121] The Euchre people [are] all dead now. They kept following those little twisted bunches of grass, the whole gang of boys and girls.

They got to that place, [and] those Mountain People got them. [The] children never showed up again.

Two years after [that], one old man put [up] a salmon fence across that creek. He made a big salmon trap of basket. He fixed [it] good. He had a little house there. He camped there. [At] nighttime he heard a fish, went there [to his trap], hit him in [the] head, [and] put him aside. [In the] daytime he cut fish. He was alone, that old fellow. [The] town was two or three miles below. He just camped there. [The] next night lots of fish came. About noon he [was] done cutting and had [the] fish all hung up. He sat down. He saw a *tall* woman coming [wading] in the creek. He saw fifteen or twenty come. They [were] all the same people that got lost. They came to see him.

"Don't cry. We're not dead. We got a good home. [The] Mountain People got us, treat us good." They [the young people speaking] wore fine feathers, arrowheads, red-headed woodpecker [feathers]. They danced for him. "Now you learn this song and dance and teach it to the people. Make the people understand they have to use this song." Near sundown, "Well, good-bye. We have to go home [now]. That's the last you'll see of us."

That's a [Euchre] people's story. Ida Bensell, [Euchre], her father knew that song.[122]

Robin

A young man packs an old woman across a creek. On the other side she refuses to get down, and nothing he does can dislodge her from his back. After three days she (Robin) transforms into a good-looking woman, compensates him with strings of dentalium for her abuse, and becomes his wife.

The story presented here is taken from Jacobs's Upper Coquille Athabaskan field notebook 3 (pp. 106–9). The title is Jacobs's.

Men always told their sons, "Anyone you see [who wants to go across the river], you [must] take across. Any old woman who wants to go across [the] creek, you help her across."

[The] fellow might say, "Oh, I don't want to bother [with] old folks."

"No, you do that. Sometimes it means good luck. Always help a woman [or] anybody who wants to go across. Once in a while that means good luck."

A young man had been told like that. One time he came to a creek [when] it was high water. There [was] an old, old lady with a cane [who stood] in [the] water looking [to see] how to get across.

This young man said, "Where do you want to go?"

"I want to go across," she said.

"Well, I'll catch [hold of] your hand," he told her.

"No, you pack me across. I don't want to swim," the old lady said. Well, he had to do it.

He thought, "Oh, I guess I can do it."

"All right, old lady." He squatted down. [The] old lady put her arms around his neck [and] her legs around his hips. Then he swam, he paddled across.

[He] took her out on [the] ground. "Now!" he said to [the] old lady.

"No, pack me around," she said. He didn't want to. Oh, he began to cry. He couldn't get her off. He fell on his back; he ran under logs trying to scrape her off. He couldn't get rid of her. All night he did everything. He couldn't get rid of her. All night he tried. She stuck right there. Oh, that young man cried.

"Something's stuck on my back now," he said. He wept. He went on [the] mountain. He didn't want anybody to see him. "If I had a knife, I'd cut her feet and arms." He couldn't even part her arms. She was getting stout, that old lady. He cried and packed her all night. He was ashamed to go back in the house. "Something is stuck on my back," [he sang repetitively].[123]

Down home they missed him. For two or three days he packed her around. [He] went under fallen logs [and] tried everything. One morning at sunrise he [was] kind of sleepy. He lay down. [When] he got up, [there was] nothing on his back. He turned around. Right there stood a woman, oh, a good-looking woman.

"How do you feel now? You abused me too much; you treated me pretty rough. I am a person, not an animal. Why did you do that?" she said.

He told her, "That isn't my fault. If you're people [a person], you ought to treat me better than that."

She told him, "Sit down and feed me. I won't do that anymore." He sat down.

"I don't know," he said. "I pack old ladies. I saw [an] old lady who wanted to go across, so I packed you like you told me. I tried to put you down over there on the ground. You wouldn't let me. That was not my fault."

"I'll have to pay you. What do you want?" She said, "I'll make it good. I know that I abused you. It's my fault—you're right about it. I've come to see you all the time, but you don't know me. I thought I'd get you that way. You pack old ladies all right. So I got you that way. But I'll pay you for that because

I know I'm in the wrong." She reached right beside her [and] got big strings of money [beads and] put them around his neck. "Now you'll take me in the house," she told him.

"All right," he said, "My mother is old and not very well."

"I'll tend to that," she said.

Now he took her home. He [had] been gone two or three days. The old folks—one [was] packing wood in [the] house. "Our son's come back, our son's come back," she called to the old man. "He's got a woman, he's got a woman."[124] They got in [the] house. They [his parents] put [mats] down.[125] They sat down on it. His folks fed him. He hadn't eaten for three or four days, just packed that old lady.[126] That's the end of that.

That woman was Robin.[127] [She was] pretty.

Coyote Jim Gives the Law on Gambling

While traveling around, Coyote encounters a village where the people have strange gambling habits, such as trying to hit one's opponent with a shinny ball and using people as bets. He defeats these folks at their game, teaches them the stick gambling game, and forbids using people as wagers.

The story presented here is taken from Jacobs's Upper Coquille Athabaskan field notebook 3 (pp. 116–22). The title is Jacobs's.

Coyote Jim was visiting different towns. He came to one big town but in only one house did he see smoke. He came to that door. He saw two girls [and] one old lady. He went in. They gave him a place to sit.

He said, "Hello, girls."

"Hello," the old lady said. "Where do you come from? Who are you?"

"I'm a man. I come from [the] south." Coyote had heard that people were gambling over there. He packed his cards [hand-game sticks] and gambling equipment.

This old lady said, "You better tell this man. You people just got back from there."

"Yes," said the two girls. "We just came back from where the people are gambling. If you go there, you'll find out how to gamble," they told Coyote. Now Coyote took his bet out. He fixed it. He showed the girls how he gambled. He sang.

"Is that the way they do it over there?" he asked.

"No," they told him. "They don't do it that way. You see all these houses here? No one [is] in them. They won all those people over there. They bet and gambled people. None of them will come back. There's just the two of us left. They didn't bet us. We wouldn't allow it. We never went into the gambling house. We saw them from outside. Oh, people [were just] thick in the house."

Coyote, "Well, they don't do it the way I do?"

"No."

Now Coyote picked up his things, rolled them up.

"I'll go there to gamble," he said. "Can you girls come with me? Don't be afraid! I won't bet you girls. I'll bet my own money. That's the law: You have to bet money, not people."

"All right, we'll go with you."

"If you go with me, you have to stay with me, on my side, not on [the] other side. I'll show them what to do with people." He told that old lady, "Don't be afraid. They'll come back." Now the old lady was satisfied. They got ready to go. They crossed a big river in a boat. [They] tied up their boat.

People who had been won had to stay in one place, just like prisoners. They [Coyote and the girls] went. They got in that big house. People [were] all just thick [there]. He [Coyote] went right in [the] house. [The] girls followed him. They knew the girls. He went to one side.

He said, "Well, I have come to gamble with you people. I have money to bet." He fixed his bets now. He took money out, [and] he put his cards there. The people were surprised.

"What's he going to do? We don't gamble that way." He was singing, shuffling the cards, did everything the right way to gamble.

"That's the way to gamble," he told the people. "I'm just showing you the right way to gamble."

Now the boss came in and sat down.

The boss said, "That's your game, the way you play?"

Coyote answered, "Yes, that's the way people gamble all over the world. That's the way to gamble. People are people and cards are cards. They never bet people. That's not allowed." The boss sat there.

He said, "Well, we don't gamble that way here. We bet people. Now, if you are going to gamble with me, you have to use my game."

"Well," Coyote asked, "what's your game?" So he brought it out—oh, a fine shinny ball, about the size of a baseball, soft.[128] Coyote said, "All right, I think I can win."

"Take your place then," the boss told him. They wanted to get those two girls. They knew Coyote Jim would bet those girls. Coyote rolled up his bets [and] told those two girls to watch them. They fixed him a fine bed to sit down [on]. They fixed for the other side. People [stood] on both sides, watching. [The] house [was] chuck-full. Coyote Jim took off what he wore [and] had those girls pile [it] up in one place.

Now that boss man said, "If I hit you, I'll get one of your girls."

Coyote said, "All right, I'll bet one anyhow."

"All right, you ready? Sit down." Coyote studied where he would be hit and how to dodge.

"All right, I'm ready." Coyote showed his breast. He [the boss] threw. He missed.

"Bring one girl or man over," [Coyote ordered]. It was his turn to throw. Coyote motioned. "You ready?"

"Yes, I'm ready," [the boss man said,] showing his breast. Coyote Jim hit him.

"Bring one man over." Now Coyote had two. All afternoon they played. It didn't take long to win back fifteen or twenty people.

Near sundown the girls said, "We got to go back."

Coyote said, "I'll go with you. But wait awhile; I have to fix it so these people can go home." He said he would come back and gamble tomorrow. They helped [the] people cross the river. He slept at the girls' house. They told the [old] lady about it.

She said, "I knew he was a different kind of man."

Across the river the people were going to get ready to kill Coyote.

The chief said, "Not yet. It doesn't hurt us to get beat. Wait—see what he can do." [The] next day he [Coyote] came back. [He] brought nothing but the girls. They trusted him now. They started [gambling] in the morning. Everything was ready. They never hit him. They think they can, but they always miss. Coyote hit wherever he wanted. By two or three o'clock a whole lot of people had been won back.

Coyote Jim asked, "Is that all the people you won?"

"Yes," the boss said. "You've won almost all back. Just three or four people I got left."

"Well, I'll play again," Coyote said. Coyote won those four. Now they talked.

"I don't want to win your people. I don't want to gamble that way." He showed them again the right way to gamble. But they didn't care for it. They'd rather bet people.

Coyote knew that they wanted to kill him so he said, "I'll be back tomorrow." He just fooled them.

Back in [the] home village, in every house people wanted to give him money, but he refused it.

"I just won you people back to do good to you."

They warned him, "Some of them are coming to kill you."

"All right. I'll be here. Let them kill me." He got ready. In the middle of the night he left. He went home.

Down there, the next day, they missed him. He didn't show up.

He told the people on this side, "Don't gamble that way anymore. You're men. You're people. Fight back if they try to force you." So it stuck that way.

Coyote Gives the Law on Death

Narrative explanations regarding the origin of death are found throughout Native North America. Thompson's version is one of two dominant origin-of-death tale types in the Pacific Northwest. The other is the Orpheus tale type. The story presented here is taken from Jacobs's Upper Coquille Athabaskan field notebook 3 (pp. 122–24). The title is Jacobs's. Harrington recorded a similar version from Thompson in 1942 (JPH, reel 027, frame 0307). M. Jacobs recorded the story from Thompson in Chinook Jargon, "The Origin of Death" (M. Jacobs 1936:26–27). For western Oregon cognates, see the Alsea story (Frachtenberg 1920:116–17), the Hanis Coos (Frachtenberg 1913:42–45; 1922:419–22; M. Jacobs 1940:135-36), the Kalapuya (M. Jacobs 1936:18–19; 1945:137–38, 226–27), and the Takelma (E. Sapir 1909a:98–101). For the wider distribution of this tale type, see Boas (1917a).

Coyote Jim had a partner. He had one boy, and his partner had one boy. They lived close by each other. His partner's boy got sick.

He told Coyote, "My boy is pretty sick. How will I take care of him?"

"You can't take care of him—no way," Coyote said. [The] next day that boy died. Oh, that fellow couldn't stand it. He came to Coyote. Coyote helped him fix him [prepare the body for burial], bury him. He can't *stand* it! In about three or four days, on the fourth day, he came to Coyote Jim.

"I come [to] see you. I can't stand it. Tomorrow [will] be five days my boy [has been] dead. I came to see you to ask: when people die, in five days let them come back. I want my boy to come back. That's why I came to see you. What do you think about it?"

Coyote said, "Well, you want [that] in five days dead people have to come back—you want it that way?"

"Yes, I want it that way. It hurts me too much."

Coyote, "Well, you want your boy to come back tomorrow?"

"Yes."

"Now I'll tell you: this is a big world, but if people all came back in five days after death, there'd be no room. You'd have to stand. There'd be no room to sit, no grub. Do you understand that?"

"Yes, I understand that," his partner said. "If you don't want it that way, I understand that." Now [the] next day, five days [were] up. That man felt a little better.

Now Coyote's boy got sick. He died. Oh, Coyote can't stand it. His partner helped him bury [the] boy, talked with him. Coyote didn't know what to do. He studied, studied what he had done. "I said wrong when I said it. It would be better if dead people returned in five days." Now he had to see his partner. It would soon be five day's time. He saw his partner. He said, "I decided my way was wrong. I remember how it hurt you when your boy died. We might as well decide to let people come back five days after death."

"Well, that's what you decided yourself, wasn't it?"

Coyote, "Yes."

"Well, you told me [there'd be] no room to sit down. You told [the] truth then. I studied it. Besides I'm getting black now.[129] It has to be like you said."

Coyote Jim had to be satisfied with his own law.

Frog Woman

A jealous Frog Woman urinates on her co-wife Redheaded Wood-
pecker Woman's firewood so it won't burn. Redheaded Woodpecker
Woman tells their husband, who orders Frog Woman to stop.

The story presented here is taken from Jacobs's Upper Coquille
*Athabaskan field notebook 3 (pp. 126–27). g*ʷəlétc'u is a "frog."*

The title is Jacobs's. Harrington recorded a version of this story
from Thompson in 1942 (JPH, reel 027, frames 0229-30).

[This is about] Frogs a long time ago when they married, and her [Frog Wom-an's] man married another woman, a Redheaded Woodpecker Woman. When they built a fire, Frog was jealous. She [Woodpecker Woman] went and got fine dry wood, way at the top of the tree on [the] mountain.[130] [But her] fire wouldn't go, just "ts-s-s-s-s"—it made a noise that way. She couldn't figure out what had happened. Frog had peed on that wood and in that [Woodpeck-er's] fireplace.[131] [She] made lots of water.

Frog, she went out [and] got green wet wood, but she fixed that fire.[132] Oh, [her] fire burned good. She wanted her man to think only she could keep a good fire. She did that all the time. Her man never noticed her because Frog was an ugly woman, whereas the Woodpecker Woman was a good-looking woman, a fine woman.

Redheaded Woodpecker caught on at last. She told her man about it. Then he whipped Frog. "Stop that! A woman goes and gets dry wood and then you do that. That's bad!" Frog had to stop that then and act like people. Her man told her, "If you want to pee, go outdoors. Don't do that. It stinks." Frog had to give up then.

Raccoon

Raccoon is ridiculed for marrying without paying the bride price.
His detractors cause him to spear a whale, which carries him and
his wife out to the ocean, where they are stranded. Coyote and the
Sky People help him return with a large boat full of whale meat
and kill those who had made fun of him. He becomes a rich man.

The story presented here is taken from Jacobs's Upper Coquille
Athabaskan field notebook 3 (pp. 130–34). The title is Jacobs's.

One man, Coon, speared salmon. He didn't care much [about appearances]. Coon married the old man's daughter across the river and fished and hunted for the old man. Those across-the-river people didn't like Coon because he had gotten a good woman. That old man let him have her [without payment].[133] So they said, "Let Coon spear a whale, and it will take him to [the] ocean to die somewhere."

Sure enough! A big fish came along. Coon's wife was steering the boat.

Coon speared him. They [the people who disliked him] caused Coon to be unable to let go of that pole. That whale went just like a streak right out to [the] ocean. [It] must be Coyote Jim [was] helping Coon. Now there they were, one day [and the] next night [with] no food [and] no water, he [Coon] and his wife. They slept a little. [The] next day the poor things were crying.

Oh! There was Coyote Jim right in the boat. "Oh, what are you laughing about, [my stepson]?"[134] Coon was *crying*. [It's] just like laughing when Coon cries. Coon didn't answer him. Coyote took his penis out [and] rubbed all over the pole [with it]. [He] got his [Coon's] hands loose from [the] pole. Now that pole got like a big tree, just standing there. Coyote told him, "[The Heaven (Sky) People] will come from heaven and help you pretty soon."[135]

Back home those people were making fun of him.

"Coon is bringing lots of whale in a boat," they said.

The old lady said, "Oh, don't make fun of him." A lot of [Sky] People came down into [the] ocean to help Coon. They made that boat grow two or three times its [original] size. They cut that whale and piled the boat full for Coon.

"Now, early in the morning when you see a heavy fog on the ground, that's us! You be ready! We'll clean up those people. We'll kill them all. They treat poor people badly, and yet they think they are men."

That old man, all of his daughters had been taken from him, without pay. This was his last daughter. He said they'd have to kill him before they could have her. She was the one Coon had. Now those helper people [Sky People] told Coon to be ready to get home.

"You talk back to those people," they advised him. "Accuse them of everything. You go home now. Your old folks feel bad for you. Don't be afraid. We'll be there." They told the woman, "Make ready some acorns, make grub ready. We'll eat lunch with you. Good-bye." Then they [Coon and his wife] saw no one. Just [the] ocean [was there].

They turned that boat [around]. [It] went just like an automobile. Those [Sky] People helped. A whole whale was loaded into that big boat.

Maybe about two or three o'clock they were hollering across river, "Coon is bringing a whale."

Those old folks heard him answer, "Yes, I am bringing a whale, you cunt's children!"[136] They were quiet. Oh, they saw that big boat, just full of whale. They [Coon and his wife] told the old lady, "Make acorns quick; we're hungry. Tell [the] old man [to] come. This whale belongs to him." [The] old man came.

Oh, he [was] glad, felt lively. Across [the] river the people were quiet. [They] hollered no more. They all got shamed. So they beat them, you see.

Four or five poor old fellows, up above [river] friends, came down and got whale, but those across-the-river people got nothing. [A] couple [of] mornings later Coon went outside. Oh, a heavy fog was on the ground. When [the] fog was all gone, he saw people just standing thick all around.[137] They helped him make a great big house. They all ate acorns. Then they cleaned up those people across the river, killed them all. They brought back the old man's daughters. Now Coon had ten or twelve wives. [He was a] rich man! Ha! Ha!

Big Head (Cannibal)

"Big Head" is a story whose dominant theme is cannibalism. A young man, after sucking blood from a wound to his foot, proceeds to eat his own body before beginning to consume fellow villagers. With the help of his sister, the community succeeds in killing this dangerously antisocial fellow. Another theme concerns the love of a sister for her formerly good-hearted brother that is offset by the community's need for survival.

The story presented here is taken from Jacobs's Upper Coquille Athabaskan field notebook 3 (pp. 134–38).[138] Harrington (1942) recorded an untitled version from Coquelle Thompson (JPH, reel 027, frames 0283–87). Melville Jacobs recorded a Miluk Coos cognate, "The young man stepped on snail's back" (1939:54–56). M. Jacobs (1935, 1938–39) also obtained a Galice Creek Athabaskan cognate titled "Nothing but the Head Left." See Edward Sapir (1909b:246–48) for a Wasco version collected by Curtin; Aoki (1979:29–39) and Aoki and Walker (1989:551–67) for two Nez Perce versions titled "Cannibal"; Boas (1918:82-85, 272–79) for two versions of the Kutenai cognate, "The Giant"; and Smith (1993:69–73) for a Western Shoshone cognate, "Cannibal Brother."

When people were starving, a young man with [who had] sisters, a father, and a brother ran around too much in the brush. Something stuck on his foot. It tickled him. He couldn't get it off. It made blood. He put his foot up and sucked that blood. He finally started in to eat his own leg. He ate till there was nothing but bone up to [his] thigh. Then he started in on the other side and ate—left nothing but bone. All around his body, his hands and arms, he just cleaned up his body. Nothing but bones left. He head [was] about that big [three or four times its original size and still] growing. His eyes [were] bulging out, big. His face and head [were] all right [not eaten], but everything below [his] neck—[the] flesh [was] all gone, just bones. I don't know about his guts. It doesn't say.

Now he started in eating other people. Half [of the villagers] he cleaned up, half ran away. Now only houses [were] standing. Now down below in a big town his sister lived. They asked her to go see about him. He'd hit a man with a sword, mash his head, clean him up in no time. She went to see him.

"If he eats me, all right. I'll die anyhow." That was a good-hearted brother, a good fellow who got to be that way. She came by boat. Only in his house was [there] smoke. She packed her baby. That fellow sat. He saw a shadow in the door[way]. He moved; his bones rattled. She opened [the] door.

"Hello, brother, brother."

"Oh, sister?"

"Yes, brother, brother, brother, brother."[139] She cried that way. She had to bring her brother down so [the] people could kill him. That's why she cried that way. She took him down. They fixed a place for him to sit in [his] brother-in-law's house.

They put a woman on each side of him [and] told him, "This [is] your wife; that's your wife." They did this to quiet him for a little while. Otherwise, he would jump on a man and eat him.

When she coaxed him to come with her, he asked, "Are there lots of people over there?"

"Oh, yes, lots of people. You'll eat good over there." That's the way she talked to him good all the time [until] she got him downriver. He jumped in the boat in one jump. He [was] nothing but bones. She put [the] baby down on [the baby] basket and paddled him over. He carried that big sword. No one knew where he got it. Right by the [river]bank she asked to pack his knife.

"Put it on the baby basket." She packed her baby in front for fear he'd grab it [from] behind.[140]

"All right," he said. He put it there. He walked in front. He'd turn around and watch her all the time.

"Go ahead. Go ahead, I'm coming," she would tell him.

He'd ask, "How far [do we have] to go?"

"Just a little ways now, brother. We'll get there pretty soon."

"Are there lots of people there, sister?"

"Yes, lots, lots of people, brother. You will eat good." They went slowly. She cried.

"What are you doing, sister? Are you crying?"

"No, I'm sweating." She hid it [from him]. She loved that boy. Oh, it hurt her. She cried.

Now they got close to [the] house. No one was around outside. They had all been ordered to keep in the house. He stopped.

"Sister, are there people?"

"Yes, *lots* of them. You'll see after a while, *lots* of them." So they came indoors [since there was] nobody around outdoors. He stood at [the] door [and] looked in. [Then] he dodged back.

"Come in, brother, come in." He looked in again. He saw the two women sitting there. He kind of smiled. He dodged back, ashamed [embarrassed]. "Come in, come in [and] sit down between these girls." Oh, he [was] ashamed, [being] nothing but bones. He went [and] sat down between those girls. Already it was fixed. Those two women were to pull back that [mat].[141] They had a plank over the hole there.

Those women got up, pulled that mat [aside].[142] [They] put a plank that had been [part of a] boat on top [of the hole, and] everyone sat on it. He jumped up against that board, [hitting it] with his big head for an hour, but he couldn't bust it. He died there. After he died, something exploded and went up through the house. It was his power. Now he was done.[143]

Skunk

During a famine, Skunk pretends to be sick and invites everyone in the village into his house to help the attending shamans sing. Skunk shoots his musk and kills everyone, but the musk spoils the taste of the meat.

The motif of Skunk's lethal musk is widespread in Northwest Indian oral traditions. The story presented here is taken from Jacobs's Upper Coquille Athabaskan field notebook 3 (pp. 139–40).[144] Harrington recorded a version from Thompson in 1942 (JPH, reel 027, frames 0394–95). For cognates and analogous stories, see the Karok "Skunk Story" (Kroeber and Gifford 1980:244) and "The Story of Skunk" (Bright 1957:246–47), the Kathlamet "Coyote

*and Badger" (Boas 1901:79–89), the Clackamas Chinook "Coy-
ote and Skunk. He tied his musk sac" (M. Jacobs 1959a:13–18),
the Wishram "Coyote and Skunk" (E. Sapir 1909b:149–53), the
Upper Cowlitz "Skunk pretends dying and with Coyote tricks and
kills animals" (M. Jacobs 1934:177–79), the Klikitat "Skunk pretends dying and with Coyote tricks and kills animals" (M. Jacobs
1934:98–100), the Lushootseed "Skunk's Important Information"
(Hilbert 1985:165–67) and "Skunk Was Living There" (Snyder
2002:89–91).*

One day Skunk claimed he got sick, sick. His belly got big, big. He wouldn't
let go of his fart. He had to hold it. He got everything to come in the house:
Bear, Deer, Elk, Jay Bird, and others. They hired Jay Bird for [as a] doctor.
Everybody sat there. This fellow was sick.

"Oh, my belly! Oh, my belly." Jay Bird danced. He danced, danced, [and]
danced. [It] didn't do anything; [he] couldn't cure him. He had to sit down. He
watched that fellow [Skunk]. He didn't know what he would do when Skunk's
belly burst. He saw a little crack in the wall.

He decided, "I'll just put my nose there in the crack." Over there [across the
room] was a little [Water Dog] or [Lizard].[145] He was going to dance now. [A]
full house [was] singing. They sang, they sang. No one watched but those two
doctors. [The] people just sat.

"I come under the riffles, come out and go under the grass. Come under the
riffles and under grass." That's how [Lizard] sang.

Blue Jay said, "Oh, I don't like that song."

Now Skunk's getting ready. "Oh, my belly, oh, oh." Presently Skunk shot
all around. Then he ran out. He got better. Deer, Elk, everything died in the
house. It was starving [famine] time. He [Skunk] had to do something. But no
one could hardly eat that meat. [It] stank like Skunk.

Snake and Money

*A poor man pities his daughters, who wear white camas shoots
instead of dentalium shells when digging camas in the spring. He
is visited by a wealth-giving power in a dream. He carefully follows his dream's instructions and is rewarded with quantities of
dentalia, which he shares with his chief and fellow villagers. At the
end of one year he has ten wives.*

The story presented here is taken from Jacobs's Upper Coquille Athabaskan field notebook 3 (pp. 141–46). Jacobs supplied the title. See Harrington (1942) (JPH, reel 027, frames 0242–48) for another rendition of this story by Thompson. For a published version of Harrington's text, see Whereat (2002:31–33).

Poor people, not upper-class people, dug camas in the springtime. When you dug in that spring, it made dirty water [down] below. [Some] poor girls couldn't dig anything because just dirty water came by them. This old fellow felt bad, sorry for those girls. They wore white camas shoots that looked like Indian money [beads]. They'd only last one day.

The old man told them he [had] dreamed that a man came to see him and told him, "Over there where [there is] deep blue water, a man [is] coming to see you. I'll tell you what you [should] do. Now, when that one comes, he'll come to [in the] smoke hole, not in the door. You fix that smoke hole. Sit in one corner, with your bow. Don't look—just hold [your] bow. When it comes close to you, circling down till it fills the house, then cut that bow string. It will snap right through that snake's belly, [and] you'll get all kinds of money piled up right there. That's the only way you can get through that snake's belly. A knife or arrow won't do it."

He sent the girls away. "You go stay at [the] chief's house [for] one or two days." They went. He cleaned the house up good now. Just as his dream had told him, he did it. In the evening he went and sweated. [He kept] no fire in the house. [He] fastened [the] door. About ten o'clock he sat in [the] corner. He heard something down below like wind. Oh, he just shook. "I believe that's it, like my dream." Something [was] blowing breath. He was told not to look or move. Now, sure enough, he heard it on top of [his] house, dripping water like rain. Pretty soon he heard something drop over on [the] floor. It didn't take long till that snake filled half the house.[146] He felt it touch his leg, now. [It was] cool, nice. It stopped dripping up above. He thought it [was] pretty well all in now. Now he cut his bowstring. Just like [as if] it burst [the] house, [the] snake went right back in [the] water. All [was] quiet. It got kind of moonlight. He felt all kinds of money. He made pitch light. Money lay around until [so thickly that] he could hardly walk.

Outside in its [the snake's] trail to [the] water, he filled baskets first. Then he came in [the] house. By noon he had them [the money beads] all in baskets.

He started working, making strings. The girls came back. They didn't know the difference [what had happened].

He told them, "Now you girls have to get to work making your own money to put on your hair [and] around your neck, [to] fix yourselves up." Oh, the girls got busy. [They] had a fine time. It's a big thing. Now the old man fixed up a big basket for his chief. His chief had always helped him. He put away lots of money. He gave a panful to everyone in the village. Now when he had filled as many baskets as he needed for himself, he divided [the] rest with his people.

The girls were busy—too busy to eat. They helped each other put it [money] in [their] hair.

He told them, "You girls take good care of that. Don't lose it. People have to see you, that you are no longer poor." Then when they were all fixed, he said, "You children done now? Well, you go tell the chief to come. Tell the chief [that your] papa wants to see him right away." They went. A woman met them.

"Oh, lots of Indian money. What is it they have got? It looks like money."

Someone said, "Oh, that's camas tails, I guess," because the girls had used them [before].

Well, the chief got ready to go. He took his first wife and took a little grub. They always did that. He got in the house. It looked different. [The] old man was working, with stringing Indian money. He told his chief what he had.

"Now, I have money for you, chief. You have helped me [for] a long time. All the time I have been poor, you have helped me. You are to get that big basket piled full of Indian money." He put it right by the chief's wife. [The] chief opened it up [and] looked.

"That's money, all right. Now we have to go back and get this money fixed [sorted and strung]." Each length [of shell] had to be exactly matched. [Ones] a little shorter in one pile, [ones] a little longer in one pile—lots of work.[147] Now the chief said, "I have one wife. I have never touched her. [I have] just kept her for [the] family. I'll send her to you." [The] youngest one he [had] never touched [because] he had too many wives. So the girls went to get her.

The old man said, "Bring her quick, so she can work." They had to clean up quick what's on [the] ground. After [the money was] in the baskets, no one [would] bother them. They worked all night.

The story ends there. [It tells] how a poor man, someway, somehow gets help. They heard about him all over. People came [from] different places with women. Before one year he had ten wives. His daughters had all the money they needed. Now he had to take care of his ten wives. Now his wives helped him. His daughters both married. [Those were] good times. The people thought the girls still used camas tails.

Brown Bear and Grizzly Bear

The story presented here is taken from Jacobs's Upper Coquille Athabaskan field notebook 3 (pp. 147–50). Jacobs's original title was "Bear and Grizzly." I have altered it to its current "Brown Bear and Grizzly Bear." Thompson noted that this was a xʷɛ́cdən story. As Jacobs noted (1960:102), this popular drama of Bear and Grizzly "appears in many versions in the northwest states" and beyond, including northern California and the Great Basin. Cognates include the Klamath story "Old Bear and Antelope" (Barker 1963:7–13), the Yurok "Brown Bear and Black Bear" (J. Sapir 1928:259–60), the Karok "The Bear and the Deer" (Bright 1957:227–31), the Miluk Coos "Black bear and pack basket bear (grizzly)" (M. Jacobs 1940:152-55), the Takelma "Grizzly Bear and Black Bear" (E. Sapir 1909a:117–23), the Santiam Kalapuya "Grizzly and bear each have five daughters" (M. Jacobs 1945:115–19), the Kathlamet Chinook "Robin and Salmonberry" (Boas 1901:118–28), the Clackamas Chinook "Black Bear and Grizzly Woman and their sons" (M. Jacobs 1958:143–56; 1960:102–11), the Lushootseed "Grizzly Bear and Black Bear" (Haeberlin 1924:422–25), the Northern Paiute "Bear and the Fawns" (Kelly 1938:431–32), and the Gosiute Shoshone "Bear and Fawns" (Smith 1993:37–38). For partial cognates, see the Klikitat Sahaptin "Bear woman kills Grizzly woman's daughter" (M. Jacobs 1934:45:47), the Cowlitz "Bear and Grizzly" (Adamson 1934:211–13), the Upper Chehalis "Lion and Bear" (Adamson 1934:43–46), and the Cowlitz and Upper Cowlitz "Grizzly woman kills Bear woman" (M. Jacobs 1934:159–63). For further discussion of this tale type, see Gayton (1935b:591).

Brown Bear and Grizzly Bear had [shared] one man. He had two wives. They both had children. Grizzly got jealous. The man hunted all the time—never stayed home. Brown Bear and Grizzly Bear petted each other. Brown Bear thought they were good friends.

One day Grizzly killed Brown Bear and her children except for one boy and girl. Brown Bear's older daughter took that one boy and ran away. They got to a river. [There was] one man there, Crane.[148]

Brown Bear's daughter said, "We're in a hurry to go across. Someone is after us."

Crane said, "What's after you?"

"Grizzly Bear."

"Gosh, go over quick. I'll put my leg across." Crane stretched his leg across, and they went over. "Go in that house there. Don't be outside," Crane told them. So they went in [the] house [and] were fed and hidden. They ate quick. They had run all night. Those people hid them.

Already across [the] river Grizzly was there. Crane told her, "I have no boat. I don't know how you can go across."

Grizzly answered, "Oh, you can pack me."

"I can't pack you. There is no way I can take you across."

"You better take me across!"

"Well, if you're not too heavy, I can put my leg across."

"Oh, that's fine. I can cross on that."

When Grizzly was halfway over, he [Crane] yelled, "Oh, my leg is almost broken." He pulled it back. Grizzly fell down in the water but swam back out on his side. He handled his leg, pretended it [was] very sore.

"I nearly made it," Grizzly said. "Can you try again?"

"Oh, I don't know. You nearly broke my leg."

"Well, I kind of trust you [have faith in your ability to do it]. You'd better try again."

"All right," Crane said, "if you want it." He put his leg across [the] river again. "Walk slow," he told her. "If you walk fast, you might break my leg."

"All right." She walked slow.

When she got nearly in the middle, "Oh, go slow. You are nearly breaking my leg," he called. Presently he pulled his leg back. Grizzly fell in, swam out on his side again. I don't know why. She ought to swim across if she wanted to go across so bad. She begged him to try again. He didn't want to do it.

She had asked when she first arrived, "Did you see [any] children?"

"Yes, I took them across." That's how he made a mistake in telling her he had crossed them on his leg.

Now she asked, "How far do you think those children have gone now?"

"Oh, they must be pretty far—they run pretty good." He decided the children were far enough now so he would let her get across. She begged him again to cross her. "All right, I might be able to stand it, but walk slow." She crossed, then ran off like lightning.

Grizzly opened the door in that house. "Did you see children pass?"

"Oh, they went by a long time ago," those people told her.

"All right," she said. [She] shut the door and started running. Those children had been weeping, singing, "Run, my brother, someone is chasing us."[149] They sang as they ran.

Grizzly went away. She never came back. Those children stayed right there and had a good time. The people raised them. They decided Grizzly must have killed her man, too. He never came, showed up again, and she never returned.

Sun

The text presented here is taken from Jacobs's Upper Coquille Athabaskan field notebook 4 (pp. 6–7). The title, x̣á'ci, "Sun," is Thompson's. It appears to be more of an ethnographic note than a text. It may represent a fragment of a text no longer remembered by Thompson.

Sun is a man. He was traveling. He went and came back underground.[150] He got home. He had two, three, or four dead people he was packing. He did that every day. That's why they believed Sun [was] no good for power.[151]

Sun said, "[If] you dream me, you can't do anything without my seeing it. You can't do it. Everything, whether under the ground, in the house, under the water—no matter how dark—I'm there with you. That's why if you do anything wrong, I know it. That's why even if no one saw you, it will come to light. Because I see you, you can't hide it."

Sun is a man. You can't look at his face—his eyes are just like fire! Warm![152]

Gambler and Snake

While ritually preparing for gambling power by swimming in a river, a man is swallowed by a large snake. Several snake shamans' medicines fail to kill the man as he cuts the snake's heart, eventually killing the snake. The man gets dentalium from his snake encounter. It magically multiples, and he supplies his chief and

*fellow villagers with quantities of gambling money. The snake's
dentalium is so powerful that no other village can ever defeat them
in gambling.*

*The story presented here is taken from Jacobs's Upper Coquille
Athabaskan field notebook 4 (pp. 74–83). Jacobs supplied the title.*[153] *For a probable Galice cognate, see Goddard (1903–4:no. 2).*

One man had a card's bed.[154] He [was] the last to go swim, swam right down
the middle of the river, got down to the riffles, went down—a big flat-headed
snake swallowed him.[155] He felt just like he was coming in a house. [There
was] no water [inside]. He sat down there. He had a little knife [of flint] and
that [gambling bed] with him.[156] Now he kind of realized he's in a snake's belly.
He tried to cut its heart. He wanted to get out. Oh, that snake hollered, went
[thrashed] all around. Finally the snake gave up. He came back in his house.

Big, deep water—that's snake's house. That fellow kept cutting.

The snake people talked, "What's the matter with you? You're always hungry, have to eat everything?[157] Now you've swallowed poison! Where did you
swallow that man?"

"Oh, I don't know, except one place upriver I felt something go in my
throat."

"Yes, you have to eat anything. You eat timber."

They abused him because he just ate and drank anything and never had
enough. In every river he'd watch, open his mouth, a stick [would] come in,
he'd swallow.

The snake chief said, "You go get that doctor Big-Deep-Water Chief. He
might know that [swallowing-everything] medicine."[158]

All right, one fellow went. This man had beat that snake. He knew everything the snake was doing. The snake [was] making noise; he was a pretty good
sick man. Every so often the man inside would cut a little.

"Now they're coming; make more room."

That doctor didn't come in the door. He came down the smoke hole. The
man inside had cut till he could see through. He saw everyone sitting around—
that doctor standing up there.

"What's the matter with this fellow?" the doctor said.

They told him, "Well, he's a pretty sick fellow. He ate a person at that place,
up the river."

"Uh-huh, all right, I've got medicine," the doctor said. He reached in his pocket, took out medicine, put it in a cup—a shell cup. He came; he said, "Hold his head up."

The man went under the snake's heart so he could dodge the medicine. Presently something dropped, dropped. It was the medicine. He kept out of the way. It didn't affect him in any way.

The doctor said, "Well, that's all I know, just that medicine."

The man inside cut more. It hurt more. In [that] big belly, wide as this house, he could dodge anywhere. Now he cut more.

"U‑‑‑h," the snake groaned.

Now they talked it over, talked it over, "Who knows that kind of medicine?"

The chief said, "Maybe that Along-the-River Chief knows that kind."

The doctor chief said, "Go get him. I'll go back now. I've done the best I can. I can't do any more. He ate a person all right. That person's in his belly now. It takes strong medicine to kill a person."

That [doctor] fellow left. A man had already started out to get the Along-the-River Chief.

Pretty soon that mail carrier [messenger] returned. "He's coming, make ready! Make more room, that fellow takes lots of room," he told them.

It took a long time for that doctor fellow to come down. Now the man went to one side of his [the snake's] heart. He figured the medicine [would] come down the other way. He cut, made [the snake] sick. Now that doctor was opening that medicine. The fellow inside was getting sick. "Must be strong medicine. I guess I'll get killed." He heard the medicine drop to one side. He had shut his mouth and nose. As long as the medicine didn't touch him, he's all right, but kind of paralyzed. [If] one drop touched him, he would have died.

Now that sick snake was having a little rest. They decided this new doctor had helped. He said, "That's all I do. If he doesn't get better today, he never will get better." Then that doctor left.

[As] soon as the doctor went out, that man cut a little more. Oh, that snake fellow cried.

Well, they talked, "What are we going to do?"

"Around-Gravel Chief, he knows something about it," one said.

"All right, go get him."

They went. Now the man inside got ready. They might kill him this time. [It] didn't take long, the mail carrier [messenger was] back.

"He's coming, make big room."

He came, came down tail first, winding around and around [until] the room [was] half full. "How's the sick man?"

"No better at all," the people answered.

"Did he get medicine?"

"Yes."

"Well, I've got some medicine. Maybe it'll help him." He took his medicine out.

The fellow saw it: it just paralyzed him there in the snake's belly. "I'll have to cut the whole thing," he thought, "That medicine will sure kill me." He took his knife and just cut right down. Everything spilled out. He got two or three handfuls of money. The water boiled around him; that ocean was mad. It just spilled him right up on the side hill. Now he was safe. Now he looked at his money: he [had] two, three, four, five long ones.[159] He put it away.

Down home they missed him. He had been gone a day and a half. They thought sure he drowned. Now he fixed his money: put one on the [gambling bed], put the others together.[160] Now he thought he'd go home.

They saw him. "Oh, he's come back, he's coming."

He got in the house. He went to the sweathouse, he sweat, he swam, he came back in the house. Then he ate.

Someone asked, "Where have you been?"

"Oh, I've been around all over. I've been camping somewhere." He didn't say he had been that way; he wouldn't tell.

The next day he went away again to see his money in that hollow log. Oh, he saw lots. He got, oh, maybe a basketful. In four, five days he told his wife to clean up the house. "I'm going to bring money in," he said. "We'll have to work." He fixed [a mat] in that room.[161] He brought that basketful of money, poured it right down on that [mat] so he can pick up the big ones. She helped too. They picked up the big ones, put them together in one place, in one little basket. They were busy all day, he and his wife. He told his wife that evening, "Make lots of acorns. I want to call the chief tomorrow morning."

She [was] busy that night. She mashed acorns until ten that night, with one woman helping her. By sweating-time in the morning she had everything nearly all cooked, nice. They put [a mat] down, [and] he went after the chief.

The chief said, "You are giving us a meal?"

"Yes, I made you breakfast."

"Well, how about this fellow, that fellow, that fellow, and that fellow?"

"Bring them all," the man said. "That's for you to say. I just called you; you have to say about the rest."

"All right," the chief said, "that's good."

People [were] coming in, coming in; pretty soon [there was a] full house of leaders, high[-class] people. Everybody got a little bucket of acorn soup, put his spoon in. They started in eating. They ate all morning, and in the afternoon they [were] all done eating—they had to take grub away [with them].

And they had fixed already how much money they would give away. The man said, "Sit down now before you go home; I have something to tell you folks. Now I leave it to the chief, whatever he says. I got [a gambling bed] and swam with it. I think it is all right. Now, I got a little money. You folks have to go ahead and gamble with it. So the chief has to decide when to get ready."

Everybody talked. One said, "Well, we have to do the best we can with whatever money we have. I don't know how I myself can bet. I got no money."

His wife held a basket pan.[162] He took that little pan and dipped. Each man got a panful. He issued, issued, issued money. What was left in the bottom, that [was] for the chief. That's his chief's money. Now he put the basket before the chief. "This is yours. You're my chief. I'll help you that much, help my people."

Well, they all got money. No one opened his mouth. Only the chief talked, "You people get ready. We'll go the day after tomorrow morning. I'll go with you, soon as you get ready, get your cards [gambling pieces] ready and make your money ready."

They decided it was fine. "All right, I'll be ready," everyone said.

Where people had [previously] won everything from them, that's where they were going to gamble. Come time, everyone ready, they went. This fellow [Gambler] went too. He had that [gambling bed] with him. They got there. Soon as they got in the house, "Which side shall we put our bets on?"

"Oh, over there, where you put them before."

"All right."

They got ready. The other side [was] all ready quick. They wanted to have a good time.

They started to bet, bet—bet big money. Everybody bet. They had to make one bunch [pile of bets]. Now they started to gamble. The first game, they won it. It took a long time to place bets again. Soon as [the bets were] ready, they started the game. Before twelve o'clock at night, they just had one game, a pretty tight game. The sticks went back and forth. It took all twelve sticks to make a game. Maybe [by] two o'clock they got [won] another game. They played all [through the early] morning until about six-thirty, then they got another game. They had won lots of money in three games. They played all forenoon and got another game.

Now those people [the hosts] talked it over. "We have to give up. We haven't got enough money to match what we have lost. You take it; we give up," the man said.

They took their money, went home, had supper at home. They didn't go anywhere to gamble then. That was the end of that. He sent word to two places, but they didn't go because those other people didn't have enough money to match bets.

Now when everybody [was] back in the sweathouse, that man told where he had been.

One old man said, "I just thought that's where you'd been. That [big flat-headed snake] swallows anything that swims across."

So no one could win from him. They were always lucky. No one [other group] could play against them [successfully].

Little Man (2)

Little Man steals the meat of a man's cooked fish three times but leaves him the empty skins. After the man curses him, Little Man appears, and they wrestle. The man gets Little Man in a hold from which he cannot escape until he promises the man gambling equipment and Indian money, which he cannot lose in gambling. Little Man complies, and they part.

The story presented here is taken from Jacobs's Upper Coquille Athabaskan field notebook 4 (pp. 88–92). The title is Jacobs's.

A man was cooking a fine salmon for supper. ts'əsdú·ni, that Little Man, was there. He didn't know that Little Man was there. He got his fish all ready, put [it] in [a] pan, [and] went down to swim before supper. He came back—noticed nothing [different], thought he [could] eat now. He opened that fish, nothing but skin! No meat at all.

He thought, "What's the matter?" He [was] surprised [but] said nothing. He decided he'd go without. He fixed lots of wood, went to bed. [The] next morning he cooked one fish. He got [it] ready. He put it in [a] pan, went to swim. Not long [afterward, he] came back. [The] fish [was] already that way: when opened, no meat! Oh, it made him mad. He said nothing; [it] might be dangerous. He [was] just mad and didn't know what to do. He just wanted to know who was doing that. He couldn't tell. He slung [the] salmon skin outside. That Little Man was watching him. He wouldn't show himself. [The] man caught lots of fish in that creek. He decided he [would] go [home] tomorrow. He got lots, hung them up, [and] turned them over. [About] four o'clock, [it was] getting dark; he cooked one fish, [a] good one, too.

He thought, "I'll eat [a] good one now." Little Man knew what he thought. He tried to make him forget all about [the] previous happenings. He [the man] forgot. He cooked [the] fish good, put it away right there. Soon as he left [to swim], [the] little fellow ate it right up, leaving [the] skin [to] cover it up. [The] man came back, ready to eat, saw only [the] hide [skin].

"Goddamn son of a bitch who doesn't eat any hide! Why doesn't he eat [the] hide?"[163] Now Little Man [was] mad at [the] swearing. He came up; they fought right there.

This man thought, "I'll whip him."

Little Man answered [the thought], "Yeah! You'll whip me! You'll be tired pretty soon." [He] worked hard, threw [the] man down—that Little Man got up like nothing [had happened], wrestled with [his] butt [sticking] way out.

Now that man remembered, "Oh, that kind [of] people always got [have] hair on [their] butt." He grabbed that. "Oh, oh, let me go! Let me go!" that Little Man hollered. He held him there.

"I won't let you go till you help me with something. Why didn't you ask me? I could cook you all the fish you want. But no! You have to steal. That's why I cuss you." Now he held that guy, had him paralyzed. He pulled him around [by his butt hair].

"Let me go. I'll give you something," Little Man said.

"Well, what [are] you going to give me?"

"I'll give you cards."[164]

"All right." He had it right there. He handed [him the] bundle of cards with [the] [ace] tied up nice.[165]

"Now let me go."

"Oh, I can't let you go till you give me something else."

"Well, what [do] you want?"

"Oh, I want [a gambling bed]."[166] He pulled out [a] fine [gambling bed]. He handed it to him. [The] man put [the] cards right in [the] middle.

"I want something else," he said then.

"What [do] you want now? Will you let me go if I give you Indian money?"

"Yes, I'll let you go if you give me Indian money."

"Well, I'll give you Indian [money].[167] If you bet this [Indian money], you'll never lose it. Think of me all the time when you gamble. I'll be right there, fooling around. I'll be there to help you. Now let me go."

"All right, I'll let you go now, only you have to promise me, these things you have given me, will they remain that way?"

"Yes, they [will] be like that all the time. It's yours. I have given it to you. You have whipped me. I give up now."

"All right." He let him go.

He said, "Shake hands with me." They shook hands and sat down and talked.

[The] man said, "You come around tomorrow morning. I'll cook fish for you." [The little] fellow [was] just gone, vanished. He put his [gambling bed] away, put away his fine [Indian money]. He got ready, packed up his salmon, got all fixed so he could go tomorrow morning. Early [in the] morning he got up, cooked one fish for Little Man. He himself didn't eat anything. He put that fish as he always had. He packed [it] outdoors, left that fish there and went. So he went back [home].

Wren and His Grandmother

This ribald, humorous story focuses on a naive young man, his sexually insatiable grandmother, the shame of incest, and the inevitability of wrongdoing being found out.

The story presented here is taken from Jacobs's Upper Coquille Athabaskan field notebook 4 (pp. 92–99).[168] tcats' kwísł'ɛ is a "wren," a "little red bird." The title is Jacobs's. Harrington recorded a similar version from Thompson in 1942 (JPH, reel 027, frames 0395–98). For regional cognate or analogous versions, see the Miluk Coos story "The young man lived with his grandmother" (M. Jacobs 1940:172–73), the Clackamas Chinook "Wren and his father's mother" (M. Jacobs 1958:199–207; 1960:141–52), the Lower Chinook "Wren Kills Elk" (Ray 1938:146–48), the Upper

Chehalis "Wren Kills Elk" (Adamson 1934:33–40), the Upper Cowlitz "Coon kills Grizzly swallower, whips his lewd grandmother, the Ducks scold her" (M. Jacobs 1934:179–83), the Cowlitz "Wren Kills Elk" (Adamson 1934:185–88), and the Lushootseed "Wren, Mouse, and Water Ousel" (Ballard 1929:137).

He [Wren] stayed with his grandma. He lived with her, ate with her.

Wren said to Elk, "I can kill you."

"How can you kill me?"

"I can go in your ear."

"Oh, [if] you go in my ear, I'll shake my head. You'll drop way over there; you ain't going to kill me."

"Then I'll go between your toenails, and you can't kill me. I can go there and stay right there."

"Oh, stay right there! No, you can't! I'd mash you just like mud. You can't kill me that way."

"Well, I can kill you. I would go in your nose. I can kill you that way."

"Oh, nose! You can't kill me that way. I'd sneeze and you'd drop way off."

"That's all I know. I can kill you any way I get a chance."

"All right. Kill me! Go ahead [and] kill me."

"Well, I can go in your behind."

"Yes, you go in my behind, and I'd shit you out. You'd drop way off."

"All right." He [Wren] jumped all around [Elk], between his legs, everywhere. [He] wanted to go in Elk's behind. Finally he grabbed on right alongside Elk's tail. That Elk did all he could, just shit, shit, [and] shit. Finally when the shit's all gone, now he [Wren] went in. As soon as he got inside, he cut his [Elk's] heart out. Elk had to stagger around. Pretty soon he fell down, dead. Wren felt him fall. He came up out of his [Elk's] anus hole. Now he had to cut that Elk up. It didn't take long [until] he got it all cut up. Then he went to get his grandma to help pack.

That old lady wouldn't pack the shoulder or butt.

"I don't want to pack that."

"Pack the neck."

"No, I don't want to pack [the] neck."

"Pack [the] head then; pack [the] ribs then."

To each one she would respond, "No, I don't want to pack that." She wanted to pack [the penis].[169] She saw Elk's thing still attached.

"You pack this, grandma."

"All right, grandchild, that's what I want to pack." He put rope on it, fixed it for her.

"You can go," she said, "I'll come pretty soon." He packed [and] packed. When he came back, she [was] still sitting there. She had used that Elk's thing on herself. She sat half a day there in that one place. He had made a dozen trips [and] packed all that elk alone. He began to be suspicious of her. She was always pretending to work when she saw him coming. He caught on. He didn't say a word. He packed everything home, [and] he cut the Elk.

He thought, "Let her go." At last she came home.

"I'm so tired I can hardly pack," she said.

He told her, "That's good that you can hardly pack. Now you can eat that meat yourself."

They were making a blanket [of the Elk skin]. [The] sunshine [was] warm, [and] their blanket was getting soft.

[The] little boy [Wren] said, "Oh, I wish I [could] get married and sleep under this blanket."

"What's that you say, grandchild?"

"Oh, I didn't say anything."

"Yes, you did. You said something!"

"Well, how about it? What [do] you want to know for? I just said I want to sleep with a woman under this blanket."

"Oh, I know now what you said. I kind of thought you said that, all right." Now she went back in the house. That fellow worked on the blanket [and] worked on the blanket.

That old lady—she studied [and] she studied how it would be tomorrow morning. She tried to make herself young. She couldn't get young. She couldn't do it. Wren went to the sweathouse. She fixed herself. Where she [usually] lay down, she put a little rotten wood there in her bed. She lay down elsewhere. [She] put that fine blanket down, put lots of [mats there].[170] She sat down right there [looking like] a young woman. That fellow [Wren] came in. She gave her man something to eat. Little Wren ate. He saw that old lady lying over in [her] usual place. He watched this young woman. He studied [how] not to go back to the sweathouse, but to stay with this young woman. They sat up a long time. Newly married [couples] don't go to bed right away. Finally she went to bed. That old lady [over there] never moved, just lay there [in the] same way.

He [Wren] undressed. He went to bed with [this] fresh, new woman. She wouldn't face him. He kept telling her to turn around, [but] she wouldn't do it. At last, near daylight, she turned over. Wren gave it to her.

Then she began to holler several times, "Push more, push harder, push more, push harder."[171] She hollered [and] foamed at the mouth. Old Wren gave her the dickens. When he went [over] where that old lady lay, [there was] only rotten wood there. Wren [was] mad now. He went out, sat down on top [of the] sweathouse. [It was] daylight now. Now he knew somebody would be bound to know. People always found out [about wrongdoing].[172]

He saw one boat coming. [There were] three or four men in that boat, all paddling good. They came pretty close.[173]

"Any news [from] up that way?" Wren called.

"No. Maybe [the] next boat [can] tell you something," they answered.

"All right." That boat went to turn, [but instead it] stopped. [They] got out. They knew [there would] be something [doing] when they told him. That old lady [was] alive again now. She came around, the old lady. He [Wren] never noticed her. The next boat came; he sat there.

"Any news of that way?"

"No, no news. Maybe [the] next boat can tell you something." Wren was getting [his] bow and arrow all ready. [The] old lady was getting ready too. She planned to help her grandchild when he got in that fight. He [was] bound to fight. [He would] get shamed, you know. That old woman was Pheasant.[174] She was his mother's mother. He kept asking boats. Finally [the] last boat came.

"Any news from up there?"

"Someone upriver has been staying with his grandma."[175] Oh, he got mad. He tried to hit that guy with an arrow. Those people [were] ready. They fought a long time. [The] old lady helped him. Finally he [Wren] hid in the brush, then turned up elsewhere.

Finally they [the boat people] said, "Oh, let it go. To hell with it." Shags were fighting them. Shags left then. They rode a stick [and] fooled him [Wren]. They didn't have any boat. They had been going by to fool him that way, because he's guilty.

This [is the] last [of the story].

Coyote and His Two Daughters

Coyote's attempt to seduce or marry one of his daughters is a widely distributed episode in the loosely concatenated cycle of

Coyote (or other trickster) stories. Although aided by his excre-
ment adviser powers, in this text Coyote is defeated by his young-
est, smartest daughter, who was never fooled by his faked death
and bizarre burial request.

The story presented here is taken from Jacobs's Upper Coquille
Athabaskan field notebook 4 (pp. 108–13). The title is Jacobs's. For
cognate and/or analogous texts, see the Karok story "Coyote Mar-
ries His Own Daughter" (Bright 1993:146–49; Kroeber and Gif-
ford 1980:197–99), the Miluk Coos (M. Jacobs 1940:186–87), the
Northern Paiute "Coyote and his daughter" (Kelly 1938:404–5),
the Wishram "Coyote and His Daughter" (E. Sapir 1909b:105–7),
the Cowlitz and Upper Cowlitz "Coyote pretends to die, returns to
cohabit with his daughters" (M. Jacobs 1934:146–47), the Sanpoil
"Coyote Marries His Daughter" (Ray 1933:173–75), the Okanagan
"Coyote marries his Daughter (or Niece)" (Boas 1917b:72–74), the
Nez Perce "Coyote Marries His Daughter" (Walker 1998:135–38),
and the Lushootseed "Coyote Marries His Own Daughter" (Hil-
bert 1985:87–95). For an early study of this tale type, see Schmer-
ler (1931:196–207).

I only hear Coyote Jim had two daughters. One of his daughters, the youngest, was kind of smart. She wouldn't do what the old man told her. The oldest one, she did whatever the old man told her, but [the] youngest one wouldn't trust the old fellow. Coyote Jim got sick. [The] oldest daughter, she looked after him, took care of him good. [The] one who never trusted the old fellow, she told her sister to get water. The old man may want a drink. She went to get water [and] brought [it] in the house.

[The] old man [was] pretty sick then.

He said, "When I die, you must not get a man among these people here. Maybe you [can] get one from California, [from the] mouth of the Klamath River people. That kind of people [are] good people. Get that kind of man." [That was what] he told his daughters, both of whom were sitting by him. That's how he put up a will.

"When I'm dead, you dig [the] ground about three feet [deep]. Make me sit down right there. Leave my head sit out that way [and] put a mortar over my head.[176] When I die, bury me that way."

That youngest daughter felt that that old man was tricky.

"I never heard of people being buried that way," she told her sister, who replied, "Maybe that's his way, the way he wants it." So he died that night. They dug [the] ground. That oldest daughter dug [the] ground [and] dug [the] ground. They dragged him there with rope. They could see he was dead. So they fixed him the way he left orders. They covered his shoulders, [but] his neck and head stuck out. They turned a mortar over his head.

"Lú·q, lú·q is what those people will say who come to marry you. That will mean he wants water," Coyote had told his daughters. One day and one night passed. [The] next day his older daughter went to see him. [She] took the mortar off, saw him. He's dead, of course, [so she] put it back. Two nights [passed]. [The] next day the oldest one went again. Still that younger girl didn't believe it.

She said, "I don't believe that old man died. He's around somewhere."

[The] oldest one answered, "Oh, don't talk that way about the poor old fellow. He's dead now." Two, three days after that, now going on five days, he [was] still dead. [The] oldest one went there every day. He's dead all right, she saw.

After the fifth day, [as] soon as [it was] dark, he [Coyote] got out. He fixed the cover back. He went someplace.

He shit a little [and] asked his shit, "What am I going to do? I've got two daughters."

His shit answered, "What [do] you want now?" It kind of insulted him. "What [are] you going to do about your daughters, anyhow? What [do] you want?"

"Well, I want my daughter, my oldest daughter."

"You want your daughter! Can't you find a woman anywhere else?"

"Well, I want it that way."

"All right. You'll have it that way."

"Well, I have to talk the mouth of Klamath River language."

"All right. You can talk it. But I can't do much because that youngest girl doesn't believe you died. She thinks you're just cheating."

Coyote said, "I didn't know that. What shall I wear?" His shit didn't want to help him because he's [doing] wrong. He knows that young girl [is] going [to] catch him.

"Oh, you can wear a deerskin." It was right there.

"I'll be like the Klamath people, ain't it?"

"Yes, you'll be like the Klamath people, all right. That's all I can do for you. Go in the house," his shit told him.

Those two girls saw someone coming, a man. He came right to the door.

They told him, "Come in." A long time he sat down. He didn't talk.

His shit had told him, "[If] you want it that way, don't you talk, because they can't understand what you mean. Those girls don't know."

He said, "Lúq, lúq." "Give me a drink [of] water." So they gave him a drink. He sat there like a chief. That girl didn't believe him. It [was] nearly dark now. She went out to walk around. She went to that grave, she took up that mortar, [and] she saw nothing there.

"Oh, I just know he's that way," she said. She came back in the house. She looked at him. That's their old man—that's old Coyote Jim. She punched her sister.

"Let's go out." They went in the doorway to talk. "I've been there. That's the old man. He's gone over there," she told her sister.

Now the oldest girl believed her.

She said, "We can't sleep now. We have to sit up all night." He sat there like a chief, saying nothing. About the middle [of the] night, the smallest one got sleepy. By two or three o'clock both [girls] were asleep. Maybe he [Coyote] wished them to sleep so he could get away. He didn't do anything, just got ready and went.

When they awoke, that old man [was] gone. That chief [was] gone. They missed him. They covered that grave hole good. Coyote was gone for good. He wouldn't come back. [It] must be he felt ashamed.

Coyote Becomes a Steelhead

These two short episodes from the larger cycle of Coyote stories reveal once again the lecherous side of Coyote's personality, amply illustrated in other Coyote stories in this collection. The incredibly expanding penis—whether his own or a borrowed one—is a motif closely associated with Coyote and other trickster figures in Pacific Northwest Indian oral traditions.

The story presented here is taken from Jacobs's Upper Coquille Athabaskan field notebook 4 (pp. 114–15). Jacobs supplied the title for this story. For a partial cognate text, see the Shasta

story "Coyote's Amorous Adventures" (Farrand and Frachtenberg
1915:222–23).

Two young women were digging camas. They got [their] baskets full [and]
came back [about] two, three o'clock. [It was a] warm, hot day. They came
right in the creek. They saw one steelhead right there, in low water, about a
foot deep. [It was] just a little hole there where salmon played.

"Put your pack down. We'll get him!" one said. They put their packs down
[and] took [their] dresses off. One sat at each end [of the pool]. [They] put
[their] hands out to try to catch his tail. He swam back and forth. He rubbed
one's vulva with his nose, the other with his tail. They kept him there. They
liked it. They played half an hour or more. After a while he jumped out. He ran
off. It was Coyote.

"Yoo-hooh, you girls catch salmon!" he called [mockingly].[177] Those two
girls could hardly walk. [They were] getting big bellies right there. They
stepped on each other's bellies. That stuff [seminal fluid] all came out. [It was]
half water. Then they were all right.

Coyote went [on]. He saw lots of women digging camas. [There was a] little
mountain between [Coyote and the women]. He came up on the hill. He shit
a little.

"What can I do, my shit? I want to get that woman over there."

"Run your thing [penis] along the ground. It can stick up where she's stooped
and straddled, digging." They dug in a row. He did that. He put [his] thing on
the ground. He sat down. He watched that woman, that woman digging camas.
Pretty soon she saw something rising up off the ground. She pretended she
didn't notice. Suddenly she just chopped right down hard on it. Now Coyote
fell over dead. When he began to stink, something bit him [and] he got right up.
They killed him lots of places, but he always came alive again.

Hollering-like-a-Person

A canoe builder is pursued by a one-horned creature. While stab-
bing at the man, the animal's horn gets stuck in a rotten tree,
whereupon the man knocks it off the animal's head.

The story presented here is taken from Jacobs's Upper Coquille
Athabaskan field notebook 4 (pp. 116–17). Jacobs supplied the title.
In 1942 Harrington recorded an untitled version from Thompson,
but with an epilogue not found in the Jacobs version (JPH, reel 027,

frames 0235–38). Compare with the Miluk Coos text "The person
that halloos" (M. Jacobs 1939:51–52) and an unpublished Chetco
text, "Giant Man," recorded by E. Jacobs in 1935.[178]

One man lived near [the] mouth [of the] Coquille River. A little above and
across [the] river, he was making a canoe. He went every day, making the canoe.
One day about eleven o'clock someone hollered on that mountain, "Wooooo."
That fool, he answered [the hollering]. By God that thing [was] coming. It hollered again. Now he wouldn't answer [because] he got scared. [The] first time
[it hollered] he thought maybe a woman picking berries had got lost. He didn't
answer. That thing smelled him. He went around [and] went around, on two
legs like a quail. It saw him. This fellow [was] ready. He had his wedge and
maul. It came right after him. He dodged it. It came again—he dodged. This
fellow [was a] good jumper. One time he came, [and the] man dodged behind
an old rotten tree. He hit that tree. Oh gosh, his horn went right through. He
couldn't get out. He couldn't get his horn out. He lost his horn. That fellow hit
that horn [and] knocked it off. Now he just looked at that man. He couldn't do
anything anymore. He won't hurt anybody.

Penis and Vulva: Origin of Sex Knowledge

The story presented here is taken from Jacobs's Upper Coquille
Athabaskan field notebook 5 (p. 85). The title is Jacobs's. Compare
the Santiam Kalapuya story "Penis and clitoris race" (M. Jacobs
1945:133), the Cowlitz and Upper Cowlitz "Vulva outraces Penis"
(M. Jacobs 1934:124), and the Clackamas Chinook "Penis and
Vulva race" (M. Jacobs 1959a:484; 1960:352–53).[179]

They [were] eating, the first people. [A] woman [at that time] didn't know
[about sexual intercourse with a] man and man didn't know [about a] woman.
[They were the] first people. [They were] eating all around. [There was one]
red-faced fellow [red because he was Penis].

"Come eat," [they called to him]. No, he wouldn't eat. "What do you eat?"
[they asked him].

[A] man said, "Well, maybe he eats [Vulva]."[180] Now that [red-faced] man
[was] glad. He decided he [would] do that way. He liked that. [He was Pe-
nis].[181]

Crow Eats Feces, Marries a Woman

Because of Crow's repulsive habit of eating feces, his newly acquired wife leaves him. His in-laws send him packing with a basketful of shit.

The story presented here is taken from Jacobs's Upper Coquille Athabaskan field notebook 5 (pp. 131–33). The title is Jacobs's.[182]

Crow married one woman. [He] bought her. He stayed at her home [for a] while, then wanted to take her to his home. There [at his wife's home] his father-in-law, mother-in-law, [and] two young sisters-in-law cooked for him. He sat down by his wife.

He said, "You tell your mother I want [dung] on that soup.[183] Tell her I want some." His wife wouldn't say [that] word. She got mad. He bothered her that way all the time that he stayed with her.

She said, "He wants shit on his soup; let him eat shit!" she said. Her father got mad.

"Why do you talk that way to my son-in-law? Don't do that."

"What's the matter with you? He wants it that way," she answered. That old man kept still then.

[The] next day they filled a kettle with meat and shit and brought it before him. He got up; he smelled that. He ate, ate, [and] ate. In no time he emptied that bucket. She wouldn't go with him then. She couldn't eat that [feces].[184]

Now he wanted to go home. Now everybody shit in that one big basket. They got it full. Then they told him, "Your pack [is] full now." Then he went, packing that basket.

A Girl Is Ill with Desire

This story can be found throughout the Northwest states. Typically, though, it is Coyote—or some other trickster figure—who pretends to be a shaman, rapes the young girl, and then runs away. The story often comprises one episode in the so-called Coyote cycle of stories. Thompson tells the story as a historical narrative rather than as a myth or tale.

The story presented here is taken from Jacobs's Upper Coquille Athabaskan field notebook 5 (pp. 133–35). The title is from Jacobs. For cognate texts, see the Karok story "Coyote as Doctor" (Bright 1957:196–98), the Mary's River Kalapuya (M. Jacobs 1945:240–

*44), the Alsea "Coyote's Amorous Adventures (I)" (Frachtenberg
1917:74–75), the Tillamook (Boas 1898:140–41; E. Jacobs [1959]
1990:124–27), the Cowlitz and Upper Cowlitz "Coyote pretends
to doctor a girl" (M. Jacobs 1934:102–3; 243–245), the Cowlitz
"xwáni Doctors a Girl" (Adamson 1934:263), and the Wishram
"Coyote as Medicine-Man" (E. Sapir 1909b:11–19).*

One young woman was pretty sick, sick for two, three months, getting poor.
[She] didn't eat anything. [They] got all kinds of doctors [for her]. Doctors,
each one, [would] dance, dance, and sing, [but] never saw anything, couldn't
find anything. But she [was] sick. [They] couldn't find out what [was] wrong
with her. They decided to get a different doctor, get tc'əcέnɛ.[185] The old man
[her father] went to the tc'əcέnɛ. He explained, asked if he [could] get help.

"I hired all kinds of doctors. They don't find anything, say she [is] not sick.
But she [is] sick."

That man [the doctor] said, "All right, I [will] go with you." Well, he saw
that woman, the sick girl, [but] didn't say anything, didn't touch her.

"I'll come back pretty soon. When it's getting dark, I'll come back. I know
what ails her. I know." Now her father and his wife, they [were] glad. They
[were] glad now [that] they got a doctor that knew. [When it was] getting dark,
about bedtime, that tc'əcέnɛ came in. That old lady was sitting there. [The] old
man had gone [to the] sweathouse.

He [the doctor] told the old lady, "You go somewhere for about half the
night. I don't want anyone around when I give her medicine." That old lady
was willing. She wanted her daughter to get better. So she went.

That young woman lay there at the side of the house by the fire. That fellow
fooled around, keeping [up] a good fire. [He] went to the woman [and] felt all
over her. He [was a] doctor! Well, that old man went to work. [He] climbed on
that girl. She let him have it [intercourse] quick. He did it two or three times.
She got up, felt fine. That old man [tc'əcέnɛ] went home. [The] old lady came
home. Her daughter [was] up, well! [The] old man came from the sweathouse
in the morning, [and] his daughter was up cooking. Oh, that old man [was]
glad. Everybody [was] surprised. That old man, he knew. That's the way that
story goes.

Nobody found out how he had doctored her.

Gray Eagle and Snowbird Gamble

Snowbird gambles against Gray Eagle and wins a second white tail feather.

The story presented here is from Jacobs's Upper Coquille Athabaskan field notebook 6 (pp. 9–10).[186]

Little Snowbird and Gray Eagle, they came together to gamble.

The little bird says, "What [am] I going [to] bet?"

Big Eagle says, "Well, you bet money. You got money." Well, that little Snowbird bet money.

Then Eagle said, "What do you want me to bet?"

Snowbird said, "I want you [to] bet one of your little tail feathers."

"All right." Now they gambled.

Snowbird sang,

> *"Snowbird floats down,*
> *Snowbird sits down."*[187]

Eagle shot. He hit him. Now they have to stop. Eagle has to sing now. He gets [the] cards.

He sings,

> *"A hard rock sits there,*
> *A hard rocks sits there."*[188]

They [Snowbird's side] shot. They hit him. They sing again. All day they beat him. Eagle didn't know what to do. He hated to give [up] one of his fine white tail feathers. He had to do it.

Before that, Snowbird had only one white tail feather. Now they got two, one on each side.

Weasel and His Older Brother

Mink and his immature younger brother Weasel travel all around. Weasel's loquacity, inquisitiveness, inattention, and impulsiveness land him in trouble, from which Mink rescues him. In the process Mink transforms dangerous features of the myth world for the benefit of the people who are coming.

The story presented here is taken from Jacobs's Upper Coquille Athabaskan notebook 6 (pp. 10–15). The title was added by Jacobs,

taken from the first line of the story. Compare the text recorded
from Thompson by Harrington (1942) that contains many of the
same episodes but different actors (JPH, reel 027, frames 0288–95).
For cognate and analogous texts, see the Takelma story "Daldal
as Transformer" (E. Sapir 1909a:34–42), the Kathlamet "Myth
of the Mink" (Boas 1901:103–17), the Kathlamet "Panther and
Lynx" (Boas 1901:90–97), the Cowlitz "Cougar and His Younger
Brothers" (Adamson 1934:202–9), the Upper Chehalis "Cougar
and Wildcat" (Adamson 1934: 60–64), the Humptulip "The Cou-
gars and Their Brother Wildcat" (Adamson 1934: 310–15), the
Klikitat (M. Jacobs 1929:192–96, 219–23), and the Lushootseed
"The Sucking Monster" (Ballard 1929:118–19).

Weasel had an older brother. His brother—I can't recall his name. They travel all the time. Weasel can't keep still. His brother always [tried to] make him keep still. Weasel's brother [was a] traveler, too. He's a good man; he could do anything. They came to one place. Oh, lots of people [were] there, lots of birds, Jay Birds in [the] tops of the trees. Weasel and [his] brother stand right there, look around. Something dropped, dropped, dropped.

"What is it [that] drops?" Weasel's brother's name [was] Mink.[189] They look up. Jay Bird was scratching his sore. It came down, just like snow, scabs. Weasel was going to drive the bird away. He threw a rock at Jay Bird.

His brother said, "Keep still, don't bother [it], let it alone."

"Oh," Weasel said, "that's nothing."

His brother told him, "Someday we'll come to something dangerous, and when you can't keep still, it will get you." They went.

Weasel was always asking questions. "What's this here? What [do] you call this place?"

"Oh, I don't know—[it's the] first time I come through here," Mink would answer.

Now Mink knew where there was a dangerous place right there on [the] mountain, [an] open place.

Weasel said, "What are you watching for up there?"

"Well, you'll see pretty soon. You'd better dodge him as soon as he comes down." Now a big rock came down. Oh! [It] rolled down fast! Mink stood aside, but Weasel [stood] right there playing around. It nearly got him. Another came, another, more, more, bigger and bigger rocks. Weasel played around, dodged, dodged, and dodged. Rocks were after him; [they] never noticed Mink, who [was] standing still. Finally Weasel got tired; two rocks nearly got him. Now Mink caught [one], the next time, stabbed it with [his] knife. It was cooked camas!

Weasel wanted to know, "What is it?"

"Here, eat some," Mink said. Then he told Camas, "You'll just be camas. People will eat you. You don't have to kill anybody." Now Camas had become camas of today.

They went on. Weasel kept asking [a] whole lot of questions. They traveled.

"What's this creek's name?"

"Oh, that's just a creek, that's all. You don't need to know everything." About five, six o'clock, they cross.

In front of them someone hollers, "Ei-hhhhh, you better come here! I'm tired of laying down here," it [the voice] said.

Oh, Weasel got excited. "Somebody [is] calling us!"

Mink said, "You keep still. You don't know."

"Oh, let us go there!"

"Well, we'll go there pretty soon. I'll take my time." So they go slow. Weasel ran in front. Mink come behind, slow. Oh, there was [a] woman lying down on [her] back, legs apart.

"Come here; lie down with me." Weasel went [and] got on that woman, even though Mink told him not to. Her vagina clamped together on his penis. It was River Mussel. He [Weasel] thought it [was a] woman. Oh! He cried. It punished him good. Mink opened that Mussel, took Weasel out, sick. Now Mink threw all those open things [other mussels] into [the] water.

"You will be river mussels," he said. "You will not pretend to be women. People will eat you, when people grow in this world."

Now they go along. Weasel [is] quiet now, ha! ha! ha! He [is] sick. Now they were going to make camp.

Weasel, "What [do you] call this place where we camp?"

Mink gets mad. "I'll tell you pretty soon. Now go get a lot of wood."

"What do you want lots of wood for?"

"Well, you have to keep warm!" They sat down. Pretty soon Mink said, "You lie down on that side of [the] fire. I'll lie down over here." Weasel lay down.

He asked, "What was the name of this place where we camp?"

"Yes. Nighttime-Fire-Fights-Here. Maybe Fire will hit you. [The] name of [the] place [is] 'Fire-Fight-Place,' if you must know so bad."[190] Weasel already lay down. Mink smoked, laid down. Pretty soon Fire almost hit him [Weasel]. Another piece pretty near hit him. Fire-Fight, Weasel had to dodge all night. Sometimes it hit him right behind. He [would] see Fire come with [a] stick. All night he dodged right there. It never bothered Mink. At last it was nearly daylight. Fire quit fighting then.

[It was] daylight now. Weasel sat there, never opened his mouth. Mink made ready.

He said, "We'll go now. The sun is rising up." They went along, don't say anything, don't see anything. [They] keep on going. Finally [they] see one house [with] smoke. Weasel was hungry. He wanted to get in that house. He sneaks [up] to [the] door. There two blind women mashed [Indian oats].[191] Weasel got a handful [to] eat.

One old woman says, "What's the matter? [Indian oats] [are] nearly gone. Maybe Weasel got it." He stood right there eating. He ate it *all*. He [was] hungry. They [the women] put the mill away.

They [Weasel and Mink] went on then. They got to one place.

"Older brother! What's the name of this place?"

"Well, this place is where Spear Pole hits you and maybe kills you. I'll go in front. You come behind. Don't go [in] front." They walk along, hear it coming. Mink was packing [a] little stick. He hit that Spear. It came off. He got it.

"What [are] you going [to] do now?" Weasel asked.

"Oh, I'm going [to] get fish." They go down to [the] river. He gets fish. He put [the] Pole right there.

Mink said, "You will stay here. When people want to get fish, they'll use you. You will be pole." Now they built [a] grass fire and cooked steelhead. It cooks so quick. They ate there.

That's as far as I remember.

Coyote Jim and His Neighbor Crane

Crane won't share his fish catch with Coyote, so Coyote transforms himself into a large steelhead and causes Crane to lose his fishing spear. Transformed back into Coyote, he returns the spear to the unsuspecting Crane in exchange for dried and fresh fish.

> *The story presented here is taken from Jacobs's Upper Co-*
> *quille Athabaskan field notebook 6 (pp. 37–40). Jacobs provided*
> *the title. For partially cognate texts, see the Yurok story "Coyote*
> *and Crane" (E. Sapir 2001:1017–22), the Karok "Coyote and*
> *Great Blue Heron" (Kroeber and Gifford 1980:186–87), and the*
> *Santiam Kalapuya "Coyote and the one legged man" (M. Jacobs*
> *1945:92–96).*

A fellow lived across the river from Coyote Jim, by a dam. They [were] not good friends. This fellow caught fish all the time and never gave Coyote any. Coyote saw all kinds of fish lying around there, but that man never offered him a one.

Coyote thought, "All right, you don't want to give me any fish, I'll fix you." He went back home.

It was getting low water, now. There were a whole lot of steelhead, close where they can be speared. Coyote saw that fellow spearing. Coyote defecated [for] quite a while. [He] got very little.

[He] asked [his feces], "What [am] I going to do? That fellow never gives me any fish."

His feces said, "Well, what do you want?"

"I want to be like steelhead. I want to get in the water."

"All right. Have you got a knife?"

"Yes, I've got a little [flint knife]."[192]

"All right." He jumped in the water. He became a big steelhead. [He] went right over where that man was spearing. That man saw him.

"Oh, a big steelhead. I'm going to get it." He fixed his spear good. He stood right there, ready. Coyote came [swam] around, went back, went around. That man didn't bother [with] small steelhead; [he was] just watching that big one. He [Coyote] came closer to the man. Now he speared. [The] fish [Coyote] cut that string on the spear [and] swam away! Oh, that fellow lost his spear! He cried. He didn't know what to do.

Coyote went ashore down below, became a man again, [and] put that spear right in a rotten log there. That man left his pole [and] went home to get a bone wedge. He wanted bone out of the front of his own leg.[193]

Coyote said, "Oh, what [do] you do that for?"

"Well, I don't know. That's [the] best I can do," the man answered. "I can't get a spear anywhere. That's [the] best I can do."

Coyote said, "I'm going to look for that steelhead. Maybe he died some-where." He went. Crane's wife patted her man.

"Don't cry. We can starve," she said. Coyote went and got the spear. He took it back.

"I told you that. That fish died right there. You wanted this spear?" Oh, that fellow [was] glad!

"I'll do the best I can for you," he said.

"Oh," replied Coyote, "I don't charge anything."

"But I'll do anything for you." Then he ordered his wife to make him a big pack of dried fish, salmon. That's all Coyote wanted. "Come around tomorrow [and] get fresh fish, too." Coyote went once in [a] while for fresh fish too. That Crane [was a] good neighbor now. He [would] holler across river to Coyote, "Come, get fish."

Grizzly Wants Red-Headed Woodpecker Scalps

Desiring Red-Headed Woodpecker scalps, Grizzly Bears challenge Woodpeckers to a shooting contest (?), but supply them with worth-less arrowheads. After seven Woodpeckers are killed, Woodpeckers obtain good bullets (arrowheads) from Rattlesnake and kill one Grizzly Bear. Grizzly Bears give up and quit.

The story presented here is taken from Jacobs's Upper Coquille Athabaskan field notebook 6 (pp. 41–43). The title is Jacobs's. For cognate texts, see the Santiam Kalapuya story "The woodpeckers and grizzlies kill each other" (M. Jacobs 1945:119–25) and the Nez Perce "The Five Grizzly Bear Sisters and the Five Woodpecker Brothers" (Aoki and Walker 1989:197–203).

Grizzly Bears, the first time they saw people dance, all the people had [wore] yellowhammer heads.[194] [The] Grizzly Bear boss of the whole bunch said, "We can start in and make a big fence and put a man there in the corner [for them] to kill him. And [but] Grizzly Bear will kill him [a Woodpecker]." Now a Wood-pecker sat there [to shoot Grizzly].[195] Grizzly took his head off [and] went away. It didn't hurt Grizzly to be shot. Lots of them were Woodpecker people. They wanted to shoot. They did, but [their] arrows [were] no good.

Grizzly Bear said, "We'll fix it [again] tomorrow. We'll have to kill another." They wanted ten Woodpecker heads, good ones. [The] next day he did it again. He [Grizzly] caused all those arrow points to be soft. [He] put a [Grizzly] man in there. [Woodpecker people] shot [and] shot, but it never hurt Grizzly. He [had] killed five now, five Woodpecker people. [He] killed seven by seven days.

Oh, those Woodpecker people felt bad. "What's the matter with these arrows?" [the] Woodpecker boss said. "What's the matter [that] you fellows get killed? What's the matter [with] your arrows?" [Then the] boss said, "You fellows come [in the] house. We'll talk over who has to go." This Woodpecker boss said, "They'll give you fellows that little soft bark [for arrow points]. Who[ever is] the best runner, who [is the] best traveler, he'll have to go all night. I want to send you to the man who's got the best bullets. The minute his bullet touches you, you die. He has that kind of bullets. [He is] Rattlesnake. Who will go? This man has to be back before [the] break of day."

Fish Duck was picked out.[196] He was a good traveler. He started off. He got back at just daylight. So they made ready. He hadn't put that arrowhead on yet. That big Grizzly boss came around [and] told [the] Woodpecker to stand on one side. [He] gave him bullets. Everybody got ready. So Woodpecker took off that poor bullet the boss gave him [and] put on the good one. Now Grizzly Bear came roaring. That Woodpecker fellow [was] ready. [As] soon as he [Grizzly] got within five, six feet, he let go of that bullet. Grizzly dropped right there. Oh! Everybody [was] surprised. Everybody went to examine it.

[The] Grizzly Bear boss said, "What kind of bullet did you shoot it [with]?"

Woodpecker said, "Well, you put me in here [and] tell me to shoot. I have to do the best I can."

Now they didn't [any longer] call that dead one a Grizzly. They called him just bear.

"Drag away that bear. Burn him, cook him," the Grizzly Boss said. None of the Grizzly Bear people would touch it. They pretended smoke got in their eyes, but they were really crying.

[When it was] getting evening, "Go see what the people are doing." [A Woodpecker] man went to see. [It was] quiet. All those Grizzlies were quiet. But they smoked, and all sat crying. They hated to try [risk] another Grizzly.

"We'll have to stop now. They've got [a] different kind of bullets, now."

The boss said, "Why, I gave every one the same kind of bullets."

"Yes, but you don't know. Maybe they threw [them] away [as] soon as you went and put on a good kind of bullets. We don't want to lose another man just for a Woodpecker head. We got seven."

Now that man went back and reported to his people that the Grizzlies had given up. They were going to quit now. They were scared.[197]

Afterword

I would like to close this volume of Coquelle Thompson's myths and tales with a few thoughts about the value and importance of Native stories told directly in English.

For many years in American anthropology, there has been a bias against the authenticity of Native stories recorded directly in English or some other European language. Franz Boas ([1914] 1940:452) argued that texts recorded only in English translation were inadequate, especially for the investigation of folklore style. Melville Jacobs, one of Boas's students, often denigrated the value of most text collections in English (1967, 1969–70). Among other limitations, most texts in English were thought to be "contaminated" by the expressive style of English narrative discourse. As such they perhaps best reflected cultural breakdown and acculturation.

Neither Boas nor Jacobs entertained the notion that Native storytellers telling stories in English may have developed their *own* expressive style over time, a style in English—different from but not necessarily inferior to—that of texts dictated or recorded in the Native language. Gradually, English-language Native texts have come to be more highly regarded. The examples that follow document this change of attitude.

In 1980 Grace Buzaljko edited E. W. Gifford's Karok folklore text manuscript for publication. The texts originally had been transcribed by Gifford in Indian English. "After considerable debate" with folklorist Alan Dundes, Buzaljko agreed to preserve the consultants' nonstandard English, apparently not for any intrinsic stylistic or aesthetic worth but "for the historical approach. He [Dundes] wished to give readers, and especially folklorists, the opportunity to read an unvarnished text just as it was taken down by an anthropologist. Specifically, he wanted readers to be able to identify Gifford's later emendations, as well as [Buzaljko's] own" (Kroeber and Gifford 1980:xliv).

Related to the issue of stories told in English is the use of Indian or Red English as translations of Native-language versions. According to Tony Mattina, Dorothea Kashube's (1978) *Crow Texts* were published with Red English translations, which Mattina described as "perfectly beautiful poetic language," a "witness to the legitimacy of Red English" (Mattina 1987:11). Mattina discussed his preference for Red English translations in the introduction to his volume *The Golden Woman* (1987), where he explains, "I translated *The Golden Woman* into the Red English of Madeline DeSautel, because a Red English translation matches better than another kind of English the function of the original Colville narrative." DeSautel translated the story "into the English she normally spoke," that is, "the slowly emerging tradition of artistic (hence respectable and appropriate) published Red English" (Mattina 1987:9–10). Although Mattina preferred DeSautel's colloquial English translations, he does not discuss their distinctive stylistic features.

In 1989 Wendy Wickwire published a collection of Okanagan storyteller Harry Robinson's narratives, *Write It on Your Heart*, just as he told them in English. It was Wickwire's opinion that "[a]s more and more of [Robinson's] listeners, native included, understood only English, Harry began telling his old stories in English to keep them alive. By the time [she] met him in 1977, he had become as skillful a storyteller in English as he had been in his native tongue" (1989:15). Three years later Wickwire published a second volume of Robinson's stories, *Nature Power* (1992), again attempting to "remain as true to Harry's originals as possible." As Wickwire explains, "Because Harry had translated his own stories to perform them in English, editing was unnecessary. Here was an opportunity for readers to experience storytelling straight from the source" (1992:17). It remains for someone to describe the ethnopoetic style of Robinson's stories.

Coquelle Thompson could—and did—tell his stories in his ancestral language of Upper Coquille Athabaskan, as evidenced by the dozens of records made by John P. Marr in 1942. But as fewer and fewer speakers of his language were left to hear the stories, Thompson by necessity turned to English as his medium.[1] By the time Elizabeth Jacobs came along in 1935 to record his repertoire, Thompson, like Harry Robinson, was more comfortable telling the stories in English, especially for purposes of slow transcription by the hand of the visiting anthropologist. Over the years he had developed his own English style, some aspects of which I have discussed in chapter 3. More research on the style of these texts, as well as on his unpublished historical and personal experience texts, needs to be done.[2]

Melville Jacobs argued that a stylistic characteristic of Native-language versions of texts is laconicism: "All the evidence points to an extreme of laconicism in depiction of action, movement, travel, feelings, relationships, and personalities, with great speed in plot action" (1972:16). This is especially the case in the older collections Jacobs consulted. Preliminary analysis of more recent texts, though, indicates some changes in expressive style in Native-language texts. For example, Nez Perce narratives recorded in the Nez Perce language by Aoki (1979) and Aoki and Walker (1989) between 1960 and 1967 provide examples of at least three broad categories of innovations in expressive style absent from texts recorded in Nez Perce by Archie Phinney (1934) in 1929–30: cultural explication, presumably for the sake of the cultural outsider; allusions to or analogies with modern European American culture; and back-translations of English idioms (Seaburg 1997b).

One of the stylistic characteristics of Native texts in English is their frequent *inclusion* of depictive details, as illustrated in chapter 3 for Coquelle Thompson. This is true of other storytellers in the region as well, for example, Clara Pearson (Nehalem Tillamook) and Sophie Smith (Cowlitz Sahaptin). Clara Pearson, who dictated her stories in English to Elizabeth Jacobs ([1959] 1990), often gave voice to a character's thoughts, informed us about how a character was feeling, sometimes provided personality characteristics, evaluated a character's actions, provided Tillamook cultural background, and provided descriptive details and explanations not required by the plot or necessary to understand the plot.

Rather than see such depictive detail as a defect, as a corruption of, a falling away from precontact style, I suggest that we see it in a positive light, as providing important clues about how the storytellers felt about the stories, the actors, and the actors' actions. We could regard this oral literary criticism—in Alan Dundes (1975) apt phrasing—as embedded within the text itself. Folklorists and anthropologists ought to take full advantage of this wealth of Native interpretation and evaluation. We can't go back and ask all the questions we wish would have been asked of such marvelous storytellers as Sophie Smith, Clara Pearson, and Coquelle Thompson, but we can learn something of Native exegesis if we only take the time to look and to analyze.

Appendix 1
A Comparison of Jacobs's and Harrington's
Text Transcription Styles

Below are reproduced verbatim transcriptions of two versions of the same text, one recorded by Elizabeth D. Jacobs in 1935 and the other by John P. Harrington in 1942. Coquelle Thompson is the storyteller. Both were recorded at the Siletz Reservation, Oregon. Comparison of the two texts illustrates the different transcription styles of the two recorders and reveals interesting differences in textual details between texts told to different investigators seven years apart. I have added the endnotes.

This first text comes from Elizabeth D. Jacobs's Upper Coquille Athabaskan field notebook 3, pages 127–30. Jacobs supplied the title. I have enclosed Jacobs's phonetic transcriptions in square brackets. I have also spelled out or explained her abbreviations, also enclosed in square brackets, after the abbreviation in the text.

Good, White Bird

[gałáł'ɛ] crow (no story)
[gasátcʼu] (Raven) big black hawk
[ándjac] "buzzard" (not here)[1]

When anything dies on beach, a good bird, white as snow, [ántcac] will come down from mt. [mountain] and circle around & eat that dead seal or whatever it is. [Gasátc'u] comes down afterward. One day a man cut himself all over, blood running down—it dried on him. He lay down on beach at low tide, early in a.m., he wanted to get that white bird. That [gasátc'u] came, the man saw him. The big crow went back to get his people. [Ándjac][2] came down—came right by his foot—blood all over—never move—[ántcac] went to get his people. About 1 hour later—oh, lots of people, real *people* come down, they were talking. "We'll build a big fire, get all ready, soon as boss comes, we'll cut him, and boil him." He heard them, heard them moving their buckets. He saw that boss come now, oh white as snow. Then that chicken hawk (black) boss came, he was shiny black, fine. Now he wanted to get the eye, first; that was their law. He came by the foot. The man looked at him, the hawk saw his eye move. He did that so he wouldn't lose his eye. So the hawk left, and they asked "What's matter," "oh that [tc'i·lti] move his eye, some bad luck somewhere.[3] He went again. Now the boss came, the white boss. He came, oh fine man, good bird. He go round, come round to his feet and stand right there. The fellow lay very still, now that boss stepped on him. The man grabbed him. All the others got excited, tried to run away, but didn't want to leave their chief. The man stood up, holding on to that bird. He (the bird) said, "You've got me all right. I'll have to take you home." They all got ready, the boss sent so many ahead, so many to come behind & they started home. The boss said, "I've got a good daughter, I'll give you my daughter—you've got me all right." That man was satisfied; that boss said, "Now you'll come with me, but you shut your eye." The man didn't know how they'd come to heaven up there. They went, he felt himself going, just like he stood in one place holding that fellows hand. Pretty soon they opened door—it was up in sky. They let him go in chiefs house. Oh, lots of people. They lived there as people but come down here as bird. He got a home there, married. He came down & notified his father & mother—They gave him power to come down & tell them not to feel bad, and he had to come right back. That's all.

That man knew that white bird was chief or something, that's why he wanted to get that bird. (They're, those birds over at R. [Rogue] River on mt. [mountain] when they kill elk they'd see that bird sit on tree—must be vulture, Coq. [Coquelle] unfamiliar with word vulture or buzzard.)

This second text was copied from John P. Harrington's Upper Coquille Athabaskan fieldnotes, JPH, 27:0220–28. I have enclosed Harrington's phonetic transcriptions in square brackets. I have also spelled out or explained his abbreviations, also enclosed in square brackets, after the abbreviation in the text. The story title is mine.

['ɑ́ndʒɑʃ]

A man lay on the beach & waves came at low tide, the chief of the kind of birds called ['ɑ́ ndʒɑʃ] is snow white.[4] That man gashed his body at many places & lay on the beach, blood was all over his body. That man lay there bec[ause] he wanted to catch an ['ɑ́ ndʒɑʃ]. The waves came & pusht [pushed] him & one of those birds came & beheld him. He went back, & notified, & soon 15 or 20 ['ɑ́ndʒɑʃ] came. These birds brought with them buckets for fetching water & all parap[h]ernalia or utensils. Pretty soon raven came to near the man, but neither he nor any of the ['ɑ́ndʒɑʃ] were allowed to touch that dead man until the ['ɑ́ndʒɑʃ] chief (who was white as snow) & his wife came. This chief notified Raven that Raven cd [could] pick the eyes out of the dead man. Raven edged around the man & looked the dead man in the face—whereupon the dead man moved his eyes. Raven went away, & told the chief: no good, that dead-one moved his eye. Ye [you (plural)] come! (These birds were people as they came.) Let me go! they said. "All right. 3 men went over there & were about to take his eye out, whereupon suddenly the man grabd [grabbed] the chief. It was just like thunder from the ['ɑ́ndʒɑʃ]. The chief hollered: Ye [you (plural)] keep still! Then he said to the man: You've got me. What do you want. I have a daughter, I have all kinds of money. How much money do you want, how do you want it. The man said how much.

I['] m g. [going] to go back, I'll take you along with me (to heaven or wherever those stay, they were Inds. [Indians], not birds now.) You got me, but I'll take you along with me. I've got a daughter. That's what you wanted money. The man did not deny it, that chief knew without the man saying. "Now ye everybody go home." He took the man with him.

He walk up—just like a bird, they see lots of house, and chief's house in middle. Some 5 houses this side, some five houses that side. Chief's house right in the middle. The chief said: This is my house now. He opened the door. Oh, a fine house. Just earth for floor, everything nice. And yellowhammer feathers on everything—on arrows & bows. The chief said: Here's your husband I have got for you. The daughter was married right there, she had to become married.

They cookt [cooked] acorns, dry elk meat, everything they eat. The chief and his wife ate together with the man. This was maybe in heaven—a fine place. That fellow stayed there one month. The ['ɑ́ndʒɑʃ] flew around as a bird where the aged f. [father] and m. [mother] were crying for that man, whom they deemed lost. They reported this grief to the chief—maybe the old couple die? What are y[ou] g[oing] to do about it?

"I am g. [going] to send him home for a visit," the chief said. If the chief cd. [could] get the man down to the ground, the man cd [could] walk home.

They had to pack (carry) that man down to the ground. Then the man walkt [walked] home. Oh everybody was glad to see him. He stayed there 2 mos. [months], then he told the people: Now I have to go back, my wife is lonesome for me. I live up there with those people. They are not birds—it's people, not birds. They are rich people, much food, many things. My wife has 2 or 3 sea-otter skins that she sleeps on. Ye [you (plural)] must not cry any more. He told his mother esp. [especially]: Don't cry any more, just eat what you have. "We are all right now," the old folks said, we know you are alive, you not die, all right, they said.

He climbed back home, his wife gave him power to do it, nobody knows how he traveled.

That was the last—maybe he come back again, maybe not, they knew where he is, he had talkt [talked] to them, no use to come back any more. All through.

Wd [would] call the place they stay ['ɑ́ndʒɑʃ wæhmæ'], flicker-staying-place

But n [doesn't know] the name of the man nor of what village. But it was an Ind. [Indian] & on the beach of the U.S. The Inds [Indians] were training all the time, & he trained to get that flickers' chief.

Appendix 2

A Note on Orthography and Pronunciation

*The following phonetic alphabetic symbols occur in Upper Co-
quille Athabaskan words that appear in the texts and endnotes to
the texts. The first column lists Jacobs's 1935 transcription symbols. The second column lists modern linguists' transcription symbols but only where they differ from Jacobs's.*

1935	Modern	Approximate Pronunciation
a		the *o* in English *lot*.
b	p	no equivalent in English; similar to the *p* in English *spot*.
c	š	the *sh* of English *sheep*.
d	t	no equivalent in English; similar to the *t* in English *stop*.
dj	č	no equivalent in English; similar to the *ch* in English *church* but without the aspiration.

ɛ	ɛ, æ	probably sometimes the *e* of English *met* and sometimes close to the *a* of English *mat*.
ə		the *u* in English *but*; the *a* in English *sofa*.
g	k	no equivalent in English; similar to the *k* in English *skull*.
gʷ	kʷ	like g above but with lip rounding, indicated by the raised *w*.
γ		no equivalent in English; similar to x below, but with voiced pronunciation.
h		the *h* in English *hill*.
i	i, ɪ	probably sometimes the *ee* of English *beet* and sometimes the *i* of English *bit*.
k		no equivalent in English; similar to the *k* in English *skull*.
k'		the k of English *keep*.
kʷ'		the *qu* of English *queen*.
k'	k̓	no equivalent in English; similar to the *k* of English *keep* but with an explosive release, indicated by the apostrophe.
kʷ'	k̓ʷ	no equivalent in English; similar to the *qu* of English *queen* but with an explosive release, indicated by the apostrophe.
l		the *l* of English *leap*.

ł		no equivalent in English; similar to the Welsh pronunciation of *ll* in *Lloyd*.
m		the *m* of English *moon*.
n		the *n* of English *neat*.
q		no equivalent in English; similar to the *k* in *skull* but made further back in the throat.
q'		no equivalent in English; similar to the *k* of English *cod* but further back in the throat.[1]
q'	q̇	no equivalent in English; similar to the *k* of English *cod* but further back in the throat and with an explosive release, indicated by the apostrophe.
qʷ'		no equivalent in English; similar to the *qu* of English *quote*, but further back in the throat.
qʷ'	q̇ʷ	Eno equivalent in English; similar to the *qu* of English *quote*, but further back in the throat and with an explosive release, indicated by the apostrophe.
s		the *s* of English *seen*.
t		no equivalent in English; similar to the *t* in English *stop*.
t'		the *t* of English *team*.
t'	ṫ	no equivalent in English; similar to the *t* of English *team* but with an explosive release, indicated by the apostrophe.

tł'	ƛ̓	no equivalent in English; a combination of the t and the ł above, but with an explosive release, indicated by the apostrophe.
tc'	č'	the *ch* in English *church*.
tc'	č̓	no equivalent in English; similar to the *ch* of English *church* but with an explosive release.
ts'	c̓	no equivalent in English; similar to the *ts* in English *cats* but with an explosive release, indicated by the apostrophe.
u		the *oo* of English *boot*.
w		the *w* of English *wet*.
x		no equivalent in English; similar to the *ch* in German *Ich*.
x^w		same as x but with lip rounding, indicated by the raised *w*.
x̣		no equivalent in English; similar to the *ch* in German *Ach*.[2]
x̣^{w}		same as x̣ but with lip rounding, indicated by the raised *w*.
y	j	the *y* of English *yet*.
'	ʔ	a brief glottal stop or pause, represented by the hyphen in English *uh-oh*.
'	h	a brief aspiration (puff of air) after a vowel sound.

Notes

Foreword

1. Sadly, the sound recordings of Coquelle Thompson made by the Jacobses in 1935 and by John P. Marr in 1941 are of such poor acoustic quality that they only imperfectly reflect his performance style. See chapter 3, this volume.

2. Reading the stories aloud, however, can enhance one's understanding and appreciation of them, and I urge the reader to do so.

3. In a draft of an unpublished paper written late in Melville Jacobs's career, he wrote: "A further thought, indeed a worrisome one, is that, as fieldworkers, we tended to be regarded as if we were early morning youngsters, uninformed poor things to be sure, who had to be subjected to lectures and careful explanations as much as we were to be granted esthetically fine readings that would appear in a book that later generations of Indians would see. Therefore we found ourselves writing, at dictation, 'that's why' and ethical admonition statements some or most of which also graced early morning but not night sessions" (Jacobs 1969–70).

4. Since we have no comparable body of texts from a female Upper Coquille Athabaskan speaker, we do not know if or how they may have differed from stories told by men, who told stories primarily in the exclusively male domain of the sweathouse.

5. See Sven Liljeblad's (1962) review of Melville Jacobs's *People Are Coming Soon* on this score.

1. Introduction

1. For lack of space, Thompson's personal experience stories and historical narratives have been omitted from this volume. I hope to publish them in a future collection.

2. For a book-length biography of Coquelle Thompson, see Youst and Seaburg (2002).

3. Seven anthropologists if we include the physical measurements Thompson provided Franz Boas's anthropometric fieldwork at Siletz in 1890.

4. For a fuller biographical sketch of Elizabeth D. Jacobs, see E. Jacobs (2003).

5. The Jacobs Research Fund is administered by the Whatcom Museum of History and Art, Bellingham, Washington.

6. Melville Jacobs (1902–71) was a professor of anthropology and linguistics at the University of Washington, whose career at the university spanned the years 1928–71. See Seaburg and Amoss (2000) for a biographical sketch of his life and work.

7. The reference is to Professor Bernhard J. Stern (1894–1956).

8. Terry Thompson, a longtime friend who had been visiting Elizabeth, had read her the story.

9. Unfortunately none of Jacobs's fieldnotes or drafts of her write-ups is dated.

10. See M. Jacobs (1968) and E. Jacobs (1977).

11. These elicitation questions are copied from Jacobs's notes in my possession.

12. Notes on the Upper Coquille Athabaskan recordings can be found in UC nbs. 120 and 121, Melville Jacobs Collection, University of Washington Libraries. A few additional notes on the recordings are in my possession.

13. I have identified several additional personal and historical narratives from the field notebooks that were not included in Jacobs's compilation.

14. Both the first and second edited versions of Elizabeth Jacobs's Upper Coquille Athabaskan texts are in my possession.

15. These asides and explanations hint at the dynamics of Indian-white relations on the Siletz Reservation—just one of many facets of Siletz culture that has not been explored by anthropologists.

16. The first number refers to the microfilm reel number; the second number refers to the frame number on that reel.

17. To study Coquelle Thompson's Indian English one needs to consult Jacobs's original notebook transcriptions and listen to the John P. Marr recordings (see chapter 3).

2. A Cultural Sketch

An earlier version of this chapter appeared as appendix 1 of Youst and Seaburg (2002). It has been revised and greatly expanded for publication here.

1. Unfortunately, the anthropologists who worked with Coquelle Thompson and other Indians of the southwestern Oregon region did not ask probing questions about

cosmology and world-view, value ideals, or humor in their fieldwork sessions. Lacking relevant independent ethnographic materials, I have had to rely on the texts themselves for insight.

2. Thompson told E. Jacobs (1935) that men dressed or cured elk skins. Barnett (1937:165) notes "skin dressing by men" for the Tolowa, Chetco, and Galice Creek Athabaskans.

3. One exception may be the tale "A Girl Is Ill with Desire."

4. Because Coquelle Thompson told stories learned from other southwestern Oregon Athabaskan culture groups, deductions about cosmology and world-view, value ideals, and humor probably apply to all these groups and not just to the Upper Coquille.

5. sx̣áiyɛł'a is rendered as "God" here. In an early editing of the text "Coyote and God," in the editor's possession, Jacobs translates the Upper Coquille word as "he-sends-children."

6. Jay Miller notes that many Northwest Coast Native peoples have "separate words for 'myth' as distinct from 'stories' in" their languages (1989:125). Boas says, "For our purposes it seems desirable to adhere to the definition of myth given by the Indian himself. In the mind of the American native there exists almost always a clear distinction between two classes of tales. One group relates incidents which happened at a time when the world had not yet assumed its present form, and mankind was not yet in possession of all the arts and customs that belong to our period. The other group contains tales of our modern period. In other words, tales of the first group are considered as myths; those of the other, as history" ([1914] 1940: 454–55).

7. Panther here refers to the mountain lion or the cougar.

8. Wayne Suttles (1981, 1987) argues that the Coast Salish did not recognize a distinction between a "natural" world of humans, plants, and animals and a separate and transcendent "supernatural" world of nonhuman beings. The salient distinction was between human beings and nonhuman beings or people. I believe this distinction is equally applicable to the southwestern Oregon Athabaskans.

9. M. Jacobs (1964:245) offers the following list of worldwide factors:

incongruity, lack of fit	understatement
slapstick	exaggeration
regressive behavior	language error
unusual physical prowess	language misunderstanding
cleverness	pun
foolishness	vocal mannerism
faulty perception	musical error
forbidden behavior	dance error
evil-doer comes to grief	repetition
falsehood	progression
hypocrisy	saturation
irony, sarcasm	mimicry
onomatopoeia	

10. Berger's (1996:73) forty-five basic techniques of humor:

Logic	*Language*	*Identity*	*Visual*
absurdity	allusion	before & after	chase
accident	bombast	burlesque	speed
analogy	definition	caricature	slapstick
catalogue	exaggeration	eccentricity	
coincidence	facetiousness	embarrassment	
comparison	insults	exposure	
disappointment	infantilism	grotesque	
ignorance	irony	imitation	
mistakes	misunderstanding	impersonation	
repetition	overliteralness	mimicry	
reversal	puns/wordplay	parody	
rigidity	repartee	scale	
theme & variation	ridicule	stereotypes	
	sarcasm	unmasking	
	satire		

11. nx̱at, "a little" (?).

12. isá, "shit."

13. M. Jacobs claimed that for the Clackamas Chinook, Coyote's feces were "regarded as two spirit-powers," advisers that "proffered information to him on several occasions when he was nonplussed" (1959b:238). I believe that Coyote's excrements functioned in a similar way in Upper Coquille Athabaskan oral literature, where they not only advised Coyote but were able to physically transform him and outfit him with the accessories that he needed for his disguises—almost always as a means of fooling or tricking someone.

14. Jay Miller suggests that constipation may indicate poor diet or health (personal communication, 2004). In many Coyote stories in the Northwest states, Coyote is a notoriously poor hunter. "Finally there came a little tiny bit" may also hint that Coyote's power was reluctant to help him, yet another source of humor.

15. "Yoo-hooh" is said like kids patting their mouths.

16. nícniỷəɬ súnli⋯, "she whipped me, my grandma."

3. Features of Style and Performance

1. I have been unable to locate Skeels's Nez Perce wire recordings. He told me in an interview in the 1980s that he had given them to the Washington State Museum (now the Burke Museum of Natural History and Culture) on the University of Washington Seattle campus. The museum has no record of the recordings.

2. Reichard said much the same thing over ten years earlier: "[A] fine distinction between [stylistic] elements and episodes cannot be made, for elements which may

consist of only a phrase or two may have an important bearing on the plot, or a formal combination of elements which might from its length be called an episode may play little or no part in plot development" (1947:10).

3. I believe Jacobs overstates his case here. I have found plenty of instances where storytellers put sentiments into words in Native language texts, in the earliest transcribed texts as well as later ones. My impression is that negative more than positive sentiments or feelings were likely to be expressed in the stories.

4. Although, as Hymes has shown, covert evaluations may show up in the structure of the texts themselves (2003:203–27).

5. For some reason when Thompson originally told the story to Jacobs, he did not sing these songs nor explain that Coyote chose his traveling companions on the strength of their power songs. Later, during the phonograph recording sessions (see chapter 1), Thompson sang several of the myth actors' songs, including those of Raccoon, Red Squirrel, and Beaver (Seaburg 1982:71). Coyote's assessment of Beaver's song and Jacobs's comments on Thompson quoted here are from Jacobs's first editing of this text, in the editor's possession. The original fieldnotes regarding Beaver's song read: "Coy. don't like [Beaver's song]. Coy. Jim mad, give him dickens. Coy. 'What's the matter with you[.] are you drowning. If I take you cross ocean, oh I be shame. That ain't no song, that's sound of people drowning—so I don't take you, you stay home.'"

6. Throughout the Northwest—probably throughout all of North America—there were cultural taboos against telling stories, especially myths, in the summertime.

7. Glenn ([1991] 1994); and Preliminary Partial Inventory to the John P. Marr Recordings at the National Anthropological Archives, June 22, 1990.

8. That is, he was talking to himself.

4. Analyses of Four Stories

1. The analysis of "A Man Grows a Snake in a Bucket" was first drafted by Elizabeth Jacobs; I subsequently added to and considerably reworked it. The result, which appears in this volume, is an amalgam of both of our interpretations. The interpretation of "Panther and Deer Woman" is based largely on unpublished notes by Elizabeth Jacobs. I have edited her comments and added my own commentary throughout as well as an overall summary of themes and stylistic features at the end.

2. Sven Liljeblad objects to the term *precultural*, noting that Melville Jacobs "equates the Myth Age with a 'precultural era,' a somewhat puzzling term, since he actually recognizes cultural determinants and makes good use of them for cultural reconstruction" (1962:96).

3. k'əmá, "a split-stick tonglike implement, used for cooking; something like a large pair of tweezers."

4. Money, probably in the form of strings of dentalium shells, sometimes called money beads or Indian money.

5. Thompson probably heard this story told by a man in the company of other men and young boys in the men's "dormitory" or sweathouse.

6. Note that betting people is specifically interdicted in the text "Coyote Jim Gives the Law on Gambling," in this volume.

7. ts'istú·ni, "Little Man." A free translation of the cognate Chetco text is in the editor's possession.

8. sxáyu, "brother-in-law."

9. ɣiyał, "Come on."

10. cádɛ' disnɛ́łá nanícłti, "Sister, I have brought one man."

11. By "cards" Thompson is referring to stick game gambling equipment. Shinny is a game played with long, heavy sticks or clubs and a ball. See Drucker (1937:240); Culin ([1907] 1975:616–47).

12. nxats'ənɣita, "they think you drowned."

13. nxats'intɛ, "they look for you."

14. nxɛsta'i', "they hunt for you."

15. tɛ·tc'əlɛ́c, "stout man."

16. See the text "Coyote Jim Gives the Law on Gambling," in this volume.

17. ts'ín tc'ən t'i, "Up-from-the-Ocean."

18. tc'əxɔ́n, "ace," the marked stick in the stick gambling game.

19. Perhaps in answer to questions by Jacobs, Thompson added at the end of the story: "He couldn't get his first wife back. He couldn't buy her back.

"Snakes didn't bother him because he swam too fast and didn't smell good. He was clean because he practiced all the time. Snakes would see like fire going over water when [a] man cleaned himself lots in practice.

"A man just swam. He wouldn't tell anybody how he trained. If you tell somebody, it makes your training no good.

"Men only trained for gambling, shinny—pack shinny at nighttime. Hunter training, one just sweats, swims in [the] morning, not like cards people. Don't believe women ever trained except for [becoming a] doctor."

20. From Jacobs's Upper Coquille Athabaskan field notebook 4, pp. 119–21. The story is unpublished.

21. Compare with the cannibal man in the text "Big Head (Cannibal)," in this volume.

22. It may be an areal trait to refer to one's power animal as one's "dog" or one's "pet." Cf. Yurok texts recorded by Kroeber (1976); also the Hanis Coos text "The Girl and Her Pet" (Frachtenberg 1913:85–91).

23. Thompson told Jacobs at this point in the text that this was a story from up the Coquille River.

24. dəs·ɔ́n stá daníłsi, "hungry time put grub away."

25. In response to a question by Jacobs about payment for the death of the children, Thompson replied, "[They] didn't say anything about pay. That man's snake had supported people two, three years [by] bringing a whale. The children were to blame."

26. dənɛ́ dənɔ́łyɛ·ɣɛ, "raised-by-people"; xʷɛsɛ' xuqʷ'ɛnətq'i, "ten white stripes around him."

27. In Harrington's version (JPH, reel 027, frame 0270), Thompson says, "Well, the son had to train (study) two or three weeks before going." A Native audience would have known that such a dangerous undertaking would have required ritual preparation on the part of the young man.

28. gasásł'ɛ', "crow" (?) Cf. Chasta Costa gałał'é, "crow" (E. Sapir 1914:293); Tututni ka-sásh-le (Curtis [1924] 1970:244).

29. "The watcher" is gasásł'ɛ́, "crow."

30. tł'əɣə́c dasɛq'ɛ, "you eat what Snake spits on."

31. "Watcher" is gasásł'ɛ́, "crow."

32. See M. Jacobs in Seaburg and Amoss (2000:94–102) for a discussion of features of style in Indian oral genres in the Northwest states.

33. Jacobs first translated this as "attachment of small intestines," then as "sweetbread in cattle," and finally as "pancreas."

34. "Sunday man" is an epithet for an ugly person. Indians call a government or disliked person a "Sunday man."

35. I.e., they constructed a large drying rack.

5. Oral Traditional Texts

1. ɛ·dətni, "noise-under-ground."

2. tc'ɛsə́q'łtá, "big-round-short-person."

3. Presumably an animal; Jacobs speculates that it was Panther or Grizzly.

4. sələ́s, "Squirrel."

5. Up to this point the text was dictated in Upper Coquille Athabaskan with interlinear English translation. After this point, the text was told in English only. Jacobs's translation of the Upper Coquille Athabaskan was a rather free and somewhat embellished one. I have tried to restore it closer to Thompson's interlinear translation.

6. stalyɛ, "Coyote"; dutútəní, "Tututni"; tc'ɛmətdənɛ, "Joshua"; kamásdənɛ́, "mouth of the Coquille"; məcíntc'ɛdə́nɛ, "mouth of the Coos."

7. gɛ́'lə́m, "Crawfish."

8. The Harrington version begins: "When they first made this world there were about twenty months. Coyote Jim said, 'Too many. There ought to be twelve.'" If Coyote killed "seven or eight" Moons, an original twenty Moons makes more sense than the fifteen reported in the Jacobs version.

9. sɛq'ɛhu·li, "Big-Eater." The snake, Big-Eater, also appears in the text "Gambler and Snake" (Seaburg 2004:209–25; and in this volume).

10. ł'ə́mɛ, "Mouse."

11. Thompson prefaces his rendition of the story recorded by Harrington (JPH, reel 027, frame 0333) with the following: Pitch Woman "is a tall woman, six or seven feet tall, her pack basket was lined with pitch so a person put in it stuck to it. She carries a stick called k'ámmá', a salmon spit with split ends on which salmons are roasted and she carries one of these [k'ámmá'] for the purpose of catching children. This kind of woman does not kill anyone, [she's] just after children."

12. A free translation of the Chetco text is in the editor's possession.

13. In the notebook this sentence reads: "Then this Pitch Woman hears this open door, he's mad, he say . . . ." I have reproduced what Jacobs wrote in her second edited version of the text, in the editor's possession.

14. x̣ə́n, sx̣ən, "Husband, my husband."

15. The notebook reads: "At last they pass him again, so" followed by a word that's been crossed out and then the beginning of a new sentence. In Jacobs's second edited version, she eliminates "At last they pass him again, so" and begins a new paragraph.

16. tc'ə́ɣə́sɛ x̌ʷɛt'ɛ, "big, long money."

17. Red-headed woodpecker–scalp headdresses were a valuable wealth item in southwestern Oregon–northwestern California Native cultures, displayed with obsidian blades, strings of dentalium shells, and other items in wealth dances and on other ceremonial occasions.

18. x̣ə́n, ts'ətɛ, "My man, my money."

19. dɛminɣə́ctyɛɬ, "I'm [being] followed" or "I'm [being] chased."

20. x̣ə́sx̣ɛ, "chief." Thompson's version of the story as recorded by Harrington does not end with the drowning of Pitch Woman. Instead Thompson adds the following coda (JPH, reel 027, frame 0336): "Thereupon another woman came from the other side, but she did not enter the water, but ran way down the far bank, thinking the man had gone down there. Only that woman wanted to get married—they wanted to stay with a man, a big man. Those women always went in couples—always two. Sometimes three. And nobody could open their house; they lived in a stone house [that] had a great big iron door. And she wore a pitch-dress—maybe [because it was] warm [Thompson doesn't know] why. She had her house on a little hill."

21. ts'ɛ́ɬbɛ, "Pick 'em up (with tweezers)."

22. The words of the song aren't translated.

23. Thompson added a postscript, perhaps in response to a question by Jacobs: "If a hunter builds a fire [and] stays alone away from others, they [Pitch Women] never bother him."

24. tc'ə́ntíli, "little flint knife."

25. tɬ'ɛs'ɛ́·tc'u, "Pitch Woman."

26. nənɛsɛ nənáɣal'ɛ, "he fights all the time, all around."

27. ɣ́áltc'ɛ·, "elk-skin armor."

28. tc'ə́q'ət nát'ən, "war knife."

29. tux̌ʷí·dən nax̌ʷə́txa, "there is war all the time."

30. tc'ətdu·nic, "warrior (mean person)."

31. tc'ətdu·nic, "warrior (mean person)."

32. yasi·na or yá·mɛ, "heaven."

33. In the land of the dead, dead people are not visible to live people during the day.

34. x̌ʷətdác, "Spider."

35. ts'ənu·lɣəɬ, "Evening Star" (?).

36. sənɣatdə́ł, (?); cf. Galice /sanʔ/ "star"; sənx̣ástłʼu, (?).

37. Thompson noted at the end of the story that they "started calling Coyote Jim ever since white people came in because white people didn't understand Coyote was a person. So, they tacked on 'Jim.' They really just call him Coyote."

38. sx̣áiyɛłʼa, "God." In an early editing of this text, in the editor's possession, Jacobs translates this word as "he-sends-children."

39. ádú tɛstli·la, "threw sand in the ocean."

40. sɛsəqtɛlyɛ, "Use sharp grass."

41. Thompson knew of no translation for the name.

42. si·ʼɛqɛʼə wa···, "My sons! Gone(?)," sung from a high monotone, descending to a lower pitch.

43. Gray Eagle is not an ordinary eagle, cudɛ·tcʻu, but tsʼɛɣəltcʼu.

44. saʼwə́lyɛ, "Little lizard named White Face." Thompson said that the Indians claim if a two-month-old baby is scared, it's that little lizard teasing it.

45. A free translation of the unpublished Chetco text is in the editor's possession.

46. qʼəctʻila, "alder or red whale."

47. saqʼɛni·nu tcʼunɛ mɛ́lsən, "like live people this Whale smells."

48. tcʼałdənɛ́, "travel in the morning," when a menstruating young woman was supposed to travel to go swimming.

49. "String" is si·ɣɛłmi·n, "strip of skin."

50. cisdjɛ, "my thigh."

51. cnəɣɛ́, "my eye"; cicda, "my mouth"; cyɛ́ɣəlɛ, "my chin"; cqʷʼə́s, "my throat"; cmɛcwə́l, "hollow of my neck."

52. tsʼewɛ, "breast"; cga·nɛ, "my arm"; cmət, "my stomach"; cdjɛ́, "my thigh"; cgʷə́t, "my knees"; stsʼə́nɛ sa·dɛ, "my shinbone"; sx̣ɛbíldjɛ, "my ankle."

53. ctəɣə́lsatsʼɛc, "my vagina."

54. cə́ltináltłʼat, "Come together, my stick."

55. tłʼu·mɛ́··ta tcʼiyaci···, "hollering for a bird."

56. ga·tcʻu, "Rabbit."

57. səsdəlítcʻu, "Owl."

58. tcʼác łʼɛ́cə́n, "Fisher."

59. qʼa·lɛc, "Coon."

60. gi·stcʻɛ, "Blue Jay."

61. sáʼkʷə̕ł, "Beaver."

62. nhitłʼɛ́tcʻu, "Woodpecker."

63. qʼasá·tcʻu, "Raven" [?, one would expect an initial g-].

64. ci·sánɛ, "My feces."

65. x̣əsx̣ái ɣał, "headman [is] coming."

66. Thompson didn't know what the words of the song meant.

67. di··tcʻu, "Panther."

68. ntsʼí·tnɛ, "ghosts."

69. An earlier edition of this text, with brief commentary, was published in Seaburg (2004); see also this volume.

70. The notebook version says: "She make them for ga·yu." ga·yu is the Upper Coquille word for "baby."

71. The notebook version reads: "ga·yu thing for packing baby," apparently referring to a cradleboard.

72. *Stout* in this and other contexts in this story means "strong."

73. The notebook version reads: "tc'ədətni (sənsalts'əł hammer all time—you hear long ways)." In Jacobs's editing of the text, she renders this as Thunder's name, "Hammering-all-the-time."

74. The notebook reads: "mɛ·lts'i· (to pound meal) She told that stone." mɛ·lts'i· is the Upper Coquille word for "grinding stone" or "pestle."

75. Here Thompson renders Thunder's name as "sənsəldyɛł (Thunder)."

76. In Thompson's version of this narrative recorded by John P. Harrington, Thompson notes: "The wind woman always kept her hair tied on both sides. She never let it loose" (JPH, reel 027, frame 0420).

77. Thompson uses the Upper Coquille word tł'u·dɛ', which he translates as "Indian oats."

78. An earlier edition of this text was published in Seaburg (1997a).

79. tł'u'dɛ, "Indian oats."

80. səłnə́lgi is the name of Grizzly Woman's sister.

81. tc'ə́tsi·ɣɛ, "guts"; tc'ə́matc'u, "stomach."

82. At the head of the notebook transcription, Jacobs has "wolf wife" and "si·tc`álni." In an early editing of the text, she gave it the title "Sea-Wolf Wife," while in a later editing she called it "Wolf's Wife." I have titled it "The Woman Who Married the Sea Wolf."

83. Moon-sick, i.e., menstruating.

84. si·tc'álni, "Sea Wolves"; t'a··mic, "Shag," "black bird in river." Another word for the bird "shag" is "cormorant."

85. məgə́s t'ámic, apparently another word for Shag, who is speaking here in this passage.

86. "Indian money," i.e., dentalia and perhaps other valuable shells. Another Indian English word for Indian money is money beads.

87. Jacobs indicates that "I don't know what they use it for" was an aside by Coquelle Thompson.

88. nícniłɣəł súnli···, "she whipped me, my grandma."

89. I.e., maybe Coon had a power that helped him.

90. Thompson noted that there was no name for that man.

91. Coon was called gə́ncá by some. Coon was also called níqʷ'asq'í, "striped face." This information is an indication of the kind of linguistic detail Thompson often volunteered.

92. I.e., she put it on a raised storage platform in the house.

93. i··nən'ɛ́ saqʷ'ɔ́t nú·nanícdjá dɛsícłsi·ni, "On ground I got better. You made me come alive again."

94. xʷɔ́tdac, "Spider." Thompson commented after the story: "Spider lives up in the sky. The Sky People send them down with two fish. That really means two sacks full."

95. This may be the first text Jacobs recorded from Coquelle Thompson. The two sides of the first page of the text are in phonetic transcription and English; the rest of the text is in English with occasional Upper Coquille words. It is a difficult text to decipher and has a disjointed feel, as if Jacobs and Thompson were adjusting to the practice of text dictation and transcription. Evidently Thompson did not have much patience for the slow process of phonetic text dictation. sítc'alnɛ (or sítc'alni) is Thompson's title. Jacobs gave it the title "Wolf Person."

96. I.e., a different power was in him so that he didn't think about his human family and village.

97. Or possibly: "Seven or eight Wolf brothers came in packing elk."

98. denɛ́, "people."

99. tásəł, "soup"; tc'əq'a, "grease."

100. i·łɔ́q, "piss."

101. gu·səntc'u, "Measuring Worm."

102. mɛ·'nát'ən, "acorn stirring paddle."

103. tátc'ɛ́·ts'ən, Klamath River (?).

104. cíʔɛxɛ́, cíʔɛxɛ́, "My sons, my sons." The pitch begins at a high level, then descends to a lower level.

105. q'í·yas, "quiver, arrow sack."

106. nxat, "a little" (?).

107. isá, "shit."

108. Thompson described the pipe as being made from a long piece of alder wood with the soft center poked out, with a hole about two inches deep in the end for tobacco, and about sixteen inches in length. It was smoked like a cigar, held up to keep the tobacco in.

109. Thompson explained that iron knives, a long time ago, were made from iron taken from wrecked steamers. It was hammered on a log all day long until both edges were sharp. They put on a wrapped buckskin handle, tied it with rope from the wrist, and packed it that way. It was as long as an arm, two feet or more.

110. sa, "shit."

111. metc'i, "woven mat."

112. sxáiyɛł'a, "he sends babies." Thompson noted after the story that a "little baby goes [to the] same heaven. [A] baby goes back into its water. There's baby water where sxáiyɛł'a is." A new baby might be reborn as evidenced by ear holes, but adults were not reborn as babies. See E. Jacobs (2003) for a discussion of the Tillamook concept of Babyland, from whence babies were born and to which they returned if they died before verbal age.

113. Of the approximately 120 versions of the Orpheus story examined by Hult-krantz, 16 versions have a happy ending.

114. Her dress had shells and beads sewn on it, and they rattled when she moved.

115. Things in the land of the dead are often the opposite of things in the land of the living, although the dead don't see them that way. Thus, the panful of salmon eggs is really a panful of lice.

116. x̣ə́nə́s xá'ic, "hollers for the canoe."

117. ts'ítnɛ tá'an', "dead people's land."

118. Dead people are able to smell the presence of live people in the land of the dead.

119. "Great big bird" is dəmɛ́lkɛ́·'. Cf. Chasta Costa dʌmel'kɛ́, "pelican" (E. Sapir 1914:293).

120. Apparently in answer to a question, Thompson remarks that there was no soul recovery by shamans. Jacobs notes that both old men in the story were live people, not dead people. There was no concept of soul loss, she adds.

121. yúgʷi, rendered Euchre in English.

122. Ida Bensell (1880–1983), a Tututni speaker, was a longtime resident of the Siletz Reservation.

123. ádu dɛ́icɛ níł'a hí·na·· hi·na··, "Something's stuck on my back [+ vocables]."

124. ts'áx̣ɛi nílti, "He's got a woman."

125. mətc'í, "mats."

126. "At that time, if a woman came to see me, they know my name. I don't have to buy. They'll ask where I live and say, 'I want to get him.' In those times they never buy." This concluding comment by Thompson is probably in answer to a question from Jacobs regarding whether the man had to pay a bride price when he married Robin Woman.

127. tcigá' ga'ts'ɛ, "Robin Woman."

128. See Culin ([1907] 1975:616–17, 623) for a description of the game of shinny and its equipment.

129. í·nəct.cí·', "I'm getting black (like a cockroach)."

130. This is reminiscent of Yurok men's ritualistic practices for acquiring luck, one of which included gathering sweathouse firewood from the tops of trees, "often special-izing on the topmost branches of tall Douglas firs" (Kroeber [1960] 1992:166, n. 57).

131. Wives in a polygynous household would have maintained separate fires and separate bed platforms.

132. I.e., Frog Woman used her powers to make the wet green wood burn.

133. Marriage without a bride price must have been relatively rare in southwestern Oregon Athabaskan cultures. Absent a bride payment a father-in-law might arrange for his son-in-law to live with and work for him. Such an arrangement was socially stigmatized and would reflect poorly not only on the "half-married" couple but on their children as well.

134. cmí·sε, "my stepson."

135. mi·ámεiʻ, "Heaven/Sky People." Thompson said here, "[They're] not dead people, just Sky People."

136. malú·qʼε mɛ́γεcłxɛ́ł ndjúcnε sxεxε, "I'm bringing a whale, you cunt's children!"

137. mí·ʼamεʻ, "Heaven People," Thompson explained again, were not dead people. They never intermarried with Indian people, just came down and helped young folks. He added that Coyote Jim is everywhere. He has good help because those Heaven People help him.

138. tcʼəsí· təmástcʼu, "big-round-headed-person." The -tcʼu is perhaps a mishearing for the enclitic -tcʻu, "large, big." After telling the story Thompson commented, "[There was] no dance to mock him—too dangerous. Just this one person; he stepped on something, stepped on dry bí·lε "little snail" house. It came in his foot; it poisoned him."

139. i··stcə́lʼε, "brother."

140. Normally, she would have carried the baby in its basketry cradle on her back.

141. mətcí, "mat."

142. It is understood that he fell in the hole.

143. Thompson's ending to the version he told Harrington differs enough from Jacobs's to warrant reproducing it here: "Now his sister took hold of him and seated him between the two girls, who were all beaded up nice above the waist. They suddenly jumped and tried to throw him in the pit. But he jumped and his brains popped upward. They buried him right there in the hole and all the people moved out, converting that into a burial house. The people moved to a neighboring house. He had become mere bones, only his head shot upward. They put in the grave lots of Indian money, lots of elk blankets, then covered them up. Moved to a neighboring house" (JPH, reel 027, frame 0287).

144. gʷəlsi·tcʻu, "big Skunk." Thompson explained, "When they fart at Elk, it kills him. They turn the same way to a person—[when it] wants to shoot you."

145. tcʻustεni, "Water Dog"; sí·skεn, "Lizard."

146. nεsʼátʼε, "big long thing, snake." This word also means some kind of chief.

147. tcʼətɛ́lgu or tɛ́ltʼa·s, "a $1 string"; táxəsxε, "only ten on a string, about a $100 string"; tcʻúsxula, "shortest string, $5 or $10 string."

148. saqʷʼisɛ́·, "Crane."

149. γ́ldáłε·· stcʼə́lε, "Run, my brother"; dənε qʷinγənyεł, "Someone's chasing us" (transcription uncertain).

150. I.e., he went out in the daytime and came home underground at night.

151. "If they dream *Sun* and get Sun power, Sun wants one's [own] children. It's always bad luck. He can't help it if he dreams Sun. Sun wants his children—they all die. He has to tell his dream. Sun sometimes takes his wife, too. It's pretty good for him [because] he can doctor, but it's no good for his family." Thompson could recall no case of a Sun dream.

152. Thompson added: "Sun said, 'I am light all over the world. . . . They say there were lots of suns. I heard old people talk about Suns and Thunder. They said Suns were people. Coyote never went to visit Sun. Sun must have been going to eat those dead people. They didn't say; they just said he packed them.'"

153. An earlier edition of this text, with brief commentary, was published in Seaburg (2004).

154. The "card's bed" or "gambling bed," ntɛɬ, was a buckskin blanket on which the stick or hand game was played.

155. sɛ́q'ɛ hú·li was the name for the big flat-headed snake.

156. tc'ənt'i, "flint knife."

157. ngətɛ́lsá ɣilxə́tla, "you have to eat everything."

158. The notebook reads: "ngətɛ́lsa medicine."

159. Long dentalium shells, a form of money.

160. tɛ́ɬ, "gambling bed.

161. mətcí, "mats woven from grass."

162. gása, "basket pan."

163. dɛ́dəné djic məcxɛ́ du ɬuq'ɛ tsəsya, "Why not eat skin?"

164. "Cards" = the stick game gambling pieces.

165. tcəxə́n, the "ace" or specially marked gambling piece in the stick game.

166. tɛɬ, "gambling bed." Coquelle Thompson uses the Upper Coquille word here for a flat piece of [probably deer] skin used as a blanket to gamble on.

167. nályɛ, a large and particularly valuable dentalium shell.

168. The text was told in several disjointed segments, probably reflecting Thompson's remembering parts of the story and inserting them out of order. The text in this volume follows the following notebook pages: 92–93, 98–99, 96–98, 93–96.

169. mí·tc'əní, "penis."

170. metci, "mats."

171. ɣiɬɣəɬ tcəstc'ayɛ, "push more, push more."

172. See Hymes's discussion of the news getting out in "Coyote, the Thinking (Wo)man's Trickster" (2003:278–99).

173. In Harrington's version Thompson indicated that "[w]here Wren lived was nággɑt'-xæhdɑn. This was a village on the south side of [the] Rogue River" (JPH, reel 027, frame 0397).

174. dəldustc'ɛ, "Pheasant."

175. nagətxɛ́ tdən tɬásuɬ natɛ́ lgɛt, "someone upriver has been staying with his grandma."

176. qʷ'ɛ́·si, "mortar."

177. "Yoo-hooh" said like kids patting their mouths.

178. Thompson explained that this event happened a long time ago and that it was the only time a thing like this was ever seen. The creature was called dɛctɬ'ɛ, "big one-horned-thing." It "hollered like a person" and apparently resembled a quail. "That's quail, that big one-horned thing, only bigger. Just like quail."

A free translation of the Chetco text is in the editor's possession.

179. Regarding a tale type that involves a race between Penis and Vulva, Melville Jacobs comments, "I lack field data on the source of this tale, which many Indian groups of Oregon and Washington knew and told in the 1920's. Professor Franz Boas once said to me that the story must have been borrowed only recently from Caucasians. I believe that at least the Clackamas of the later nineteenth century decades placed the tale in pre-Caucasian times" (1959a:647).

180. tcʻúc, "vulva"; dəɣwá, (?), possibly "vulva" is tcʻúc dəɣwá. Cf. Tolowa -yuušɛʔ, "a woman's genitals" (Seaburg 1976–82).

181. míˑsɛ, "penis."

182. gasátcu, "crow," "he looks for feces [sa] all the time."

183. úˑgi, "dung."

184. sa, "feces."

185. Jacobs does not provide a translation of the Upper Coquille word for this type of healer. Cf. Upper Coquille River tcucéːnɛ, "formulists, who ranked as lesser doctors" (Drucker 1937:281); also Lower Rogue River tcucénɛ, "formulists," lit. "talking doctors" (Drucker 1937:276).

186. In response to a query about stories involving Eagle, Thompson dictated this text, noting that it was their only story about Eagle: "Our only story—not so long." The title was supplied by Jacobs. cudɛˑtcu is the Upper Coquille word for "gray eagle." At the end of the text dictation Thompson indicated that he had never heard of anyone dreaming of Eagle.

187. át'ədíˑslɛ' ná' níˑts'ił, "Snowbird floats down, Snowbird sits down."

188. sɛ'silí dádi, "A hard rock sits there."

189. tɛkʷilíˑclɛ, "Mink."

190. xʷə́n məł ts'uldjasdən, "Fire-fight-place."

191. tł'úˑdɛ, "Indian oats."

192. tc'ənti, "flint (knife)."

193. The man was sa'kʷəsts'ɛ́, "Crane."

194. Presumably yellowhammer bird scalps as headdress decoration. In Jacobs's first editing of this text, she rewrote the two sentences of the text to read: "Grizzly was the chief of all the people there. The first time that they all danced, they had only yellowhammer heads to wear."

195. The first three lines of this text are problematic. Jacobs's notebook page has many crossed out words and phrases, and what we have written here is our best interpretation of what Thompson may have meant.

196. sə́gʷəstcʻu, "Fish Duck." The first vowel may be a—Jacobs either overwrote a ə or an a here.

197. Thompson noted at the end of the text: "Grizzly was [the] chief for the whole bunch there."

Afterword

1. To the best of my knowledge, no one still speaks the Upper Coquille Athabaskan language. There may be a few semi-speakers of the closely related dialect of Tututni.

2. I have not attempted a linguistic analysis of his English dialect, in part because of the uncertainties of the source materials. One could call it Red English, but in his case I'm unsure that designation tells us anything more than English spoken by an Indian. His vocabulary and idioms strike me as typical of rural, uneducated farmer English; his grammar, marked by the frequent absence of a copula, conjunctions, and determiners, to name the most frequent omissions, that of a second-language learner whose first language lacked those particular function words.

Appendix 1

1. The identity of the bird, ándjac, is not clear from the texts but probably refers to a buzzard. Compare Alsea yáⁿt'cǝc, "buzzard," from Melville Jacobs's unpublished Alsea slip file, MJC. In Drucker's interviews with Thompson (field notebook 2, p. 30), he reported: "ántcac—some kind of big bird gave good power. Land bird" (Drucker 1933–54).

2. Jacobs has written tcac above djac in the notebook original.

3. tc'i·lti, "dead thing" (corpse).

4. The word 'ɑ́ndʒɑʃ in this first line of the text is underlined, with a line drawn from the underlining to an interlinear note that says, "[used for birds]." The square brackets here are from the original transcription.

Appendix 2

1. There is no distinctive (phonemic) contrast between k' and q', k̓ʷ and q̓ʷ, or their respective glottalized counterparts.

2. There is no distinctive (phonemic) contrast between x and x̣ or their rounded counterparts.

References Cited

Adamson, Thelma. 1934. *Folktales of the Coast Salish*. Memoirs of the American Folk-Lore Society 27. New York: American Folklore Society.

Aoki, Haruo. 1979. *Nez Perce Texts*. University of California Publications in Linguistics, vol. 90. Berkeley: University of California Press.

Aoki, Haruo, and Deward E. Walker Jr. 1989. *Nez Perce Oral Narratives*. University of California Publications in Linguistics, vol. 104. Berkeley: University of California Press.

Ballard, Arthur. 1929. *Mythology of Southern Puget Sound*. University of Washington Publications in Anthropology vol. 3, no. 2, 31–150. Seattle: University of Washington Press.

Barker, M. A. R. 1963. *Klamath Texts*. University of California Publications in Linguistics, vol. 30. Berkeley: University of California Press.

Barnett, Homer G. 1937. *Culture Element Distributions, VII: Oregon Coast*. University of California Anthropological Records vol. 1, no. 3, 155–204. Berkeley: University of California Press.

Becker, A. L. 1995. *Beyond Translation: Essays toward a Modern Philology*. Ann Arbor: University of Michigan Press.

Berger, Arthur Asa. 1996. "What's in a Joke? A Microanalysis." In *Manufacturing Desire: Media, Popular Culture, and Everyday Life*, 71–81. New Brunswick NJ: Transaction.

Boas, Franz. 1898. "Traditions of the Tillamook Indians." *Journal of American Folklore* 11:23–38, 133–150.

————. 1901. *Kathlamet Texts*. Bureau of American Ethnology Bulletin 26. Washington DC: Smithsonian Institution.

————. [1914] 1940. "Mythology and Folk-tales of the North American Indians." In *Race, Language and Culture*, 451–90. New York: Macmillan.

————. 1916. *Tsimshian Mythology*. Thirty-first Annual Report of the Bureau of American Ethnology for the Years 1909–10. Washington DC: Smithsonian Institution.

————. 1917a. "The Origin of Death." *Journal of American Folklore* 30:486–91.

————, ed. 1917b. *Folktales of Salish and Sahaptin Tribes*. Memoirs of the American Folk-Lore Society 11. New York: American Folklore Society.

————. 1918. *Kutenai Tales*. Bureau of American Ethnology Bulletin 59. Washington DC: Smithsonian Institution.

————. 1935. *Kwakiutl Culture as Reflected in Mythology*. Memoirs of the American Folk-Lore Society 28. New York: American Folklore Society.

Bommelyn, Loren. 2002. "Test-ch'as (The Tidal Wave)." In *Surviving through the Days: Translations of Native California Stories and Songs*, ed. Herbert W. Luthin, 67–76. Berkeley: University of California Press.

Bright, William. 1957. *The Karok Language*. University of California Publications in Linguistics, vol. 13. Berkeley: University of California Press.

————. 1993. *A Coyote Reader*. Berkeley: University of California Press.

Clements, William. 1990. "Schoolcraft as Textmaker." *Journal of American Folklore* 103:177–92.

Culin, Stewart. [1907] 1975. *Games of the North American Indians*. New York: Dover.

Curtis, Edward S. [1924] 1970. *The North American Indian*. Vol. 13. New York: Johnson Reprint.

Darnell, Regna. 1990. "Franz Boas, Edward Sapir and the Americanist Text Tradition." *Historiographia Linguistica* 17:129–44.

————. 1992. "The Boasian Text Tradition and the History of Canadian Anthropology." *Culture* 17:39–48.

Drucker, Philip. 1933–54. Philip Drucker Papers. Manuscript no. 4516. National Anthropological Archives, Smithsonian Institution, Washington DC.

————. 1937. *The Tolowa and Their Southwest Oregon Kin*. University of California Publications in American Archaeology and Ethnology vol. 36, no. 4, 221–300.

Du Bois, Cora A. 1939. *The 1870 Ghost Dance*. University of California Anthropological Records vol. 3, no. 1. Berkeley: University of California Press.

Dundes, Alan. 1975. "Metafolklore and Oral Literary Criticism." In *Analytic Essays in Folklore*, 50–58. The Hague: Mouton.

————, ed. 1984. *Sacred Narrative: Readings in the Theory of Myth*. Berkeley: University of California Press.

————, ed. 1988. *The Flood Myth*. Berkeley: University of California Press.

Farrand, Livingston, and Leo J. Frachtenberg. 1915. "Shasta and Athapascan Myths from Oregon." *Journal of American Folklore* 28:207–42.

Frachtenberg, Leo J. 1913. *Coos Texts*. Columbia University Contributions to Anthropology 1. New York: Columbia University Press.

———. 1917. "Myths of the Alsea Indians of Northwestern Oregon." *International Journal of American Linguistics* 1:64–75.

———. 1920. *Alsea Texts and Myths*. Bureau of American Ethnology Bulletin 67. Washington DC: Smithsonian Institution.

———. 1922. *Coos*. In *Handbook of American Indian Languages*, Bureau of American Ethnology Bulletin 40, pt. 2, 297–429. Washington DC: Smithsonian Institution.

Gayton, Anna H. 1935a. "The Orpheus Myth in North America." *Journal of American Folklore* 48:263–93.

———. 1935b. "Areal Affiliations of California Folktales." *American Anthropologist* 37:582–99.

Georges, Robert. 1981. "Do Narrators Really Digress? A Reconsideration of 'Audience Asides' in Narrating." *Western Folklore* 40, no. 3:245–52.

Glenn, James R. [1991] 1994. "The Sound Recordings of John P. Harrington." *Anthropological Linguistics* 33, no. 4:357–66.

Goddard, Pliny E. 1903–4. Galice Creek Linguistic and Ethnographic Field Notebooks and Texts. Melville Jacobs Collection. University of Washington Libraries, Seattle.

Haeberlin, Herman. 1924. "Mythology of Puget Sound." *Journal of American Folklore* 37:371–438.

Harrington, John P. 1932. *Karuk Indian Myths*. Bureau of American Ethnology Bulletin 107. Washington DC: Smithsonian Institution.

———. 1942. Southwest Oregon Athabaskan. Microfilm reel nos. 025-027. John Peabody Harrington Papers, Alaska/Northwest Coast. National Anthropological Archives, Smithsonian Institution, Washington DC.

Hilbert, Vi, ed. 1985. *Haboo: Native American Stories from Puget Sound*. Seattle: University of Washington Press.

Hinton, Leanne. 1992-93. "The House Is Afire! John Peabody Harrington—Then and Now." *News from Native California* 7, no. 1:9–13.

Hultkrantz, Åke. 1957. *The North American Indian Orpheus Tradition*. Ethnological Museum of Sweden Monograph Series, no. 2. Stockholm.

Hymes, Dell. 1981. *"In Vain I Tried to Tell You": Essays on Native American Ethnopoetics*. Philadelphia: University of Pennsylvania Press.

———. 2003. *Now I Know Only So Far: Essays in Ethnopoetics*. Lincoln: University of Nebraska Press.

Jacobs, Elizabeth D. 1935. Upper Coquille Athabaskan Linguistic and Ethnographic Notes, Folklore Texts (in English) from Fieldwork with Coquelle Thompson Sr., Siletz, Oregon. Melville Jacobs Collection. University of Washington Libraries, Seattle.

———. [1959] 1990. *Nehalem Tillamook Tales*. Corvallis: Oregon State University Press.

———. 1968. "A Chetco Athabaskan Myth Text from Southwestern Oregon." *International Journal of American Linguistics* 34, no. 3:192–93.

———. 1977. "A Chetco Athapaskan Text and Translation." *International Journal of American Linguistics* 43, no. 4:269–73.

———. 2003. *The Nehalem Tillamook: An Ethnography*. Ed. and intro. William R. Seaburg. Corvallis: Oregon State University Press.

Jacobs, Melville. 1929. *Northwest Sahaptin Texts 1*. University of Washington Publications in Anthropology vol. 2, no. 6, 175–244. Seattle: University of Washington Press.

———. 1934. *Northwest Sahaptin Texts, Part 1*. Columbia University Contributions to Anthropology vol. 19, no.1, 1–291. New York: Columbia University Press.

———. 1935, 1938-39. Galice Creek Athabaskan Linguistic Field Notebooks, Lexical File, Folklore Texts, Based on Fieldwork with Hoxie Simmons, Logsden, Oregon. Melville Jacobs Collection. University of Washington Libraries, Seattle.

———. 1936. *Texts in Chinook Jargon*. University of Washington Publications in Anthropology vol. 7, no. 1, 1–27. Seattle: University of Washington Press.

———. 1939. *Coos Narrative and Ethnologic Texts*. University of Washington Publications in Anthropology vol. 8, no. 1, 1-125. Seattle: University of Washington Press.

———. 1940. *Coos Myth Texts*. University of Washington Publications in Anthropology vol. 8, no. 2, 127–260. Seattle: University of Washington Press.

———. 1945. *Kalapuya Texts*. University of Washington Publications in Anthropology 11. Seattle: University of Washington Press.

———. 1955. "A Few Observations on the World View of the Clackamas Chinook Indians." *Journal of American Folklore* 68:283–89. Reprinted in Seaburg and Amoss (2000).

———. 1958. *Clackamas Chinook Texts, Part 1*. Indiana University Research Center in Anthropology, Folklore and Linguistics Publications 8. Bloomington: Indiana University.

———. 1959a. *Clackamas Chinook Texts, Part 2*. Indiana University Research Center in Anthropology, Folklore and Linguistics Publications 11. Bloomington: Indiana University.

———. 1959b. *The Content and Style of an Oral Literature: Clackamas Chinook Myths and Tales*. Chicago: University of Chicago Press.

———. 1959c. "Folklore." In *The Anthropology of Franz Boas*, ed. Walter Goldschmidt, 119–38. American Anthropological Association, memoir 89. Menasha WI: American Anthropological Association.

———. 1959d. Unpublished manuscript on Northwest States Indian folklore. Melville Jacobs Collection. University of Washington Libraries, Seattle.

———. 1960. *The People Are Coming Soon*. Seattle: University of Washington Press.

———. 1962. "The Fate of Indian Oral Literatures in Oregon." *Northwest Review* 5, no. 3:90–99.

————. 1964. *Pattern in Cultural Anthropology.* Homewood IL: Dorsey Press.

————. 1967. "Our Knowledge of Pacific Northwest Indian Folklores." *Northwest Folklore* 2, no. 2:14–21.

————. 1968. "An Historical Event Text from a Galice Athabaskan in Southwestern Oregon." *International Journal of American Linguistics* 34, no. 3:183–91.

————. 1969–70. "Spread of Features of Style in Indian Oral Genres in the Northwest States." Unpublished manuscript. Melville Jacobs Collection. University of Washington Libraries. Seattle.

————. 1972. "Areal Spread of Indian Oral Genre Features in the Northwest States." *Journal of the Folklore Institute* 9:10–17. Reprinted in Seaburg and Amoss (2000).

Kashube, Dorothea. 1978. *Crow Texts.* Native American Texts Series no. 2. Chicago: University of Chicago Press.

Kelly, Isabel T. 1938. "Northern Paiute Tales." *Journal of American Folklore* 51:363–438.

Kroeber, Alfred L. [1960] 1992. "Comparative Notes on the Structure of Yurok Culture." In *The Structure of Twana Culture*, by William W. Elmendorf. Pullman: Washington State University Press.

————. 1976. *Yurok Myths.* Berkeley: University of California Press.

Kroeber, Alfred L., and Edward W. Gifford. 1980. *Karok Myths.* Ed. Grace Buzaljko. Berkeley: University of California Press.

Leeds-Hurwitz, Wendy, and James M. Nyce. 1986. "Linguistic Text Collection and the Development of Life History in the Work of Edward Sapir." In *New Perspectives in Language, Culture, and Personality*, ed. William Cowan, Michael K. Foster, and Konrad Koerner, 495–529. Philadelphia: John Benjamins.

Le Guin, Ursula K. 1989. *Dancing at the Edge of the World: Thoughts on Words, Women, Places.* New York: Harper and Row.

Liljeblad, Sven. 1962. "*The People Are Coming Soon*: A Review Article." *Midwest Folklore* 12, no. 2:93–103.

Lüthi, Max. 1986. *The European Folktale: Form and Nature.* Bloomington: Indiana University Press.

Malcolm, Janet. 1987. "Reflections, J'Appelle Un Chat Un Chat." *New Yorker*, April 20.

Mattina, Anthony. 1985. *The Golden Woman: The Colville Narrative of Peter J. Seymour.* Tucson: University of Arizona Press.

Miller, Jay. 1989. "An Overview of Northwest Coast Mythology." *Northwest Anthropological Research Notes* 23, no. 2:125–41.

Miller, Jay, and William R. Seaburg. 1990. "Athapaskans of Southwestern Oregon." In *Handbook of North American Indians*, vol. 7, *Northwest Coast*, ed. Wayne Suttles, 580–88. Washington DC: Smithsonian Institution.

Mills, Elaine L., ed. 1981. *The Papers of John Peabody Harrington in the Smithsonian Institution, 1907–1957.* Vol. 1: *A Guide to the Field Notes; Native American*

History, Language, and Culture of Alaska/Northwest Coast. Millwood NY: Kraus International.

Mithun, Marianne. 1999. *The Languages of Native North America*. New York: Cambridge University Press.

Murray, David. 1991. *Forked Tongues: Speech, Writing and Representation in North American Indian Texts*. Bloomington: Indiana University Press.

Phinney, Archie. 1934. *Nez Perce Texts*. Columbia University Contributions to Anthropology 25. New York: Columbia University Press.

Ramsey, Jarold, ed. 1977. *Coyote Was Going There: Indian Literature of the Oregon Country*. Seattle: University of Washington Press.

———. 1999. *Reading the Fire: The Traditional Indian Literatures of America*. Seattle: University of Washington Press.

Ray, Verne F. 1933. "Sanpoil Folk Tales." *Journal of American Folklore* 46:129–87.

———. 1938. *Lower Chinook Ethnographic Notes*. University of Washington Publications in Anthropology vol. 7, no. 2, 29–165. Seattle: University of Washington Press.

Reichard, Gladys A. 1947. *An Analysis of Coeur d'Alene Indian Myths*. Memoirs of the American Folklore Society 41. New York: American Folklore Society.

Roemer, Michael. 1995. *Telling Stories: Postmodernism and the Invalidation of Traditional Narrative*. Lanham MD: Rowman and Littlefield.

Rooth, Anna Birgitta. [1957] 1984. "The Creation Myths of the North American Indians." In Dundes (1984), 166–81.

Sapir, Edward. 1909a. *Takelma Texts*. University of Pennsylvania Anthropological Publications vol. 2, no.1, 1–267. Philadelphia: University of Pennsylvania Press.

———. 1909b. *Wishram Texts*. Publications of the American Ethnological Society 2. Leyden: E. J. Brill.

———. 1914. *Notes on Chasta Costa Phonology and Morphology*. University of Pennsylvania Anthropological Publications vol. 2, no. 2:271–340. Philadelphia: University of Pennsylvania Press.

———. 2001. *The Collected Works of Edward Sapir*. Vol. 14: *Northwest California Linguistics*. Ed. Victor Golla and Sean O'Neill. Berlin: Walter de Gruyter.

Sapir, Jean. 1928. "Yurok Tales." *Journal of American Folklore* 41:253–61.

Schmerler, Henrietta. 1931. "Trickster Marries His Daughter." *Journal of American Folklore* 44:196–207.

Seaburg, William R. 1975. Tape-recorded interviews with Elizabeth D. Jacobs, summer 1975, Seattle.

———. 1976–82. Unpublished Tolowa (Smith River) Athabaskan linguistic and ethnographic fieldnotes from Smith River and Crescent City, California.

———. 1982. *Guide to Pacific Northwest Native American Materials in the Melville Jacobs Collection and in Other Archival Collections in the University of Washington Libraries*. Seattle: University of Washington Libraries.

————. 1997a. "Expressive Style in an Upper Coquille Athabaskan Folktale Collection Recorded in English." *Northwest Folklore* 12, no. 1:23–34.

————. 1997b. "Areal Features of Style in Pacific Northwest Folklore." Paper presented at the AAAS Annual Meeting, February 13–18, 1997, Seattle.

————, ed. 2003. *The Nehalem Tillamook: An Ethnography*, by Elizabeth D. Jacobs. Corvallis: Oregon State University Press.

————. 2004. "Two Tales of Power: 'Gambler and Snake' and 'Wind Woman'." In *Voices from Four Directions: Contemporary Translations of the Native Literatures of North America*, ed. Brian Swann, 209–25. Lincoln: University of Nebraska Press.

Seaburg, William R., and Pamela T. Amoss, eds. 2000. *Badger and Coyote Were Neighbors: Melville Jacobs on Northwest Indian Myths and Tales*. Corvallis: Oregon State University Press.

Skeels, Dell. 1949. "Style in the Unwritten Literature of the Nez Perce Indians." PhD diss., University of Washington.

Smith, Anne M. 1993. *Shoshone Tales*. Salt Lake City: University of Utah Press.

Snyder, Sally. 2002. *sgʷaʔčəł syəyəhub, Our Stories: Skagit Myths and Tales*. Ed. Laurel Sercombe and William R. Seaburg. Seattle: Lushootseed Press.

Spier, Leslie, ed. 1938. *The Sinkaietk or Southern Okanagon of Washington*. General Series in Anthropology 6. Menasha WI: George Banta.

Suttles, Wayne. 1981. "The Coast Salish Need for Wilderness." In *Inventory of Native American Religious Use, Practices, Localities and Resources*. Ed. Astrida R. Blukis Onat and Jan L. Hollenbeck, 699–716. Seattle: Institute of Cooperative Research.

————. 1987. "On the Cultural Track of the Sasquatch." In *Coast Salish Essays*, 73–99. Vancouver BC: Talonbooks.

Thomas, R. Murray. 2001. *Folk Psychologies across Cultures*. Thousand Oaks CA: Sage.

Thompson, Stith. 1929. *Tales of the North American Indians*. Cambridge MA: Harvard University Press.

Wales, Katie. 1989. *A Dictionary of Stylistics*. London: Longman.

Walker, Deward E., Jr. 1998. *Nez Perce Coyote Tales: The Myth Cycle*. Norman: University of Oklahoma Press.

Whereat, Patty. 2002. "Cultural Legacy: Traditional Athabaskan Legends of Southwest Oregon." In *Changing Landscapes: Sustaining Traditions, Proceedings of the Fifth and Sixth Annual Coquille Cultural Preservation Conferences*. North Bend OR: Coquille Indian Tribe.

Wickwire, Wendy, ed. 1989. *Write It on Your Heart: The Epic World of an Okanagan Storyteller*. Vancouver BC: Talonbooks/Theytus.

————, ed. 1992. *Nature Power: In the Spirit of an Okanagan Storyteller*. Seattle: University of Washington Press.

Youst, Lionel, and William R. Seaburg. 2002. *Coquelle Thompson, Athabaskan Witness: A Cultural Biography*. Norman: University of Oklahoma Press.

Index

In the Native Literatures of the Americas series

Pitch Woman and Other Stories:
The Oral Traditions of Coquelle Thompson,
Upper Coquille Athabaskan Indian
Edited and with an introduction
by William R. Seaburg
Collected by Elizabeth D. Jacobs

CPSIA information can be obtained
at www.ICGtesting.com
Printed in the USA
LVHW040838270422
717286LV00002B/313